THE STORY OF LIBRARIES

THE STORY OF
LIBRARIES

*From the Invention of Writing
to the Computer Age*

FRED LERNER

Continuum • New York

1998
The Continuum Publishing Company
370 Lexington Avenue
New York, NY 10017

Printed in the United States of America

Library of Congress Cataloging-in-Publication Data

Lerner, Frederick Andrew, 1945–
    The story of libraries : from the invention of writing to the
computer age / Fred Lerner.
        p.   cm.
    Includes bibliographical references and index.
    ISBN 0-8264-1114-2 (alk. paper)
    1. Libraries—History.   I. Title.
Z732.L565   1998
027'.009—dc21   98-22748
                                                              CIP

To
SHERYL AND ELIZABETH

CONTENTS

Illustrations may be found between pages 108 and 109.

LIST OF ILLUSTRATIONS

PREFACE

The Story of Libraries is a history of one of the most enduring of human institutions, one nearly as old as history itself. Though writing may have been invented to record land ownership and keep track of debts, it was not long before poets, priests, and prophets found other uses for it. Perhaps the first writers addressed only themselves, recording their thoughts and compositions merely as an aid to their own memory. But they soon realized that writing offered a way to transcend both space and time: to reach an audience beyond the range of the author's voice and the span of his years. And some in that audience understood that the written record put at their disposal the thoughts and experiences of men and women from other places and times. The wisdom of the past, the learning of the present, the hopes and fears of the future—through the written word, all could be preserved and called upon whenever needed. In this realization lay the birth of libraries.

Over the centuries more and more uses were found for the written word. It could memorialize the greatness of emperors and preserve unaltered the contents of sacred texts. It could proclaim the laws of the realm and teach the cures of disease. More subtly, it could sustain a common vision of the past and uphold an order of things in the present. Knowledge was power, and whoever controlled the storehouse of knowledge owned treasure indeed.

In this book we shall explore the ways in which men and women collected and organized the records of the human experience. *The Story of Libraries* is a brief historical narrative, not an exhaustive statistical survey. No doubt there are documented exceptions to every generalization it contains. I have made no attempt to describe every important library, nor have I tried to explain every significant development in the evolution of library science. My aim in *The Story of Libraries* is to trace the evolution of libraries and to explore the role they played in society, from the invention of writing to our own day and beyond. I have tried to show the library as an aspect of the culture in which it operated: to explain how the major societies in world history used libraries and the ways in which those societies were affected by the libraries they created or inherited.

In doing this I have drawn upon the work of archaeologists and cultural historians as well as that of specialists in library history. I have examined learned journals and monographs and consulted standard historical references. Although it is based on the work of scholars, *The Story of Libraries* is not meant to be a scholarly book. It forgoes the apparatus of footnotes that a scholarly study would require, though direct quotations are properly referenced. The reader desiring to delve further into library history will find many titles to choose from in the list of works consulted at the end of this volume.

To avoid confusion over dates, I have followed the practice of Joseph Needham and George Sarton, using the + and - signs to indicate dates during or before the common era; that is, C.E. (A.D.) or B.C.E. (B.C.), respectively. The + sign has been omitted for dates in the present millennium, or when it is obvious from context that the common era is meant.

1
THE EARLIEST LIBRARIES

So FAR AS we know, it was the Sumerians who first invented writing. They lived in the valleys of the Tigris and Euphrates, two rivers flowing through the land we now call Iraq, during the -3rd millennium; but we know nothing of their origin. Philologists cannot find in their language the roots of any modern tongue. It survives only in the literature its speakers left behind. Their civilization, though glorious in its achievements, did not spread beyond the valleys of Mesopotamia; and in time it was absorbed by the Semitic peoples that surrounded Sumer.

It may be that some earlier culture in a wetter environment wrote with ink on leather or palm leaves long before the Sumerians took reed stylus to clay tablet. But such documents are much less likely to last five thousand years than baked clay in a dry climate. As we study the records of the past, we must always remember how little of that past has come down to us, how many peoples and cultures have arisen, flourished, and declined without leaving behind any tangible remains.

Wet clay takes excellent impressions from seals or styli and when dried in a kiln or under the sun it bears permanent witness. Reeds grew abundantly in the Mesopotamian marshes. Splitting them produced inexpensive styli which, pressed into the clay, left a wedge-shaped mark. We call this writing "cuneiform," from the Latin word for wedge. Tens of thousands of these tablets have come down to us, to be read, studied, and translated by generations of scholars.

The oldest writings to survive to our time were inscribed five thousand years ago by temple bureaucrats recording economic transactions. The signs they impressed with reed styli onto wet clay represented concrete objects: crops, animals, manufactured goods. They were at first pictographic in character, stylized representations of the objects or actions they denoted. These evolved into ideograms, figurative representations of concepts related in some way to the subject of the picture. As writing became more widely practiced, many ideograms were used as phonograms, each one representing a syllable rather than an object. The conservative scribes used both types of character, a complicated arrangement that made scribal training difficult and perpetuated the power of the priesthood.

The Sumerian economy was based on cultivating grain. This, in turn, depended upon an elaborate system of irrigation and upon a centralized government to maintain it. The cities of Sumer were unwalled, testimony to the strength of their rulers. Manufacturing occupied a numerous class of artisans, and traders imported wood, stone, and metals from distant lands. Much of this economic activity was managed by the temples. The ruler of Sumeria was both high priest and king, and the Sumerian economic structure has been described as a "theocratic socialism."

The temple administrators needed to record the details of their landholdings and harvests. While the temples were immortal, their servants weren't. The memory of interested parties and the testimony of neighbors might serve to fix the details of a family's affairs from one generation to the next, but the temples needed a more permanent way to keep track of what they owed and what they owned. This the scribes provided.

The temples did not discard their old business records, but deposited them in storerooms. These were intended for preservation rather than for frequent consultation; often the storerooms had no doorways and could be entered only by descending a ladder. Within these rooms, tablets were kept in wooden boxes, reed baskets, or brick receptacles. Attached to each container was a clay tablet serving as a label, listing the contents of the tablets within each container and the dates they covered. Like modern organizations, the temples often generated more records than they had room for. Archaeologists excavating the temples have found tablets stored on floors and in corridors.

Besides business records, the temples preserved the texts of hymns, prayers, and incantations. These were used in the education of scribes, but also served a more solemn purpose. The welfare of the Sumerian people depended upon the goodwill of the gods, making it essential to assure that praise and petition alike were offered in the prescribed form. Even after the decline of Sumerian as a spoken language, it retained its liturgical use.

Around -1900, Sumerian was replaced by Akkadian, a Semitic tongue, as the speech of daily life. The Akkadian scribes were careful to preserve Sumerian religious texts as well as historical and legal records. They compiled lists of signs and bilingual glossaries, both for their own use and for training future generations of scribes. Similar activities characterized other times of cultural change: the advent of the Assyrians around -1100 and the coming of the Persian and Macedonian rulers who absorbed Mesopotamia into their empires.

In ancient Iraq, books did not have titles. The incipit (the first few words of the text) was used to identify a tablet, just as the first line is used to identify an untitled poem in a present-day anthology of verse. The incipit identified a physical object—a clay tablet—rather than a literary work. When a book occupied more than a single tablet, each carried at its end the incipit of its successor, much as early printers used catchwords to help guide readers from one page to the next.

Mesopotamian collectors kept catalogs of their libraries. These too were clay tablets, on which were inscribed all the incipits for a single group of tablets. (One of the earliest of the Sumerian catalogs, compiled five thousand years ago in the city of Ur, instead uses key-words selected from the first two lines of text, but this complicated system was not used by later catalogers.) One such catalog, of a collection of hymns, begins like this:

> Honoured and noble warrior
> Where are the sheep
> Where are the wild oxen
> And with you I did not
> In our city
> In former days
> Lord of the observance of heavenly laws
> Residence of my God
> Gibil, Gibil [the fire-god]
> On the 30th day, the day when sleeps
> God An, great ruler [the sky-god]
> A righteous woman, who heavenly laws and commandments
> The King whom you bore. . . .[1]

Little wonder that some scholars mistook these catalogs for poems!

WHEN AN ITALIAN archaeological expedition excavated the mound of Tal Mardikh, forty miles south of Aleppo in northern Syria, they did not know that they would uncover the city of Ebla. Mentioned in Sumerian and Akkadian inscriptions, the city was destroyed by the Akkadians around -2250 and again by the Hittites in -1600. The Akkadians came with fire and sword; their burning of the city may have assured the survival of thousands of clay tablets until our own time.

Ebla was a large city, with a quarter million inhabitants, the capital of an empire extending into Palestine and the Phoenecian coast. Ebla's dynamic economy was based on international trade; it maintained commercial and cultural contacts with eighty kingdoms, including states in Anatolia, Babylonia, Egypt, and Persia. Two storerooms in the royal palace contained over fifteen thousand tablets, most of them commercial, legal, and administrative records. These were arranged on wooden shelves, supported on wooden posts sunk into the floor. When they were needed by the palace staff, the tablets were brought to their users on wooden boards. A portion of this archive served as a library for reference use by those working with business records: along the northern wall of the larger room was shelved a collection of dictionaries and syllabaries. These were also used by scribes editing definitive versions of literary texts. The library's collection included epic narratives, myths, hymns, incantations, rituals, and proverbs, as well as manuals of botany, zoology, mineralogy, and mathematics.

The Eblaites were prodigious makers of lists. Their catalogs of words, of objects, of place names, of species approached encyclopedic proportions. They compiled grammars and vocabularies of their own and neighboring languages, including bilingual Sumerian/Eblaite glossaries arranged on principles similar to those of today's dictionaries. One document, which archaeologist Giovanni Pettinato calls a "Gazetteer of the Ancient Near East," lists 288 place names in Syria, Palestine, and Mesopotamia.

To some extent the palace library at Ebla was a school library. It served as an academy for the training of scribes. But, like a modern university, this academy existed to create and preserve knowledge as well as to propagate it. The scholars of Ebla studied and extended the knowledge of the Sumerians. Scribes and scholars from Mari and the cities of Mesopotamia visited Ebla, bringing texts from their native lands and returning with texts from Ebla.

Ebla was not unique. At Mari, a city in what is now northwestern Iraq, and at the Hittite capital of Boghazkoy (Hattusha) in what is now Turkey, archaeologists have discovered similar archives. There are doubtless other sites in the Fertile Crescent, as yet unexcavated, from which we will learn more about the literary culture of the ancient world, and the libraries that preserved it.

UNLIKE THOSE OF ancient Mesopotamia, the libraries of Egypt and the Holy Land did not survive the civilizations that produced them. All that we know about them is what we can deduce from archaeological evidence, cultural history, and their literary remains. Where the Babylonians and Sumerians wrote on clay, the Egyptians used papyrus and the Hebrews leather, neither medium as durable. Some Egyptian writings have survived to our own time, inscribed on tombs and monuments, written on discarded shards of pottery, or inscribed on sheets of papyrus that have escaped the vicissitudes of climate and war. Practically no writing survives from the centuries of the Hebrew Bible; but the reverence accorded the word of God ensured the utmost attempts at faithful transmission of ancient texts, so that we can feel some assurance that the words we read today are substantially those of the authors of Scripture. But despite our lack of ancient manuscripts, we can make some reasonable attempts at describing the libraries of ancient Egypt and Israel: for the very survival of their cultures depended upon the careful preservation of the written word.

The traditions of art and learning that arose during the Early Dynastic Period (-3000 to -2500) played a major part in stabilizing Egyptian politics and society. Its bureaucracy was large and well organized, requiring an extensive network of scribes. These men were held in high regard: "As for those learned scribes from the time of those who lived after the gods, they who could foretell what was to come, their names have become everlasting, (even though) they are gone, they completed their lives, and all their relatives are forgotten."[2]

The ancient Egyptians had several uses for writing: they had to keep track of property ownership and tax payments, record the annual floods of the Nile, and extol the exploits of their kings. The palace maintained an extensive foreign trade, which would have required the keeping of accounts as well as the acquisition and preservation of geographic information, foreign language vocabularies, and records of military campaigns. Domestic administration depended upon census lists and civil service reports and memoranda. Surviving temple documents include duty rosters for priests and guards, inventories of temple equipment, and land and income records.

(For monumental inscriptions the Egyptians used hieroglyphics, pictures representing words or parts of words. Most Egyptian documents were written in the hieratic script, which combined hieroglyphics with syllabic signs descended from pictographic and ideographic symbols.)

The Egyptians revered tradition. The educated Egyptian saw himself as a link in the maintenance of tradition through the ages, and hoped to continue this work in the afterlife. He held in awe the power of the written word. "A man is perished, his corpse is dust, all his relatives are come to the ground—(but) it is writing that makes him remembered in the mouth of a reciter."[3] Perpetual fame would adhere to the king whose deeds were written down in hieroglyphs; and it was to deny them this fame that their successors would sometimes deliberately efface their signs.

"Copy your fathers who were before you; achievement is determined by knowing. See! Their words are made lasting in writing. Open the writings that you may read and emulate what is known. So the expert becomes the one who is instructed."[4] With these words an Egyptian scribe urged his son to prepare himself for a career in administration, an occupation for which literacy was an indispensable prerequisite. The education of scribes consisted of two parts. At first they learned the rudiments of writing and studied ancient literature. They inscribed their lessons on *ostraca* (potsherds and limestone flakes), writing out short selections from religious texts and models of correspondence. Surviving examples, which are full of mistakes, testify to the difficulty of learning hieroglyphic writing. Upon leaving school and taking up his first post, the young scribe continued to learn on the job. Now he wrote out his exercises on papyrus. These were corrected for calligraphy and style by his superiors.

Papyrus was made from the stem of a common reed, *Cyperus papyrus*, that grew extensively in the marshes of the Nile delta. By gluing sheets of papyrus together a book could be made as long as its author desired. (Manuscripts of up to forty meters have survived.) Papyrus rolls were stored in jars or in wooden chests, facilitating their use by traveling officials. To identify rolls, their owners would have the title or a description of the contents inscribed on the blank outer side, or would have a small papyrus or parchment label pasted to the roll. Thus it could be identified quickly with minimal handling.

Physicians and surgeons required ready access to written materials. During the early years of the fifth dynasty (-2750 to -2625), King Neferrirrkere's vizier, a man called Weshptah, suffered a stroke. An inscription on Weshptah's tomb records that "His Majesty [had] brought for him a case of writings."[5] One of the books in this portable library might well have been the *Book of Surgery*, which describes forty-eight cases and their recommended treatment. Its contents were incorporated into the much later *Secret Book of the Physician,* which has come down to us in the Edwin Smith Surgical Papyrus. This document has been dated to the Hyksos period (-1788 to -1580), but it is a copy of a much earlier work. It is now part of the New-York Historical Society's library.

The archives of Imperial Egypt (-16th to -14th centuries) were located in the temple compounds. In addition to records of military campaigns and business transactions, they preserved vital legal materials. "All their laws were written down in eight volumes," reported a Greek historian fifteen hundred years later.[6] The Egyptian civil service was headed by a *tjaty* (vizier), who was usually a relative of the king. One of his primary reponsibilities was the administration of justice, in connection with which he was enjoined to render decisions fairly and in accordance with precedent. Thus the records of previously decided cases would be consulted to determine the appropriate punishment for a criminal; and events far in the past could be recalled to settle a disputed inheritance or land claim. The archives of the vizier's office contained an extensive library of case law. Each of these documents bore the seals of the judge who decided the case and the scribe who wrote down the decision. We do not know how these were organized, or how the vizier would know which documents to consult. But consult them he did. After the vizier examined one, he placed his own seal upon it. Some documents were considered confidential; these were not released by their curators except under special circumstances.

The first explicit reference to an ancient Egyptian library dates from -1788. On a stela, King Neferhotep recorded his desire "to see the ancient writings of Atum." So "His Majesty proceeded to the library. His Majesty opened the rolls . . ."[7] This library (the Egyptian word means, literally, "house of writings") was part of the temple of Heliopolis.

The most famous library of ancient Egypt was that established in the -13th century by Rameses II, the "Ozymandias, king of kings" of Shelley's poem. It was part of the Rameseum, his funerary temple complex at Thebes. Like other Egyptian temples it contained a "House of Life," in which a picture gallery, library, and dining hall awaited the king's pleasure in the afterlife. Above the entrance to this "sacred library" was inscribed the phrase "Healing-place of the Soul." Its contents included both literary and practical works: poetry, fiction, history; agriculture, astronomy, engineering. Even in the prime of the Alexandrian Library, more than a thousand years later, men remembered the sacred library of Rameses II.[8]

ACROSS THE TIGRIS River from the Iraqi city of Mosul lie the twin mounds of Quyunjiq and Nabi Yunus, beneath which were found the ruins of the ancient Assyrian capital of Nineveh. The excavations of the 19th-century British archaeologist Austen Henry Layard at Quyunjiq uncovered more than twenty-five thousand tablets, which are now in the British Museum. They contain inscriptions identifying them as part of the Library of the Temple of Nabu, the god of wisdom in the Assyrian pantheon. Nabu served the gods as their scribe, and was patron of men of learning. In most Assyrian cities his temple contained a book collection. A library existed in the temple of Nabu in Nineveh during the reign of Sargon II (-721 to -705); but it reached its peak under Assurbanipal (-668 to -627), the last great king of Assyria.

Assurbanipal's father, Esarhaddon, had been fascinated by magic and astronomy. He collected old texts of rituals, oracles, and omens, sending messengers to find them in the temples of southern Mesopotamia. He was not only a collector; he made practical use of his library. There survives a record of his request to the palace official Ishtar-shum-eresh that he look up some curses. (We do not know precisely what Ishtar-shum-eresh's role was. Might he have been the first known librarian?)

The study of magical texts was an essential aspect of statecraft. Oracles and omens predicted disasters to come, but prayer and ritual could avert them. Future events might be revealed by the livers of sacrificial sheep, whose shape or markings could be interpreted by experts. These specialists referred to clay models of livers from previous sacrifices in preparing their predictions. Inscriptions on the models explained the omens they embodied.

Essarhaddon saw to it that his son was trained in scholarship as well as statecraft. Assurbanipal had received scribal training as part of his princely education, and he was himself a learned man with a taste for literature. One historian described him as "the sort of man who was never so happy as when curled up with a good clay tablet."[9] Assurbanipal claimed mastery of all the scribal arts: not only reading and writing, but also the making and baking of clay tablets. He collated, revised, and edited the texts collected for him by the scribes he sent to schools and libraries throughout his dominions.

Assurbanipal also received many texts from the private libraries of scribes and scholars. As students these men—physicians, exorcists, interpreters of omens—copied the scientific and literary texts that contained the basic knowledge of their professions. In later life their reading often extended into other learned fields. These texts, too, they copied in school and temple libraries, for there was no organized book trade.

The king was none too scrupulous in his methods. After a civil war led to Assyria's subjugation of Babylon, Assurbanipal seized the opportunity to augment his library with tablets confiscated from Babylonian collectors. He instructed a provincial governor to "bring forth all the tablets that are in their houses," and named several titles that he was especially eager to obtain. "And in case you should see some tablet or ritual which I have not mentioned to you and which is suitable for the palace, examine it, take possession of it, and send it to me."[10] But there were limits to the king's rapacity: he allowed his unwilling contributors to retain those texts essential to the practice of their professions.

Assurbanipal's library was a well-organized operation. It had its own factory for making tablets and its own kiln for baking them, to ensure high quality. These were inscribed carefully in a uniform script, with high standards of accuracy. In size they ranged from less than a square inch to the size of a legal pad; they were usually rectangular, and an inch thick.

They were arranged in series, so that all material on the same subject was gathered together. Literary works, such as the creation epic *Enuma elish* or the *Epic of Gilgamesh*, might occupy a dozen tablets or less. Mathematical, astrological, or magical collections included as many as a hundred tablets. Each tablet ended with a colophon giving its incipit and that of its successor in the series, as well as the series title (which was the incipit of the first tablet) and the tablet's number within the series. Many colophons included the owner's name and his instructions concerning the treatment of the tablet; others included the scribe's name and details of its compilation. Some colophons were grandiose in the extreme:

> Palace of Assurbanipal, King of the World, King of Assyria, who trusts in Ashur and Ninlil, whom Nabu and Tashmetu gave wide-open ears, and who was given profound insight: the finest of the scribal art—among my royal predecessors no one had grasped this message—the wisdom of Nabu, the signs of writing, as many as have been devised, I wrote on tablets, I arranged (them) in series, I collated (them), and for my royal contemplation and recital I placed them in my palace.—Your lordship is without equal, Ashur, King of the Gods!—Whoever removes (the tablet) and writes his name next to mine: may Ashur and Ninlil, angry and embittered, cast him down and erase his name, his seed in the land.[11]

Assurbanipal's collections were wide-ranging, and included approximately fifteen hundred tablets (not including duplicates). According to the British Museum, in which most of them repose today, "The principal subjects dealt with in the tablets are history, annalistic or summaries, letters, despatches, reports, oracles, prayers, contracts, deeds of sale of land, produce, cattle, slaves, agreements, dowries, bonds for interest (with impressions of seals, and fingernails, or nail marks), chronography, chronology, canons of eponyms, divination (by astrology, the entrails of victims, oil, casual events, dreams, and symptoms), charms, spells, incantations, mythology, legends, grammar, law, geography, etc."[12]

For hundreds of years, the Mesopotamian scribes had been standardizing the wording and the arrangement of their texts. The scribes of Assurbanipal's library continued this work, gathering multiple copies of documents to prepare definitive editions. (This has greatly helped today's Assyriologists to assemble coherent texts from surviving fragments.)

Their overriding concern was with the supernatural: predicting the future, averting evil, placating the gods, exorcising demons. Hundreds of "omen texts" recorded objects or events and the predictions derived from them. Each tablet contained between eighty and two hundred short entries. It must have been a formidable task to find the relevant omens from the tens of thousands in the collection. Meteorological and astronomical phenomena provoked queries to the royal astrologers; hundreds of their replies are preserved in the palace library. Spells, charms, prayers, and hymns were preserved in carefully-edited versions. And the letters sent by the kings to the omnipotent god Ashur and sealed within the library provide us with an account of their accomplishments more honest than those they intended for mortal readers. (These reports to the deity were not limited to annals and chronicles. Summaries of legal cases were included, to demonstrate the king's maintenance of traditional law and order during his reign.)

Fewer than five percent of the tablets at Nineveh contained what we would call literary or historical material. There were some king-lists and chronicles, but these were mere enumerations of rulers or events, devoid of any geographical, social, or economic context. Epic narratives and wisdom literature were preserved not for their literary merit but because they formed part of the curriculum of scribal education. There were poets in Mesopotamia, but we have not found their lyrics in Assurbanipal's library. Perhaps they wrote on wax-covered writing boards rather than on clay; perhaps theirs was strictly an oral tradition. Or perhaps we have yet to uncover the libraries that house their legacy.

For us, the most significant documents preserved in Assurbanipal's library were the legends of a great flood, known to us today as the *Epic of Gilgamesh*. These legends were collected from older Sumerian texts, and may have their origins fifteen hundred years before the time of Assurbanipal. This would make them older than the poems of Homer or the Bible: and there are hints that a version of the Gilgamesh story might have been known to the early authors of the books of the Bible. "Written down according to the original and collated in the palace of Assurbanipal, King of the World, King of Assyria," they have come down to us.[13]

It is fortunate that they did. In -612 the Medes and Babylonians so completely destroyed Nineveh that it was never rebuilt, and Assurbanipal's great library was buried beneath the rubble of the city.

> "The making of many books is without limit
> And much study is a wearying of the flesh."
> (Ecclesiastes 12:12)

WE CAN TRACE the books of the Hebrew Bible to various parts of the -1st millennium. As the *Encyclopedia Judaica* observes, "it is clear that the books that make up the Bible cannot possibly have comprised the whole literary production of ancient Israel." Throughout the Bible there are references to other books now lost to us. The *Book of the Wars of the Lord*, mentioned in Numbers 21:14, was apparently an anthology of poems celebrating Israelite victories over their enemies, as was the *Book of Jashar* (cited at Joshua 10:13 and II Samuel 1:18). These books, compiled in or before the -10th century, were consulted and quoted by the authors of the earlier books of the Bible.

The priests who maintained the Tabernacle at Shiloh collected legal, historical, and literary texts. From these they compiled the Deuteronomic narrative that has come down to us as the books of Deuteronomy, Joshua, Judges, I and II Samuel, and I and II Kings. The historian who wrote the Book of Kings in the -6th century cites as source material two sets of royal annals, the *Book of the Chronicles of the Kings of Judah* and the *Book of the Chronicles of the Kings of Israel*. Bible historians consider these to have been edited annals rather than actual records of the kings' own scribes; they were probably compiled in the -7th century. The biblical Book of Chronicles, written during the -4th century, similarly refers the reader to more than twenty books containing more detailed information than its author sees fit to include in his own account.

We know of these books because they are mentioned by name in the Bible. But what is the Bible? It is a collection of texts considered to be sacred, selected by priestly and rabbinical consensus for preservation, study, and liturgical use. This selection process ("canonization") took hundreds of years, beginning in the Babylonian exile (-6th century) and reaching completion only in the +2nd century.

A process of canonization implies not only a considerable body of literature from which works were chosen but also some means by which this literature was preserved and made available to those undertaking the selection. We know very little about this process. But from clues contained within the Bible itself we can make some educated guesses.

"When Moses had put down in writing the words of this Teaching to the very end, Moses charged the Levites who carried the Ark of the

Covenant of the LORD, saying: Take this book of Teaching and place it beside the Ark of the Covenant of the LORD your God, and let it remain there as a witness against you." Deuteronomy 31:24–26 is echoed by I Samuel 10:25: "Samuel expounded to the people the rules of the monarchy, and recorded them in a document which he deposited before the LORD."

The holy books were kept in holy places: the Ark of the Covenant, the tabernacle at Shiloh. This tradition continued in the days of the Temple. During the reign of King Josiah of Judah (-639 to -609), less than half a century before the Babylonian exile, the priest Hilkiah "found a scroll of the Teaching in the House of the LORD" (II Kings 22:8).

These scrolls were written on animal skins, a medium readily available to a pastoral people. Neither textual nor archaeological evidence exists to tell us how they were stored and retrieved for use. One possibility is that scrolls were kept in clay jars, which were used to preserve important legal records. ("Take these documents, this deed of purchase, the sealed text and the open one, and put them into an open jar, so that they may last a long time," Jeremiah 32:14.) Several hundred years later at Qumran the Dead Sea Scrolls were stored this way. If such jars were used to house treasures belonging to the Temple priests, Hilkiah's discovery of a long-lost "scroll of the Teaching" becomes easy to understand. Some priestly families or scribal schools may have stored their books in wooden or metal chests fashioned after the Ark of the Covenant.

Some Bible scholars believe that the offices of prominent scribes served as repositories for historical, literary, and prophetic texts. In Jeremiah 36:10 we are told that his disciple Baruch read Jeremiah's words from a scroll "in the chamber of Gemariah son of Shaphan the scribe, in the upper court, near the new gateway of the House of the LORD." A room in the Temple complex would have been a secure place in which to store sacred texts—and a most appropriate one.

But these are merely guesses; and unless biblical archaeologists make some fortuitous discoveries we may never know the truth.

2
LIBRARIES OF CLASSICAL ANTIQUITY

IF THE JEWS were the People of the Book, then the Greeks were a people of many books. But one of these books dominated the Greek view of the world and of themselves.

The central event in the historical traditions of the ancient Greeks was the Trojan War. Greek bards built a cycle of heroic poems around it, and several centuries after the event a great poet shaped from these lays an epic poem that to this day is regarded as a masterwork of world literature. The *Iliad* inspired and informed generations of Greek poets, and for centuries was regarded as a source of definitive knowledge and wisdom. No wonder, then, that the establishment and preservation of a definitive text of Homer was the primary concern of Greek scholars through the centuries.

The poems of Homer were transmitted orally, recited to audiences by professional rhapsodists. But were they also composed orally, or did their maker shape them in writing? Did those who recited them do so from memory, or did they have written texts to prompt them? The scholars of our century cannot agree. But that is little wonder: Homer was always the occasion for controversy among the learned.

When the -6th-century tyrant Peisistratus ruled Athens, one of his concerns was the establishment of a complete text of Homer. Legend has it that he offered a bounty for any lines missing from the *Iliad* and *Odyssey*. Legions of forgers seized the opportunity that this presented, leaving behind them work enough for generations of editors yet to come.

Peisistratus was not devoted only to Homer. He embraced the cause of letters in general. Aulus Gellius, admittedly not the most scrupulous of historians, recalls that:

> The tyrant Peisistratus is said to have been the first to establish a public library of books relating to the liberal arts at Athens. Then the Athenians themselves added to this collection with considerable diligence and care; but later Xerxes, when he took possession of Athens and burned the entire city except the citadel, removed that whole collection of books and carried them off to Persia. Finally, a long time afterwards, king Seleucus, who was surnamed Nicanor, had all those books taken back to Athens.[1]

The great philosophers of the -4th century assembled private libraries for their own use and that of their students. Plato was a poor man, but he managed to find the money to purchase the books of Philolaus of Croton, one of the Pythagorean philosophers, as well as a copy of the poems of Antimachus. His colleague Speusippus also had a small collection, some books from which were purchased at his death by Aristotle.

Aristotle's own books were produced with the aid of a personal reference library. His writings on the drama required the abstracting of performance records from the Athenian archives, and his comparative study of civic constitutions similarly depended upon access to a collection of these documents. It was Aristotle, and the Lyceum in which he taught, that made reading an essential part of education.

Upon Aristotle's death, leadership of the Lyceum passed to his pupil Theophrastus, to whom he bequeathed his library. Theophrastus, in turn, left it to Neleus, who had come from his native Scepsis to study under both Aristotle and his successor. As the geographer Strabo reports,

> Neleus took it to Scepsis and bequeathed it to his heirs, ordinary people, who kept the books locked up and not even carefully stored. But when they heard how zealously the Attalid kings to whom the city was subject were searching for books to build up the library in Pergamum, they hid the books underground in a kind of trench. But much later, when the books had been damaged by moisture and moths, their descendants sold them to Apellicon of Teos for a large sum of money, both the books of Aristotle and those of Theophrastus. But Apellicon was a bibliophile rather than a philosopher; and therefore, seeking a restoration of the parts that had been eaten through, he made new copies of the text, filling up the gaps incorrectly, and published the books full of errors.[2]

All this led, Strabo tells us, to a lot of worthless philosophy; and when the Roman general Sulla carried off the books to Rome as spoils of war, a plague of bad copies of Aristotle spread through the city.

But Aristotle had a more positive impact on library history. As tutor to the young Alexander of Macedon, he helped to shape the future king's character, an influence which was reflected in Alexander's success as general, ruler, and colonizer.

Of all the cities he founded—and historians know of at least sixteen certain Alexandrias—the greatest was the one that he created on the Egyptian coast. The architect Deinocrates' plan to carve Mount Athos into a heroic bust of Alexander never came to pass, but he produced a greater memorial. The Alexandria that Deinocrates laid out on the Mediterranean shore of Egypt was to become the metropolis of Hellenic culture.

A GREAT LIBRARY is a monument to permanence, and the greatest library of antiquity was a monument to the permanence of Hellenic culture. The classical culture of Greece—from Homer to Aristotle—did not rely upon libraries for its preservation. Classic Greece looked inward, despising other peoples as "barbarians" and having little use for such learning as they might possess. The Greek settlements along the shores of the Black Sea and the Mediterranean were seen as outposts in the wilderness, not points of contact with other civilizations.

The conquests of Philip and Alexander were conquests of Greeks by Macedonians, not the other way round. For all his veneration of Greek wisdom—remember that he was Aristotle's pupil—Alexander could recognize the accomplishments of the civilizations that he conquered. A man who carried along a copy of Homer wherever he traveled, he could appreciate the literary achievements of other nations. As he drove through the Fertile Crescent, across Persia, all the way to the shores of the Indus, he would have come into contact with their books—and their libraries.

To the ancient Greeks the nine Muses—daughters of Zeus the all-father and Mnemosyne. goddess of memory—personified the arts and sciences. Epic poetry, lyric verse, erotic poetry, sacred hymns, choral dance and song; comedy, tragedy, history, astronomy each had its Muse. In their schools the Greeks built *mouseia*, temples to the Muses, and there they were served and worshiped.

In the leading city of the new Hellenistic world arose the grandest of all these shrines to the Muses. Around -300, Ptolemy I, who had inherited the richest part of Alexander's empire, founded the Museion (Museum) of Alexandria. It was a religious institution, and its head was a priest appointed by the king. Its members were devoted to serving the Muses by advancing the arts and sciences. They were not contemplative or speculative philosophers, whose theories might lead to political unrest, but rather active scientists and literary men. They were scholars, not teachers, and they were meant to keep themselves aloof from mundane concerns. One modern historian of scholarship describes their situation enviously: "They had a carefree life: free meals, high salaries, no taxes to pay, very pleasant surroundings, good lodgings and servants. There was plenty of opportunity for quarrelling with each other."[3] And they had at their disposal the greatest library the world had ever known.

The museum was not only a center of scholarship and an ornament to the kingdom. It served a political purpose as well. Plutarch relates that its librarian Demetrius advised Ptolemy to "collect together books on kingship and the exercise of power, and to read them."[4] Alexandria was a new foundation, a Hellenistic outpost in an ancient land. Egypt measured its history in millennia, and its royal cities and pyramids displayed the grandeur of its past. One of Ptolemy's purposes in founding the museum was to Hellenize his new dominion. Toward this end he had the wealth of all Egypt at his disposal.

But the library was never limited to Hellenic literature. It collected the classic books of Greek poetry, and its scholars edited and arranged them. (Master copies of Homer's poems, edited by the scholars of Alexandria, were made available for copying by the public, and were used as exemplars by professional scribes who produced copies for the book trade.) The Alexandrian age was a time of creative and scholarly activity, producing original prose and verse, commentaries on earlier works, and a considerable scientific literature. There were books by native historians on the countries that Alexander had conquered, and translations of the Hebrew Scriptures, Egyptian chronologies, and the teachings of the Persian mage Zoroaster.

Archaeologists have not identified any remains that can unequivocally be assigned to the museum or the library; so our portrait must depend on circumstantial evidence, and on the arrangement of other libraries in the Hellenistic world. The scholarly consensus is that the library did not occupy a separate building, but was housed within the museum. Part of that building contained the library's administrative offices and workrooms for its staff, as well as the storerooms in which book-rolls were shelved. There may have been a reading room, but in the equable climate of Alexandria that would not have been a necessity.

The museum was part of the royal compound (the Brucheion), linked to the palace by a colonnade. Along the colonnade were "spacious exedras within three porticoes with seats, where philosophers, rhetoricians and all others who take delight in studies can engage in disputation."[5] In addition to this seating area, the courtyards of the museum offered ample room for reading and discussion, and made it possible for the peripatetic tradition of Athens to be maintained. Indoors there was "the common mess-hall of the men of learning who share the museum," and perhaps living quarters and study rooms as well.[6]

The library obtained its books in many ways. It had substantial funds at its disposal, and its emissaries must have been frequent visitors to the bookshops of Athens and Rhodes, the centers of the Greek book trade. So eager were they to complete their collections that they often fell victim to forgers, who found the counterfeiting of texts a lucrative business. There was a certain justice to this, for the library was itself none too scrupulous about how it filled its shelves. Ptolemy III Euergetes I, who reigned from -246 to -221, ordered that all ships calling at the port —and Alexandria had inherited Tyre's dominance of Mediterranean trade—be searched, and any books or manuscripts found aboard brought to the library. There copies were made and given to the owners, while the originals were added to the library's collections. It was this same monarch who borrowed from the Athenians their official copies of the plays of Aeschylus, Sophocles, and Euripedes, depositing fifteen talents—equivalent to well over a million dollars in our money—as security for their return. He kept the manuscripts, returned copies of them to Athens, and cheerfully forfeited his deposit.

Some of its books were produced by the library itself. The scholars of the museum wrote many volumes of prose and verse, and especially of commentaries on earlier works; these were deposited in the library. Translations were commissioned of important works in other languages. A famous legend attributes the *Septuagint* to the initiative of the royal librarian Demetrius of Phaleron. At his instigation, the king asked the High Priest to send seventy scholars from Jerusalem to translate the Hebrew Scriptures into Greek. Sequestered in a remote part of the city, the scholars worked in isolation from one another, each translating the entire work. When their completed translations were compared, they were found to be identical, proof to Jew and Greek alike that the scholars had been working under divine inspiration. (To this day, the *Septuagint* is the version of the Hebrew Scriptures used in the Greek Orthodox church.) This story is an embellishment of the truth: the Hebrew Scriptures had been translated into Greek for the everyday use of Alexandria's large Jewish community. But there can be no doubt that so important a book was well represented in the library.

When a shipment of books arrived in Alexandria it was marked with the name of the person who had brought them and then stored in a warehouse until the library staff had time to process the books. When they were brought to the library, the accession staff would label each roll either with its physical origin (where it came from or who had owned it) or its intellectual pedigree (who had edited or corrected the particular copy). This information would enable the catalogers to add the bibliographic details of each new book to the list of those by its author already in the library. Users could then consult the catalog to determine which versions of a particular work the library owned.

The library staff faced a difficult task, for the books they received were in every state of completeness and preservation. They had no title-page, table of contents, or index, no chapter headings or running titles; sometimes not even the name of the author or the title of the book. Threefourths of them were mixed rolls, containing more than one work; and larger books, such as the poems of Homer, would occupy several rolls. Unrolling a scroll in the hope that an incomplete volume might be identified from internal evidence was a time-consuming business.

The Librarian was appointed by the king, and had to be courtier as well as scholar. He served as tutor to the children of the royal family, and selected books for the king's reading. Chosen from among the leaders of Alexandrian intellectual life, the librarians often advised the king on political as well as literary matters. This sometimes got them into trouble; but for the most part they devoted their energies to science and literature. Their library duties left them time to make substantial contributions to scholarship.

The first librarian, Zenodotos of Ephesus, began the work of establishing an authoritative text of the *Iliad* and the *Odyssey*. Over the next century and a half the project was continued by two of his successors,

Aristophanes of Byzantium and Aristarkhos, who compared newly received Homeric manuscripts with texts already in the library. Zenodotos' immediate successor, Apollonius of Rhodes, wrote the *Argonautica*, an epic treatment of the Medea legend. He was followed in office by the polymath Eratosthenes of Cyrene, nicknamed *pentathlos* and *beta* because "he attained distinction in many fields, and ranked second only to the best in each."[7] He was poet and philologist, geographer and literary historian, whose book on ancient comedy was based on a careful comparison of manuscripts and performance lists; but it is as a mathematician that we remember him today. He calculated the circumference of the Earth, and his reckoning varies from ours by less than two hundred miles. The "sieve of Eratosthenes" is a method for determining the prime numbers.

Although some historians list him among the librarians of Alexandria, it is doubtful that Callimachus ever held that post. But he was among the greatest scholars to work at the library, where he produced the *Pinakes*. These "tables of persons eminent in every branch of learning, together with a list of their writings" occupied 120 books, of which only small fragments have survived. Such a literary encyclopedia made it possible for the student to plan for himself a rational course of reading in whatever subject interested him, offering opportunities for independent learning to anyone who could come to the library. It was not a catalog of the library's collection, being selective where the library tried to be comprehensive. But it could not have come into being without having the library and the work of its catalogers to draw upon. And, in turn, it served as the basis for many subsequent scholarly bibliographies.

Other eminent users of the library included the geographer Strabo, whose *Geography* borrowed from and corrected the books of Polybius, Poseidonius, and Eratosthenes. When the historian Diodorus Siculus visited Egypt to gather material for his book *On Egypt*, he conducted much of his research in the Alexandrian Library. Some used the library indirectly. Both Diogenes Laertius' *Lives and Opinions of the Eminent Philosophers* and Plutarch's *Lives* drew upon the *Bioi*, a literary encyclopedia compiled by Hermippus of Smyrna in the Library of Alexandria.

WHAT BECAME OF this greatest of libraries?

Like many another institution of the Hellenic world, the Library of Alexandria came to a lingering end. No single disaster destroyed its collections. A series of mishaps, combined with the attrition of centuries, put an end to the greatest library of the ancient world.

In -48, during Julius Caesar's brief Alexandrian War, the Royal Library was accidentally destroyed, or at least much diminished, by fire, with a loss of four hundred thousand rolls. The smaller collection of the Serapeum remained intact. With its resources, and the two hundred thousand books from the Pergamene Library that Plutarch tells us were Mark Antony's gift to Cleopatra, Alexandria still had library resources adequate to the needs of scholarship.

These needs were anyway diminished. By that time the library had lost much of its importance as a center for scholarly activity. The persecutions of Ptolemy VIII forced many scholars out of Alexandria, to the benefit of learning elsewhere in the Hellenic world and in Rome. After the Roman conquest of Egypt, the museum and library continued to exist, and scholarly work continued to be done in Alexandria. But Rome was now the center of intellectual life, and the leading thinkers and writers gravitated there.

Another more gradual conquest had its impact on Alexandria. With the triumph of Christianity, the pagan humanistic culture of the Hellenic world gave way to the theocentric worldview of the Church. Christians, so long persecuted by the state, now revenged themselves on their adversaries. Science and literature were of little value to the fanatics who dominated the city; and with the lynching of the philosopher and mathematician Hypatia by a Christian mob in +415, secular scholarship came to an end in Alexandria.

The Christians did not confine their fury to pagans. Arians fought with Athanasians; Monophysites and Monothelites battled those of Orthodox belief. In +391, Bishop Theophilus led a mob attack on the Serapeum, which they destroyed. Secular politics also brought strife to the city. The emperors Aurelianus in +272 and Diocletian in +295 sent troops into Alexandria to suppress revolts. By the time the Arab general 'Amr ibn-al-'As invaded Egypt in +641, the people of Alexandria were ready to accept both the rule and the faith of their new masters.

'Amr, so the story goes, sought the advice of the Caliph Omar, leader of the faithful. What should be done with the books of the infidels? The answer came back from Medina: see if they agreed or disagreed with the teachings of the Koran. Books in accord with the teachings of the Prophet were unnecessary; those contradicting them were iniquitous. The four thousand bath houses of Alexandria were heated for six months with the great library for fuel.

Is there any truth to this 11th-century legend? It was the Arabs who preserved the learning of the Greeks through the Dark Ages of the West. Would they wantonly destroy the literary treasures of Alexandria? Or should this crime against humanity be laid against Christian fanatics? Apologists for both religions have argued the point.

But by the time that 'Amr came to Alexandria, how much of the library remained to be destroyed? With its scientific tradition extinguished by religious fanaticism, and its rulers no longer interested in poetry and philosophy, the library was endangered as much by apathy as by outright attack:

neglect is as sure a destroyer of libraries as arson. How many of its rolls were eaten by mice or rotted by damp? How many were stolen, or abstracted by scholars to rescue them from the consequences of official indifference?

Despite the best efforts of bishops and generals, fanatic mobs and invading armies, the glory of the Alexandrian Library did not vanish in any single disaster. Over the centuries it faded away.

ALEXANDRIA'S WAS NOT the only great library of the Hellenic world. The Attalid rulers of Pergamon, a city near the Mediterranean coast of Asia Minor, aspired to surpass their Ptolemaic rivals. Attalus I, who reigned from -241 to -197, was himself a writer who enjoyed the company of literary men. He and his successors imported prominent Athenian scholars to their court, and surrounded themselves with masterworks of Greek art. They maintained a botanical garden and a zoological collection. And they built themselves a magnificent library.

Pergamon was built on a hill rising nine hundred feet above the surrounding plain. The upper part of the city was laid out in the form of four terraces, descending from the royal palaces to the *agora* where craftsmen and merchants plied their trades. On the second-highest of these terraces stood the precinct of Athena Polias, Pergamon's patron deity. Its west side was open, affording a view of the valley of the Selinus. On the other three sides it was enclosed with *stoas,* covered walkways attached to the surrounding buildings. These were adorned with columns and statuary. Where they opened into the courtyard, hangings protected visitors from the sun.

Behind the north *stoa* lay a series of rooms housing the Pergamene Library. In the largest of these stood a twelve-foot-high statue of Athena, who was goddess of wisdom as well as patron of the city. This copy of Phidias' famous sculpture looked out over a mosaic floor and the high windows that illuminated the room. Holes drilled into the walls supported wooden shelves, while in adjoining rooms bookcases occupied the walls. The largest of the library rooms held almost eighteen thousand rolls, visible to the public but accessible only to the staff. Smaller chambers served as reading areas, as well as workrooms for the preparation of newly acquired rolls.

At its maximum the collection may have included as many as two hundred thousand rolls. Its holdings in Greek literature and history were extensive, but in non-Greek materials Pergamon's collection was far inferior to that of cosmopolitan Alexandria. Pergamene scholarship was strongest in Homeric studies, geometry, and art criticism; there was little imaginative writing, and Pergamon produced no great literature. Erudition rather than creativity flourished in Pergamon.

Crates of Mallos, born around -200, is a leading figure in Pergamene scholarship. His biographical details are uncertain, but he is thought to have served as head of the library and to have compiled a catalog of the writers represented in its collections. A geographer as well as a literary critic, he built the first known globe. He was a traveler as well; and we shall see the impact that he had on libraries in Rome.

The rivalry between Pergamon and Alexandria was a fierce one. The Ptolemies discouraged scholars from removing to Pergamon. (One of the Ptolemies threw Aristophanes of Byzantium into prison to prevent his leaving the librarianship of Alexandria for Pergamon.) The Roman historian Varro would have us believe that the Ptolemies prohibited the export of papyrus, forcing the Pergamenes to invent parchment as an alternative. This story cannot be true; the ancient Mesopotamians occasionally wrote on parchment instead of baked clay. But Pergamon certainly was the chief center for the manufacture of parchment. The Pergamenes improved the preparation of animal skins for writing to such an extent that they became known as *charta pergamena*.

Soon after the city came under Mark Antony's rule in -41, he presented the Pergamene Library to Cleopatra, presumably to make good the losses suffered when Julius Caesar invaded Egypt. So came to an end the one library that aspired to competition with Alexandria.

This is not to say that other Greek cities did not have their libraries. Pella, the capital of Macedonia, was an active center of scholarship. Antioch in Syria had a public library by the end of the -3rd century; and the historian Malalas reports that a century later a *museion* "was built by Antiochus Philopator with the money left in his will by Maron of Antioch, who had emigrated to Athens and had then stipulated that there should be built with his money the shrine of muses and a library."[8]

ROME CONQUERED GREECE, and at the same time Greece conquered Rome. Rome first involved herself in Hellenic affairs to protect the Greek city-states from Macedonian domination; but she soon grew accustomed to interfering in the internal affairs of her Greek clients. Closer to home, she annexed the Greek cities of the Italian peninsula and Sicily. But Rome was not content to be acknowledged the most powerful state in the Mediterranean world; she coveted recognition as a civilized nation, heir to the Greek tradition. For two hundred years, Roman letters and Roman culture were modeled on Greek originals.

After Rome subjugated Greece, many Greeks from the Aegean cities as well as from Italy and Sicily found their way to Rome. Many served as tutors to Romans with cultural pretensions, for a knowledge of the Greek language and its literature soon became the hallmark of an educated person. Not only Greek teachers but also Greek books came in abundance to Rome, some through purchase and some as spoils of war.

In -168 Eumenes II, the king of Pergamon, sent Crates of Mallos on a diplomatic mission to Rome. He was detained there by a broken leg; during his enforced stay he gave a series of lectures which created an interest in literary studies among the Romans. It is likely that he told his audiences of the Pergamene Library and its treasures, for it can hardly be coincidental that the establishment of libraries in Rome began shortly after his visit.

When the battle of Pydna (-168) placed the Greek peninsula firmly under Roman rule, the Roman general Aemilius Paullus chose as his portion of the booty the library of the defeated Macedonian king Perseus. Paullus, who had been educated in the Greek tradition, carried this collection to the city of Rome. Other Roman generals brought their booty to their country estates. Lucius Cornelius Sulla moved the library of Apellicon, which contained books that had belonged to Aristotle and Theophrastus, from Athens to his villa at Cumae. The Roman statesman Cicero later used this library, and may have added some of its treasures to his own when Sulla sold his books at auction. And Marcus Licinius Lucullus, conqueror of Asia Minor, whose name has become identified with the enjoyment of fine food and luxury of every kind, was equally devoted to literature. His villa at Tusculum contained an enormous library, much of it taken from king Mithridates of Pontus. Lucullus placed his collection at the disposal of visiting scholars, and it became a home away from home for Greek scholars in Rome. Their host would often join in their discussions. His fellow Romans also used Lucullus's library; Cicero records encountering the younger Cato there.

Cicero's letters give abundant testimony to his bibliophilic interests. He maintained libraries at his palace on the Palatine Hill and his country estates, and made extensive use of them. He hired the Greek scholar Tyrannio to organize the library at his villa at Antium. "Since Tyrannio arranged my books," Cicero wrote to his friend Atticus, "the house seems to have acquired a soul."[9] Not every Roman library was so heavily used. Fashionable Romans assembled libraries in their town houses and country homes; the architect Vitruvius gave detailed instructions on their construction. "Among cold baths and hot baths a library also is equipped as a necessary ornament of a great house," complained the philosopher Seneca, disparaging the man "who seeks to have book-cases of citrus-wood and ivory, who collects the works of unknown or discredited authors and sits yawning in the midst of so many thousand books, who gets most of his pleasure from the outsides of volumes and their titles." In such a library the books might be inscribed on colored papyrus, wound on rollers tipped with ivory knobs, and the rolls covered with brightly colored cloth. Such ostentation disturbed Seneca, who asked "What is the use of having countless books and libraries, whose titles their owners can scarcely read through in a whole lifetime?" He urged his readers to "let just as many books be acquired as are enough, but none for mere show."[10]

Seneca would have approved of one Roman collector. The villa of Pisones at Herculaneum, buried when Vesuvius erupted in +79, contained a library of over eighteen hundred volumes. Most of the scrolls dealt with Epicurean philosophy, evidently a hobby of their owner, who housed them in a little room whose walls were lined with wooden shelves decorated with inlays of contrasting woods. A reading table in the middle of the room gave evidence that this was a library for use rather than ostentation.

Julius Caesar, who had visited the library of Alexandria at the invitation of Cleopatra, commissioned the eminent scholar Marcus Terentius Varro to organize a public library in Rome. It was to contain a temple and two book rooms, one for Greek books and one for Latin. Thus Rome would proclaim itself the equal of Greece in literary attainment. Caesar's untimely death prevented the realization of this plan. But during the reign of his successor Octavian (known to history as Augustus) Roman public libraries came into existence.

The first was founded in -39 by Gaius Asinius Pollio, a friend of the poets Vergil and Horace. He used the booty he captured in his Illyrian campaign to build a library in the Atrium Libertatis next to the Forum. It included both Greek and Latin books, but only one living writer was represented in its collections. Varro's portrait as well as his books graced the Latin section.

Augustus boasted that he had "found Rome a city of brick and left it a city of marble." He was determined to shape the city's form to reflect Rome's greatness, and his own. To this end he established two great libraries, one in the Portico of Octavia in the Campus Martius, the other in the Temple of Apollo on the Palatine Hill near the imperial residence. Following Julius Caesar's plan, each contained a temple and separate chambers for Greek and Latin books. The Palatine Library was renowned for its law collection, and was heavily used until its destruction by fire in +192.

It became customary for emperors to found libraries: Tiberius, Vespasian, and Trajan built them at Rome, while Hadrian's sumptuous library at Athens brought forth this encomium from the +2nd-century Greek travel writer Pausanias: "Gold and alabaster glittered from the ceiling of the great hall. Wonderful frescoes decorated the walls. Everywhere stood statues of great writers of prose and verse."[11]

The great hall of an imperial public library served as reading room and lecture hall. Some were brightened by artificial lighting, which not only facilitated reading on dark days but also showed off to advantage the fine marble and expensive woods with which they were decorated. In the storerooms the scrolls lay on open shelves, with parchment labels hanging from wooden rollers. Codices, kept in chests, were few in number; the papyrus scroll remained dominant. Scientific works were produced in large format, while smaller rolls were used for poetry. Books were brought to the reading rooms for use there; they did not circulate except to the emperor and his intimates.

Roman libraries were not limited to the capital; they were found in provincial cities and resort towns across the empire. Many were located within public baths, which served as social and cultural centers. In the larger ones care was taken to keep the scrolls well away from the steam baths, lest the highly absorbent papyrus be damaged by moisture. Tivoli, where wealthy Romans often summered, maintained a comprehensive Greek and Latin library which even lent out books for home reading.

THE PAPYRUS SCROLL remained the dominant medium for book publication. During the +1st century parchment was coming into use, but only as a medium for composing literary works before copying them to papyrus for distribution to the reading public. It would be several hundred years before the parchment or vellum codex replaced the papyrus scroll. (Properly speaking, parchment is made from sheepskin, while vellum comes from the skins of calves; but the two terms are often used interchangeably.)

That transition did occur, and there were several reasons for it. Parchment and vellum are stronger than papyrus, allowing longer works to be produced in one volume. They were more widely available than papyrus, which grew only in warm climates; vellum and parchment could be had wherever people ate meat. Their surface lent itself to calligraphy and illustration, offering the possibility of the book as a work whose physical beauty might equal—and even transcend—its literary content. True, they were more difficult to prepare than papyrus. But in the monasteries of Europe there arose a class of men who had the time and the skill to devote to that task.

It was in fact the rise of the Christian Church that stimulated the evolution of the book as we know it today. Just as animal skins replaced plant fibers, so the sewing of folded sheets between covers replaced the pasting together of flat sheets into rolls. The new medium made it possible to use both sides of the writing-surface, and more sheets could be sewn between two covers than could be fastened to a roller. So it was possible to include all of Scripture within one volume; and it was easy to read that volume and find specific passages in it, an advantage that will be evident to anyone who has ever struggled with microfilm. There was another reason for Christians to embrace the codex: it surved further to differentiate them from the Jews, for whom the Torah scroll was increasingly emblematic of their faith now that their Temple was destroyed.

By the beginning of the +4th century, the codex might be encountered as frequently as the roll. Two centuries later it had displaced the roll almost completely. By the end of the +4th century the imperial library had begun the conversion of its collections from papyrus rolls to vellum codices. Other libraries and bibliophiles did the same. This was a substantial project, and it required librarians to decide which books were worth the labor and expense of transcription. No doubt there were many writings that were not judged worthy. But the transition to the codex did not work entirely to the diminution of letters.

The codex, by making possible the inclusion within one volume of a writer's entire works, tended to increase the chances of a famous writer's lesser works surviving. Its large capacity encouraged the production of anthologies and other composite works; some of these contain the only extracts of important classical texts to have survived into our own time.

3
LANTERNS OF THE DARK AGES

IN FOUR HUNDRED years a messianic cult from the east had become the dominant religion of the Roman empire. The persecution of Christians ceased, and martyrdom was reserved for missionaries bringing the gospel to the heathen peoples at the fringe of the empire and beyond. A life of prayer and renunciation came to replace a martyr's death as the ideal of Christendom. As the Church began to imitate the pomp of empire, the simplicity of the monastic life attracted an increasing number of Christian men and women.

Christian ascetics had gravitated to the deserts of Egypt and Syria since the beginning of the 3rd century, imitating Jesus who was "led away by the Spirit into the wilderness" (Matthew 4:1). The most eminent of these anchorites attracted disciples to their hermitages, some of which grew into substantial communities. By the end of the century there were monastic societies in most of the Mediterranean lands.

The first monasteries were devoted to the mortification of the flesh and meditation on the word of God. Literature was of no importance, except as an aid to prayer: Scripture, sermons, and service books were the only books to be found in them.

Rules for the governance of monastic communities were promulgated by their founders and by the bishops in whose dioceses they were situated. One of these codes, written by St. Benedict of Nursia for his monastery of Monte Cassino, was gradually adopted throughout western Europe. Benedictine monasticism has flourished into our own time, and has exerted a substantial influence on the intellectual life of Europe.

BY THE END of the 5th century the might of Rome no longer dominated the West. The barbarians who invaded the Italian peninsula were at least nominally Christian; their rulers were at least nominally literate. But they had little use for, and little interest in, the literary culture of Rome. The public libraries of the city and the provinces disappeared: some to the sack, some to the torch, many to the neglect of those who, for lack of imagination or surfeit of piety, despised the treasures they contained.

The empire did not fall overnight; indeed, a remnant of Rome held out in Constantinople for another thousand years. And Roman culture did not vanish from the western Mediterranean in an instant. Though the intellectual life of the cities might have declined, the countryside was not a cultural desert. Roman aristocrats had always spent much of their time on their country estates, where literature was considered a pursuit excellently suited to a gentleman.

During the reign of Theodoric (493–526), who brought peace to northern Italy, both Romans and Ostrogoths read and collected books. Wealthy collectors, especially men of the senatorial class, were scholars as well as bibliophiles; they were responsible for the preservation and textual revision of many of the Greek and Roman classics. Their libraries contained Christian writings as well as those of Greek philosophers, scientists, and historians. (At the beginning of the 7th century, Virgil the Grammarian spoke of the common practice of maintaining two separate libraries, one for Christian books and one for pagan literature—an echo of the Roman custom of maintaining separate libraries for Greek and Latin books.) It was to these libraries that cultivated men turned to escape the turmoil of the barbarian invasions.

But we must realize that these "barbarians" had been in contact with Rome for hundreds of years. They were literate, and they were Christian—even if their Arian beliefs differed in some essentials from those of the established church. They regarded themselves as the legitimate heirs of the Roman cultural patrimony. The 5th and 6th centuries saw a widespread production of books—pagan and Christian, legal and literary—in Italy, Spain, and Gaul.

As scholarly institutions disappeared, secular learning declined. This happened at an uneven rate in western Europe: by the second half of the 7th century, the Frankish invasions had left no remnant of scholarship in Gaul, while the Spanish royal library at Toledo contained profane as well as sacred works. The Spanish aristocracy was widely read; even Bishop Isidore of Seville read Vergil as well as Christian poets. Many monks came from noble families; their piety did not extend so far as to require them to abjure secular literature. They often devised eloquent apologies for pagan letters, and were ingenious at finding in them prefigurations of Christian truth.

Toward the end of the 5th century, Flavius Aurelius Cassiodorus was born to an aristocratic family in northern Italy. For most of his life he served the empire, now seated at Ravenna, in various bureaucratic capacities. After fifteen years' service in Byzantium, he returned to his native land; in his sixties he became a monk, founding a monastery of his own at Squillace on the Italian peninsula's southern coast. The Vivarium owed its name to the ponds in which its monks kept fish alive, and its fame to the intellectual and literary activities that flourished there.

In his younger days, Cassiodorus dreamed of founding a Christian university at Rome, and began to gather books for its library. The Gothic War of the 530s put an end to both library and university. His dream was realized, on a smaller and more transient scale, at the Vivarium. By the 560s the abbey's library contained a substantial collection of scriptural texts and commentaries, as well as grammars and ecclesiastical histories. But secular literature was held in low esteem at the Vivarium, and was valued only to the extent that it could be used as an aid to the study of Scripture.

The most important use made of the Vivarium library was in the preparation of authoritative texts of the Bible. The study of God's word was central to Cassiodorus's idea of the monastic life. He emphasized the importance of establishing and preserving the most authoritative of the ancient texts, and was reluctant to discard any potentially useful material. Even in the case of so unorthodox a writer as Origen, he preferred to mark doubtful passages with a warning sign rather than expurgate them. He was not unique in this. Many medieval librarians surreptitiously helped to preserve writings condemned by the Church by obliterating the authors and titles of heretical books, or attributing them to writers whose orthodoxy was unquestioned.

THE VIVARIUM DID not long outlast its founder. Its impact on medieval cultural life was a limited, and in some ways negative, one. The manuscripts copied there were primarily religious books for the monastery's own use. Very few found their way to other monasteries during the Vivarium's existence; after its demise most of the books were sent to the Lateran Library, the papal library in Rome. From there they gradually spread across Europe, as papal gifts to eminent visitors or new foundations, or as exemplars from which copies were made for other libraries. Cassiodorus's insistence on the primacy of Christian literature helped to put an end to the translation of pagan classics commissioned by wealthy laymen, a practice that did not resume until the days of Charlemagne.

Cassiodorus wrote the *Institutiones*, "an introduction to divine and human readings," which combined a manual of monastic practice with a syllabus of theological study. Scripture itself and the commentaries of the Church Fathers were the main elements of Cassiodorus's program, but grammar and history, science and mathematics contributed to the understanding and appreciation of God's creation. The *Institutiones* guided the curriculum of many monastic and cathedral schools and served later monastic libraries as a list of desiderata.

The Vivarium was not the only center for scriptural studies in 6th-century Italy. The library at Lucullanum, near Naples, contained manuscripts of the Gospels, Augustine's letters, the works of the theologians Origen and Rufinius, and Eugippius's Augustinian *Excerpta*. Monte Cassino, "the mother cloister of all western monasticism," was founded in 529—the same year in which the Emperor Justinian closed the Academy that Plato had founded in Athens. Benedict of Nursia established its system of government; this Benedictine Rule spread throughout Catholic Europe, and eventually came to govern almost every medieval monastery.

WHEN ST. PATRICK arrived in Ireland (432), he brought with him not only the Christian religion but also the Roman alphabet. These found a receptive audience. The ancient Irish love of language and literature had expressed itself in an oral tradition transmitted by the druidic schools that covered the island. Nourished by this tradition, learning flourished in the abbeys that spread across Ireland during the 6th century. (Their expansion may have been aided by refugee scholars fleeing the Frankish invasion of Gaul.) In these abbeys secular as well as Christian literature was read, so that students might improve their mastery of Latin the better to understand sacred books.

Each abbey contained a *teach screptra* (house of writings) in which books were stored in *polairi*, satchels made of embossed leather, which were hung from the walls on wooden pegs. These satchels were also used to carry books from one monastery to another, and to hold the books that accompanied Irish pilgrims on their travels.

Western Europe was familiar with the Irish monks "who, for the mortification of their bodies, and salvation of their souls, live in exile from their country, and go about visiting holy places."[1] The Irish abbeys trained many monks who traveled to Britain or the Continent, establishing new monasteries from which to spread the faith. These foundations included libraries and scriptoria. Collections brought by their founders were augmented by books brought from Ireland by newly arrived missionary monks and by pilgrims partaking of monastic hospitality on their way to Rome.

One of the first of the Irish missionaries was Columba, often known as Columcille, who was born in 521 to one of Ireland's ruling families. From childhood he combined an aristocratic temperament with a love of learning. As a student he would wander the country in search of books new to him. These he would copy, when he could get their owners' permission. In one famous instance he could not, but copied the text anyway. Columba's former teacher Finnian owned one of the finest book collections in Ireland. One of his treasures was Jerome's translation of the Bible, which though completed over a century before was little known among the Irish. Finnian was so possessive of this book that Columba knew better than to ask leave to copy it; so he did so surreptitiously, transcribing the manuscript by night. When Finnian discovered this, he demanded that Columba turn over the copy. The latter refused, and the matter was brought before Diarmit, the High King of Ireland. "Finnian's book has not decreased in value because of the transcript I made from it," Columba claimed. But Diarmit rendered a judgment based in the traditional Brehon law of Ireland: "To every cow her calf, to every book its transcript."[2] And he awarded the copy to Finnian.

This was the first copyright dispute in Western history; and it was one of the factors leading to Columba's exile from Ireland. Sailing across the Irish Sea, he founded on the island of Iona off the Scottish coast a monastery from which Christian teaching and Christian learning spread across northern Britain. At Iona the missionary monks studied and copied the Scriptures and the lives of saints, and trained generations of Church leaders and scholars.

ALTHOUGH THE IRISH abbot Columban (540–615) valued asceticism over scholarship, the monastery that he founded at Bobbio in northern Italy developed over time a reputation for intellectual activity. At first this was devoted primarily to the fight against heresy; the presence of Arian manuscripts in Bobbio's library attests to a need to know the enemy. But Bobbio's location on the way to Rome and its possession of Columban's holy relics ensured the monastery a steady stream of Irish pilgrims. By the 9th century, their gifts and the products of a busy scriptorium had made the Bobbio library the most important in peninsular Italy, with 666 titles in its catalog. Though most of these were religious books—Bibles, liturgical works, Church Fathers, canon law, theology, commentaries, homilies, and hagiographies—Bobbio also had works by Aristotle, Vergil, Cicero, Ovid, Terence, Martial, Perseus, Juvenal, Pliny, Lucan, Valerius Flaccus, Cato, Orosius, Cassiodorus, and Boethius, as well as several historical and mathematical works. We owe to the Bobbio library the texts that we have of many classics of Roman literature—texts that were copied at Bobbio from manuscripts once housed in the villas of Roman patricians. Our debt to the monks of Bobbio is philological as well. Many of its Latin manuscripts contain words glossed in Old Irish; such glosses are a valuable source of information on the history of the language. So devoted were they to the propagation of literature that they even erased biblical texts so that the parchment they covered could be reused for Latin grammars.

Unlike the monasteries of northern Europe, Bobbio's decline cannot be blamed on the depredations of the Northmen. It fell victim to Christian plunderers: its location midway between the papal seat in Rome and the cities of Imperial Germany enmeshed Bobbio in politics. By the 10th century its abbacy had become a sinecure for the emperor's favorites, and internal dissension had put an end to intellectual activity.

WHEN POPE VITALIAN sent the Greek monk Theodore to England as archbishop of Canterbury (668), he provided him with a learned assistant. The abbot Hadrian was educated not only in canon law but also in sacred literature, both Latin and Greek. Placed in charge of the cathedral school, Hadrian transformed the provincial training center into a seminary drawing students from the British Isles and continental Europe. At Canterbury students read the secular classics of Greece and Rome as well as Christian books. (In Ireland and England, Latin was not the language of everyday speech as it was in Italy, Spain, and Gaul but a foreign language that had to be studied. One result of this was that Irishmen and Anglo–Saxons wrote a purer Latin than did continental Europeans, whose language was already beginning to devolve into Italian, Spanish, and French. Another was the need to adapt existing Latin grammars and to compose new ones. Many of these were brought to the British Isles from insular—that is, Irish or English—monasteries on the Continent.)

During the lifetime of Benedict Biscop (628–690), the Celtic tradition was giving way to the Roman in Britain, and the Benedictine Rule was steadily replacing the more ascetic code of Columban in European monasteries. The twin monasteries that Benedict Biscop founded in the north of England—St. Paul at Monkwearmouth and St. Peter at Jarrow—lay at the confluence of these forces: both Iona and Canterbury helped to define their religious and intellectual life.

From his visits to Rome, Benedict Biscop brought many books back to England. Some were gifts from the pope, including manuscripts produced at the Vivarium; others were purchased. (There was still a flourishing book trade in Rome, producing religious manuscripts for ecclesiastical purposes and for the pilgrim market. Monasteries often provided their monks traveling to Rome with funds to buy books.) Many of Benedict's acquisitions went to Wearmouth and Jarrow. The Wearmouth library possessed Cassiodorus's copy of the Vulgate, the works of the Church Fathers, Christian and pagan poetry, historical and scientific books, and copies of records from the papal archives.

With these treasures at his disposal, Benedict's student Bede was the best-read and most prolific writer of his time. Among his teachers were men who had been pupils of Theodore and Hadrian at Canterbury. Bede's *Historia Ecclesiastica Gentis Anglorum* (Ecclesiastical history of England) is regarded to this day as an historiographical masterpiece; in addition he produced a wide range of scientific, historical, and theological works. He also used the library resources at his disposal to compile anthologies for the use of monasteries with more limited collections.

The life of a monastic scholar was not an easy one. Bede complained that in addition to "innumerable duties in the monastery, I have to make my own shorthand notes while reading my sources, to copy out the passages I take from these, and to write my books themselves with my own hand."[3] But it was all for the glory of God and the salvation of men's souls, and Bede delighted in it.

Another center of learning in the north of England was the cathedral school of York, founded by Bede's pupil Egbert. Like that of Canterbury, it had been established to train the secular clergy, the priests who administered the sacraments and taught the rudiments of the Christian faith to their countrymen. Egbert's successor, Archbishop Ethelbert, was especially devoted to its library, which he built into the finest in Europe. The collection was described in Latin verse by his pupil Alcuin:

> There shalt thou find the volumes that contain
> All of the ancient fathers that remain;
> There all the Latin writers make their home
> With those that glorious Greece transferred to Rome—
> The Hebrews draw from their celestial stream,
> And Africa is bright with learning's beam.
> Here shines what Jerome, Ambrose, Hilary thought,
> Or Athanasius and Augustine wrought.
> Orosius, Leo, Gregory the Great,
> Near Basil and Fulgentius corruscate.
> Grave Cassiodorus and John Chrysostom
> Next Master Bede and learned Aldhelm come,
> While Victorinus and Boethius stand
> With Pliny and Pompeius close at hand.
> Wise Aristotle looks on Tully near.
> Sedulius and Juvencus next appear.
> Then come Albinus, Clement, Prosper too,
> Paulinus and Arator. Next we view
> Lactantius, Fortunatus. Ranged in line
> Virgilius Maro, Statius, Lucan shine.
> Donatus, Priscian, Probus, Phocas start
> The roll of masters in grammatic art.
> Eutychius, Servius, Pompey, each extend
> The list. Comminian brings it to an end.
> There shalt thou find, O reader, many more
> Famed for their style, the masters of old lore,
> Whose many volumes singly to rehearse
> Were far too tedious for our present verse.[4]

Tedious as it is, this list bears witness to an important fact: the domination of Latin over Greek literature throughout western Europe.

Traveling homeward from a mission to Rome, Alcuin met Charles the Great. Impressed with the Frankish king's devotion to learning, Alcuin accepted the energetic monarch's invitation to join his court and help with his ambitious plans to spread the Christian faith throughout his dominions. In his palace at Aachen, Charlemagne established a substantial library. This supplied the books that were read aloud each day to accompany the emperor's dinner: Charles was fond of history and of Augustine's *City of God*. The court library also included ancient Frankish poetry and texts on Germanic grammar, for Charlemagne was proud of his Frankish forbears. Ancient works were collected from across western Europe—"Who could even count the books which Your Majesty's decrees have gathered from every land?"[5] exclaimed a monk on Charlemagne's staff—and copies made from them spread classic texts to cathedrals and monasteries across Charlemagne's empire. Books on practical topics—architecture, surveying, agriculture, medicine, the art of war—helped to train the bureaucracy that ran the empire. Charlemagne expanded the Palace School, which had previously existed to tutor royal children, into a training college for leaders of church and state, and placed Alcuin at its head.

Under Charlemagne's direction and Alcuin's administration, monasteries played an increasing role in the multiplication of books and the teaching of letters. Charlemagne urged bishops and abbots throughout his realm "not to neglect the study of letters, but to learn eagerly for this end, that more easily and rightly you may penetrate the mysteries of the Divine Scriptures."[6] Teachers of grammar and music were to be appointed, so that in speech, writing, and chant the message of the Church might be made as attractive as possible to all men. Acting on imperial orders, the monasteries translated the essential works of the Christian faith (the Lord's Prayer, the Creed, and the Benedictine Rule) into German, so that neither layman nor religious would be ignorant of its basic principles. Charlemagne's concern for the monastic propagation of knowledge extended to the smallest details: he even ordered that monasteries be provided with forests, where game might be hunted to furnish leather for bookbinding.

Alcuin stoutly upheld the value of secular books, maintaining that the knowledge they contained could be used to further the purposes of the Church. The liturgical calendar, for example, depended upon astronomical calculations; Alcuin declared that "they were the wisest of men who discerned these arts in Nature. It is a great disgrace for us to let them die out in our time."[7]

After Charlemagne's death, his son Louis the Pious narrowed the range of monastic education. Anthologies of excerpts from the Church Fathers dominated the monastic curriculum, and the study of belles-lettres, Christian or secular, was discouraged.

THE MONASTERY OF Fulda was one of many owing its foundation to the English missionary bishop Boniface (680–755). An ardent bibliophile and a copious epistolarian, his letters to friends in England are full of requests for books. His dedication to the Fulda library was maintained by his successors; Abbot Sturmi (744–79) kept forty monks at work in the Fulda scriptorium. To help missionaries preach to the northern pagans in their own language, Fulda produced manuscripts in the German vernacular as well as in Latin. Much of the Old High German literature that has survived to our day we owe to the Fulda scriptorium and library; and many of the Roman historians' works were preserved there as well.

Rabanus Maurus, who was abbot from 822 to 842, claimed that Fulda had the largest library in Germany. Its breadth is evident from Rabanus's own books, for he borrowed liberally from a wide range of earlier writers. That was not the only borrowing that took place at Fulda. So many books were lent to monasteries in France and Germany that an exchange catalog had to be kept. Fulda's influence was not transmitted only by the written word: Fulda trained many of the monks who later taught at St. Gall.

From the 9th-century *Plan of St. Gall* we can get some idea of what the ideal monastery should be. Though the Plan was not completely executed, it embodies the Carolingian idea of how a monastery should be organized; it influenced the design of Benedictine and Cistercian monasteries throughout medieval Europe. The monastery church at St. Gall, and the buildings joined to it, including the library, appear to have been built in substantial conformity to the Plan.

The Carolingian monastery was the hub of a self-contained community. It planted and harvested cereals and vegetables, baked bread and brewed beer, maintained fishponds, herb gardens, and orchards, and tended flocks of poultry and herds of livestock. While monks were permitted meat only in case of serious illness, milk, cheese, and eggs were important parts of the monastic diet; and the calves and lambs that they raised supplied vellum and parchment for monastic scribes, who wrote with quills supplied by the monastery's geese. By the end of the 7th century, parchment had completely replaced papyrus in books and charters. Both were expensive, but parchment could be produced locally while papyrus grew only in warm climates, and the Arab conquest of Egypt in 634 had cut off the West's supply. Parchment was more durable, providing an excellent substrate for rubrication—the use of red ink to highlight important words— and illumination—the use of miniature paintings to illustrate or decorate the text. And unlike papyrus, parchment could easily be erased and reused. This was fortunate, for the production of parchment was insufficient to meet the needs of European scribes.

The library and scriptorium were vital parts of the monastery, and the Plan called for them to be situated between the two schools that the monastery maintained. The Outer School educated the sons of the nobility as well as aspiring secular priests. Many of its graduates would serve the emperor or his vassals as clerks or scribes. The Inner School trained oblates and novices for the monastic life. Their advanced training may have taken place in the scriptorium and library.

On the northern side of the monastery church, a two-story building housed the scriptorium on the ground floor and the library on the upper level. This location provided both scribe and reader with diffused north light and protected them from the glare of the sun. The library was allotted a space of sixteen hundred square feet, but it was not the only place in the monastery devoted to the storage and use of books. While the main collection was housed there, liturgical books were kept in the church or the sacristy; each of the two schools had its collection of books used for teaching; and the daily reading of the monks was supplied from a separate collection.

The scriptorium provided books for the monastery's own use as well as for other monasteries and ecclesiastical and political leaders. Books to be copied were borrowed from other monasteries, sometimes from far away: manuscripts were frequently exchanged with Bobbio and Monte Cassino for this purpose. Sometimes a scribe would be sent to a distant monastery to copy a book needed at his own cloister; or a trade might be arranged, with two monasteries each copying a manuscript from its own library to fill a void in the other's collection. To speed up the process a borrowed book might be dismembered, allowing several copyists to work simultaneously. Manuscript copying was difficult work. The scribe Eadbeorht, a British monk at St. Gall, complained that "those who do not know how to write do not think that it is labor; it is true that only three fingers write, but the whole body toils."[8]

In the central library the books lay on their sides in *armoria* (wardrobes), where they were protected from the cold and damp of the unheated monastery. Several of these cabinets would have been needed in a Carolingian library; in the middle of the 9th century, Reichenau possessed 415 books, and St. Gall had 400. While most of these were religious works, some were medical treatises; there were at least eight of these at St. Gall. The books were in the care of the *bibliothecarius* (or *armarius*), whose responsibility extended to the scriptorium as well as to all of the monastic book collections. This was a reflection of the broadened scope of monastic libraries: in an earlier age, when the collection consisted almost entirely of service books, the choirmaster also served as librarian. The monastery's holdings were listed by subject in a catalog; this subject sequence also governed their arrangement on the shelves.

WHY WOULD A monastery need a library?

The Rule of St. Benedict made the reading of Christian literature a basic part of the monastic life. "Idleness is the enemy of the soul," declared the Rule. "Therefore, the brothers should have specified periods for manual labor as well as for prayerful reading." One of these reading periods was Sunday, when "all are to be engaged in reading except those who have been assigned various duties." As the Rule forbade private property of any sort, the brothers must draw their books from a common store. The Rule's provisions for Lenten reading make this clear: "each one is to receive a book from the library, and is to read the whole of it straight through."[9] This stipulation required a monastery to possess at least one book for each of its monks, in addition to the psalters and hymnals used in daily worship, the school texts used for classroom instruction, the saints' lives and biblical commentaries read aloud at mealtimes, and the legal, medical, and technical books used by administrators and specialists. A 9th-century commentator explained how the monks received their books:

> The librarian with the aid of the brothers takes all the books to the chapter meeting. There they spread out a rug, upon which the books are placed. After the regular business of the chapter meeting has been concluded the librarian announces from the check-out list the titles of the books and the names of the monks to whom they had been lent in the preceding year. Thereupon each brother deposits his book on the rug. Then the provost, or anyone else to whom he may have delegated this task, collects each book, and as it is being returned, he probes the brother with questions whether he has diligently studied his assignment. If the response is satisfactory, he inquires of the brother which book he considers to be of use to him in the coming year and provides him with the desired book. However, if the abbot finds that a desired book is not suited for a brother who asked for it, he does not give it to him but hands him a more suitable one. If the interview establishes that the brother was derelict in his study, he is not given a new book, but asked to study the old one for another year. If the abbot finds that the brother has studied with diligence, but is nevertheless not capable of comprehending it, he gives him another one. After the brothers have left the chapter meeting, the abbot sees to it that all books that have been entered in the check-out list are accounted for, and if they are not on record, searches until they are found.[10]

In addition to the required individual reading, the monks listened to books while they dined. Some of the codices in the library were marked *ad legendum* (for reading), and were read out in the refectory by brothers chosen for their strong voices and careful diction. Saints' lives were often chosen for this purpose; an abridged version of Adamnan's *Vita Columbae* was prepared specifically to be read at mealtimes.

The library also served the monastery's teachers and administrators. Students in the inner and outer schools learned the rudiments of grammar and composition by listening to their teachers read from the works of acknowledged masters, or from *formulae*, compilations of specimens illustrating various types of prose composition. More advanced instruction used Cicero and Quintilian as textbooks of rhetoric, and Vergil and various Christian poets as models of verse. Theology was taught from the Bible itself with the commentaries of the Church Fathers, and Pope Gregory I's *Cura Pastoralis* (Book of pastoral care). Other subjects included arithmetic and geometry, natural history, astronomy, and music. While most of the books were in Latin, there were a few Greek manuscripts; but Aristotle and Euclid were represented only in Boethius's Latin versions. Notker Balbulus ("the Stammerer"), who was abbot of St. Gall at the end of the 9th century, translated many books from Latin into German, the better to prepare his pupils for the study of Scripture and theology.

The abbot and his deputies would need to consult legal works—textbooks on canon law, collections of capitularies (imperial edicts), and the *Leges Barbarorum*, a codification of Germanic custom—and treatises on agriculture, surveying, and other aspects of estate management. Notker and other composers of hymns and liturgical works prepared themselves by studying Christian and pagan poetry and works on grammar and poetics. The needs of the infirmary were served by medical anthologies, excerpting the works of Galen and Hippocrates, and books on drugs and herbs.

Many of the books contained fine calligraphy and beautiful decorations; the Carolingian minuscule, vastly more legible than the insular scripts it replaced, forms the basis of our own writing and printing. Some books were covered in carved ivory tablets, others in leather-covered boards, still others in vellum wrappers.

Other than Cassiodorus's *Institutiones* there was no literature on library organization; nor was there any organized training for librarians. Experienced librarians sometimes shared their expertise, traveling to a neighboring monastery to catalog its collection. Monastery libraries collected catalogs of books owned by other institutions. This made it possible to locate manuscripts which might be borrowed for copying or for preparing a definitive text.

Books were often lent to outside readers: bishops, secular clergy, the local nobility. Laymen and women often borrowed books for Lenten reading; they were usually required to leave their own books, or other objects of equal value, as security against the borrowed books' return. When a book was lent, a notation would be made in the library catalog; another would be made to mark its return. Lending was done as a favor to the borrower, or as a courtesy to a powerful ecclesiastical or temporal authority. There was no recognized right to borrow books, no public libraries that either an ancient Roman or a 20th-century westerner would recognize.

In Carolingian times, monarchs, ecclesiastics, aristocrats, and scholars often owned small libraries. Books represented not only religion and scholarship but also wealth. The materials that went into a book were expensive— a 9th-century copy of the works of Vergil required more than fifty skins— and each volume represented a substantial expenditure of labor. Among the aristocracy, ownership of books, like possession of land, was a mark of wealth and social status. (It had its practical side, too: law books and treatises on agriculture and military science covered topics of immediate interest to the nobility.) Because books were so valuable—and so portable— a monastery would take the same precautions to protect its library as it would to safeguard its altar plate and priestly vestments. Among these precautions would be an inventory of its holdings; these evolved into library catalogs.

The monks who flocked to these Carolingian monasteries were not slaves or peasants—whose masters had other plans for them—but members of aristocratic families. Often well educated, they brought with them a taste for literature formed early in life, often at the very monasteries in which they took their vows. While in theory they were supposed to abjure pagan writings, they often found reasons to continue to read secular literature: as a help to understanding Scripture, or to improving their prose style. They and their families were generous with their gifts, allowing the monasteries to devote less effort to subsistence and more to intellectual works. This, along with the scholarly bent of Charlemagne, explains why Carolingian monasteries were more literary than those of earlier centuries.

But these monasteries were not attractive only to monks with a taste for literature. Their wealth was known beyond the borders of the empire, and drew the attention of the barbarians who threatened its peace now that its rulers lacked the strength of Charlemagne. Many Irish monks were driven from their island by the Northmen, whose dragon ships brought robbery and destruction to any monastery within range of a seacoast or navigable river. The Saracens burst out of Arabia to conquer the Iberian peninsula, and destroyed many abbeys along the Mediterranean coast. And Hungarian invaders nearly despoiled St. Gall, forcing the evacuation of its library to the more secure island stronghold of Reichenau.

HEIR TO THE grandeur that was Rome, the Byzantine empire was at first Roman in fact as well as in name. Constantine the Great issued his edicts in Latin, and regarded the bishop of Rome as head of the universal catholic Church. But as the Germanic tribes overran the empire's western half, the east increasingly reverted to its Hellenic roots. Though the emperor Justinian (r. 527–65) spoke Latin and issued his legal code in that language, his court and the writing it produced both were Greek.

Much of the Byzantine empire was lost to the Arabs during the first decades of their eruption from the desert. Monophysite Christianity, which though condemned as heretical had spread across Egypt and Syria, found Islam less alien that the convoluted theology of Constantinople; and the exchange of Byzantine overlords for Arab masters left the erstwhile Christians of the southern provinces none the worse off. By 647, thirty-two years after Muhammad's flight to Medina, Alexandria had fallen to the Arabs, and the Byzantine empire was reduced to Asia Minor, the Balkan coastline, and Sicily.

Like their Hellenic ancestors, the Byzantines founded both their education and their literature on the poems of Homer. Learning and beauty were universally admired among the upper classes, and offered an avenue of upward mobility to their social inferiors. Another delight of affluent Byzantines was theology; the Bible ran a close second to Homer as a literary and cultural influence.

Constantine founded a school, and Julian (r. 361–63) attached to it a public library. It contained 120,000 volumes and received enthusiastic imperial support. The emperor Valens in 372 ordered that seven antiquarians be hired to restore the library's existing Greek and Latin manuscripts and make new copies. The library maintained its own scriptorium, and also purchased books from the great monasteries of Constantinople and Mount Athos.

But after this library burned in 476, public access to books was limited. There were libraries in the major churches and monasteries, but they were of limited scope: at Patmos only 15 of the library's 330 books were of secular content, and more than half the books were liturgical. Wealthy bibliophiles easily amassed large collections; the empire had a flourishing book trade, and fine books were a celebrated Byzantine export. (This trade made its substantial contribution to the emerging Arab libraries.) Scholars often enjoyed access to private collections, but in their letters they often write of the need to borrow books from one another.

As the empire declined in strength, so did it also decline in culture. Books were scarce and very costly. The imperial library was housed in a single room; it was not a large one. Literary activity increasingly took the form of compilation and commentary. Religious controversy descended from the recondite to the riotous; in the 8th and 9th centuries the worship of images was alternately condemned and condoned, for reasons as much political as theological. A church council called in connection with this dispute relied for texts on the patriarchal library of Constantinople; its collection did not contain many of the books required, which had to be sought in the libraries of churches, monasteries, and private collectors.

During most of this period the patriarchate was controlled by the Iconoclasts. The Orthodox opposition, who incorporated into their worship the veneration of images, were denied access to the patriarchal library. They built up their own libraries in the monasteries, obtaining many of the books they needed from their fellow monks in Palestine and other parts of the Arab dominions.

Though the 'Abbasid civilization of Baghdad inspired a brief cultural renewal during the reign of Theophilus (829–42), Byzantium never fulfilled the promise of its Hellenic origins. Norman adventurers in the west and Seljuk Turks from the east closed in on the empire; but it was the Crusaders who destroyed the Byzantine achievement. They sacked Constantinople in 1204, dispersing and destroying the treasures of centuries. When the city fell to the Turks in 1453, it was almost an anticlimax.

4
LIBRARIES OF THE ORIENT

THE CHINESE INVENTED writing so that they could talk to the gods. When a sacrifice was offered, a blessing sought, or the future foretold, a written record accompanied the transaction. These "oracle bones," written on ox bones or tortoise shells, are the oldest surviving Chinese writing; some of them date from the Shang dynasty of the -2nd millennium. It was during the Chou dynasty (-1122 to -256) that Chinese literature truly began. Communication among the royal and subordinate governments, and among government agencies, produced large quantities of documents, which led to the establishment of archives at royal and feudal courts. These were so highly prized that chroniclers recorded as a major event the defection of an imperial archivist.

A group of books produced during this period came to be known as the Five Classics. Later generations often called them the Confucian Classics, identifying them with the great moral philosopher K'ung fu-tzu (-551 to -479), known to westerners as Confucius. His precepts for harmony and righteousness within the family and the state have shaped Chinese culture for twenty-five hundred years; they are set forth in a collection called the *Analects*, which quotes frequently from the Classics.

The *I Ching* (Book of changes), a handbook for interpreting the future by casting stalks of milfoil and observing the patterns into which they fell, was the oldest of these. The *Shu ching* (Book of history) collected speeches and other oral records of early rulers and their advisors. The *Shih ching* (Book of odes) was an anthology of lyric poetry. The *Li chi* (Book of rites) was the most important of the Ritual Texts that governed Chinese ceremonial life. The *Ch'un ch'iu* (Spring and autumn annals), ascribed by tradition to Confucius himself, chronicles his native state of Lu between -722 and -481; a voluminous body of commentary grew up around it to amplify its terse account of those years.

Chinese historians believed that these books dated from pre-Confucian times, a claim not always upheld by modern scholarship; later generations believed them to have been improved by the master's own hand. Confucian teachings greatly influenced the way in which these books were read by later generations, and they formed the basic subject matter for centuries of scholars and civil servants.

Chou aristocrats were trained from childhood for careers in state service. In addition to the arts of war they studied the ancient literature. Some specialized in scribal work, serving as court historians. It was upon their accounts that the future reputation of kings and dukes would rest, which assured that these rulers would take a lively interest in the creation and preservation of literature. Some of the members of this new intellectual class owned extensive book collections. The diplomat Su Ch'in owned several dozen trunks of books, and the philosopher Mo Ti traveled with enough books to fill five carts.

During the Chou dynasty the first Chinese libraries came into existence. The minister of religion, who supervised the performance of rites and ceremonies, "was entrusted with the custody of books of the three great sovereigns and the five rulers."[1] A similar responsibility for books relating to his duties was laid upon the minister of education, whose work included the compilation of the calendars that guided the planting of the kingdom's farmers. Other officers, called recorders (*shih*), were detailed to maintain the court archives. One of the curators of these archives, Lao-tse, is traditionally considered to be the first Chinese librarian.

CHINA WAS UNIFIED under the Ch'in dynasty (-221 to -207), which gave its name to the country. As part of its program to centralize political power, the Ch'in government simplified and standardized the writing system, and undertook to eliminate books subversive to its unification efforts, which were opposed by Confucian scholars. To this end, Grand Councilor Li Ssu sent a memorial to the emperor:

> Your servant suggests that all books in the imperial archives, save the memoirs of Ch'in, be burned. All persons in the empire, except members of the Academy of Learned Scholars, in possession of the Book of Odes, the Book of History, and discourses of the hundred philosophers should take them to the local governors and have them indiscriminately burned. Those who dare to talk to each other about the Book of Odes and the Book of History should be executed and their bodies exposed in the market place. Anyone referring to the past to criticize the present should, together with all members of his family, be put to death. Officials who fail to report cases that have come under their attention are equally guilty. After thirty days from the time of issuing the decree, those who have not destroyed their books are to be branded and sent to build the Great Wall. Books not to be destroyed will be those on medicine and pharmacy, divination by the tortoise and milfoil, and agriculture and arboriculture. People wishing to pursue learning should take the officials as their teachers.[2]

This "burning of the books," which one historian calls "China's first cultural revolution,"[3] was not totally effective. Books were hidden by their owners, often in the walls of their houses; enough were preserved to assure the survival of the Confucian Classics.

The Ch'in empire was succeeded by the Han (-206 to +220), which defined the cultural life of China to our own century. The emperor

convened great meetings at which scholars determined the correct interpretation of the Five Classics, and professors were maintained at court to
expound them. The Han founded an imperial training school to educate
candidates for high office; lower positions were filled by competitive examinations administered by the court scholars. An imperial library was formally established, to collect the officially approved versions of the Classics.
Private possession of the Classics was once again permitted, and efforts
were made to establish proper texts of these books and disseminate them
through the empire.

This task was made difficult by the format in which books were produced. Each page was a narrow strip of bamboo, on which a single verti-
cal line of characters, each representing an entire word, was inscribed. Its
light weight and smooth finish made the under surface of the bamboo stem
an excellent writing substrate. Bamboo tablets were prepared by cutting the
hollow stem into cylinders, which were then split lengthwise into tablets.
The green skin that covered them was scraped off and the tablets dried over
a fire. Bamboo was a forgiving material: mistakes could be corrected or
tablets reused by planing down the surface. There were several standard
page sizes, ranging from eight inches to the two-foot-four-inch tablets used
for the Classics, which held thirty characters each. The tablets were strung
together with silk, hemp. or leather cords to make a book that could easily be rolled up for storage or travel.

The Han emperor Wu Ti, who reigned from -140 to -87, "set plans for
restoring books and appointed officers for transcribing them, including
even works of various philosophers and the commentaries, all to be stored
in the imperial library."[4] Rewards were offered for the loan of books from
private collections, and imperial agents scoured the country in search of
texts, this time to preserve rather than to destroy them. As was the case in
Alexandria, the generous bounty offered provided many with incentive for
the forging of books.

Wu Ti's successor Ch'eng Ti, who reigned from -33 to +7, appointed a
commission of experts "to examine, compare, revise, and collate the contents of the repositories."[5] Royal advisor Liu Hsiang led the effort; his fellow commissioners included a commander of infantry, the grand historiographer, and the imperial physician. Liu's report of the commission's work,
the Pieh lu, was a catalog of the imperial collection, annotated to record
differing versions of texts. It was the first of its kind in China. His son, Liu
Hsin, devised the first Chinese book classification, dividing books into
seven categories: general; Six Classics; philosophy; poetry; military science;
astronomy and mathematics; and divination, medicine, and trades.

The Han emperors were not motivated purely by a love of learning.
Their reliance upon Confucian doctrine to justify their claim to rule China
made it prudent to ensure control over the details of that doctrine. By using

the Imperial Library to canonize the version of the Confucian Classics most amenable to their pretensions, and by making Confucian scholars dependent upon governmental largesse, they succeeded in harnessing the teachings of Confucius to their own purposes. Later rulers emulated this strategy, some going so far as to rewrite the Classics to serve the needs of the state.

> *Silk will decay,*
> *Bamboo is not permanent,*
> *Metal seems hardly eternal,*
> *And vellum and paper are easily destroyed.*
> —Juan Yüan[6]

TOWARD THE END of the Han dynasty, between +175 and +180, the Five Classics and the *Analects* of Confucius were carved on stone steles on the grounds of the Imperial University. This was done in order to preserve the standard text that had so painstakingly been established since Wu Ti's time. It took both sides of forty-six stones to contain the more than two hundred thousand characters. Curious onlookers crowded to see the stone tablets, while scholars used them to make copies for study. The prospective user would stretch a thin sheet of moistened paper across the stone, brushing it into every character carved into the stele. After the paper was dry, ink was applied across it; this would leave blank the places where the paper had been pushed into the carved stone, producing a sheet of white writing on a black background. Government officials called "makers of rubbings" would provide copies upon payment of a fee.

This practice long survived the introduction of printing, as succeeding dynasties incorporated the latest textual criticism into their stone texts: an edition of the Classics was carved between 1791 and 1794. Nor was it confined to Confucian literature. Buddhists undertook similar projects so that their sacred writings might survive periods of religious persecution. In a grotto near Hopei a library of 105 Buddhist sutras was started in +605; when the work was completed in +1091, over four million words had been carved on more than seven thousand steles. Taoists also used stone carving to preserve their literary canon. (It was during the latter part of the +5th century that Buddhist and Taoist books began to appear in the catalogs of the imperial collection.)

During the +3rd century, under the leadership of its curator Hsün Hsü, the Imperial Library copied bamboo books onto paper. Paper had been invented in or before the -2nd century, but was not used for writing until early in the +1st century. It was a cheap writing material: a single worker could make two thousand sheets of paper in a single day. (Compare the cost of one day's wages to the value of the two hundred animals whose skins were required to make one parchment or vellum codex in Europe.)

It was the same Hsün Hsü who compiled a catalog of the Imperial Library that set a bibliographical standard that lasted for fifteen hundred years. The books were divided into four main classes: classics, histories, philosophers, and collected works. (The first of these categories included philology, lexicography, and music as well as the Confucian Classics and the extensive writings about them. "Histories" included geographical and legal works, while "Philosophers" extended to astronomy, divination, medicine, botany, horticulture, and military strategy. "Collected works" included most forms of imaginative writing. This division of knowledge, though unusual to Western eyes, was in accordance with the Chinese scholarly tradition.) Each of the four classes was denoted by one of the first four cyclical letters of the Chinese notation, creating the first book notation system. The catalog, written on fine silk and stored in silk bags, listed 29,945 *chüan*. (The *chüan*, the basic bibliographical unit in traditional Chinese literature, corresponds to a chapter, in the same way that a "book" in the *Iliad* or *Odyssey* does. It represents the capacity of a scroll or folded book.)

As dynasties came and went, amid invasions and rebellions, both the Imperial Library and private collections suffered heavy losses. So important were books to the Chinese that every interval of peace saw attempts to re-create the collections that had been destroyed.

DURING THE FOUR centuries (+220 to +589) between the fall of the Han dynasty and the rise of the Sui, China was frequently divided into mutually hostile states. When the country was reunified under the Sui (+581 to +618) and the T'ang (+618 to +907), scholars at the imperial court justified the new political order in Confucian terms. Thus the Sui and T'ang emperors, like their Han predecessors, had an interest in the text of the Confucian Classics and in the commentaries and dynastic histories that accompanied them on the shelves of Chinese libraries. Precedents were sought in earlier dynasties for T'ang policies; creativity in finding appropriate precedent was a quality much valued in a court scholar.

Even during the "Six Dynasties" period between Han and Sui, when China was divided into northern and southern states, the Imperial Library was maintained and cherished by China's rulers. When China was reunified under the Sui dynasty, the library was maintained in a style befitting a great empire. A bounty was offered for rare books: a bolt of silk for each *chüan* lent for copying. A chronicler records its splendors in the reign of Yang Ti (+605 to +617), the last of the Sui emperors:

> Fourteen rooms in front of Kuan-Wen Court served as imperial reading-rooms. The doors, windows, beds, mattresses, bookcases and curtains in these rooms were all lavishly ornamented. For every three rooms, there was a square opening with brocade curtains hanging down and two figures of flying fairies atop. A mechanical device was placed on the ground outside of the rooms. When the Emperor visited these reading-rooms, a servant holding a

censer would precede. As he stepped on the device, the flying fairies would come down and pull open the curtains up to the top of the doors. The doors of the bookcase would also open automatically. When the emperor left, the doors would close and the curtains come down again.[7]

Such an establishment required a large staff: in one year (+615), 120 people were added. They were responsible for the Kuan Wen Tien at Lo-yang, with two wings housing the library, as well as two buildings, one each for antiques and paintings. The books were treated as works of art, their quality indicated by the rods around which they were rolled. The finest were given red glazed rods, the medium grade rolled on rods of dark blue, and those of inferior quality rolled on lacquer rods.

Much of the collection was lost in +622 while being shipped by boat from Lo-yang to Ch'ang-an, the new T'ang capital. But, as had been done under the Han, a search was made throughout the empire for books to replace those that had been lost. Twenty collators and over a hundred copyists toiled to restore the collection, and a T'ang chronicler reports that "after a few years the imperial library was gloriously and wholly complete."[8]

"Though the empire had been won on horseback, it could not be governed on horseback."[9] As the imperial bureaucracy became more elaborate in its structure and more pervasive in its influence, the role of the Imperial Library and of other scholarly institutions became more clearly defined. Advisory colleges, consisting of one to two dozen scholars together with support staff, were created to provide the emperor with counsel based on a sound knowledge of history and precedent. They also produced and compiled documents for the state: law codes, collections of imperial rescripts, literary anthologies, and commentaries on the Classics. This activity commanded more prestige than such worldly topics as law, medicine, and mathematics, subjects also studied in the imperial court. The advisory colleges usually had their own libraries; that of the Chi-hsien Yüan (College of Assembled Wise Men, founded in 725) grew to become second only to the Imperial Library itself.

The Court of Sacrifices was in charge of the extensive program of state ritual that secured the dynasty's relationship with the ancestral spirits. Changes in the rituals, which were proposed from time to time in order to increase the prestige of the emperor or to restore usages extant in past dynasties, required scholarly justification, which was sought in the Confucian literature. Thus an important part of the Court of Sacrifices was its library.

Another new scholarly institution was the History Office, which was responsible for compiling the official dynastic history, a task that under earlier dynasties had often fallen to the Imperial Library staff. The dynastic histories were deposited in the Imperial Library, along with necrologies of important functionaries and official chronicles. These histories were compiled for political as well as scholarly purposes: by recounting the Chin dynasty's (+265 to +420) successful rule of a united China, and by tracing the auspicious origins of the present dynasty, they helped to demonstrate the legitimacy of T'ang rule. They went beyond dynastic origins and achievements in scope, including monographs on such topics as ritual, music, the calendar, astrology, the five elements, economics, law, offices and posts, geography, and bibliography.

The main task of the Imperial Library was to collect, preserve, and catalog the best of Chinese literature. Acceptance of a new work into the Imperial Library bestowed upon it a seal of approval that was eagerly sought after. The ability to compose prose and verse was highly prized among scholars and rulers alike, and the best compositions were collected in extensive encyclopedias. Earlier works, too, were collected to inspire T'ang writers. In order to make such compilations possible, it was necessary to catalog the library. Surviving catalogs from previous dynasties served as checklists of books to be searched for and recopied into the library collection.

New commentaries on the Classics were added to established ones, providing that they respected the limits of permissible dissent. A subsidiary office, the Bureau of Compositions, wrote prayers for the state rituals whose proper performance sustained the dynasty's legitimacy, and supplied texts for official functions. The library's responsibilities embraced the future as well as the past: the Bureau of Astrology came within its purview.

By the end of the +7th century, the Imperial Library contained tens of thousands of scrolls. Staff members—some of them women—were deployed to edit and to repair its books. Special care was taken to prepare and preserve the paper on which they were written. Fine paper was brought in from Szechuan, as was ink from Hopei and fifteen hundred rabbit skins each year for brushes. The imperial government took an active interest in papermaking. During the +8th century, the Imperial Library had ten papermakers on its staff, a practice emulated by other scholarly agencies. Private collectors took an active interest in preservation, and many of the books that they collected have survived in remarkably good condition to our time. With such demanding customers, manufacturers designed paper for longevity and durability.

During the peaceful T'ang years, literacy increased, more books were produced, and private collectors accumulated large libraries. In the early 8th century at least two private libraries rivalled the Imperial Library in size. A catalog of the Imperial Library in Ch'ang-an compiled in +721 listed 3,060 titles in 51,852 *chüan*. Ten years later the collection had grown to 89,000 *chüan*. In addition to the libraries at Ch'ang-an, substantial collections were maintained at the eastern capital of Lo-yang. Posts at the Imperial Library were greatly coveted, and were awarded to some of the brightest young civil servants. These were selected by competitive examinations that tested knowledge of the classics and talent in literary composition.

The civil service examination system, with its emphasis on scholarship rather than high birth as a qualification for high office, stimulated the development of private collections. As the T'ang educational system deteriorated in the late +8th and +9th centuries, leading families anxious to preserve their role in the bureaucracy established *shuku*—clan libraries—to collect the books their sons would need to master. These evolved into private colleges for family members. Examination candidates without access to *shuku* had to resort to private lending libraries.

In the middle of the +8th century, military setbacks abroad and a revolt at home substantially reduced the authority and prestige of the T'ang dynasty. The Imperial Library suffered damage during the rebellion of renegade general An Lu-shan; once again it became necessary to scour the empire for lost works. The library became a sinecure for ailing and elderly bureaucrats, so much so that it acquired the nickname of "sick ward for chief ministers."[10] But its junior staff continued to be recruited from the most able examination graduates.

THE 10TH CENTURY was an unsettled period, known to historians as the Ten Kingdoms period (in the south) and Five Dynasties (in the north). As the T'ang dynasty came to an end at the beginning of the 10th century, the Imperial Library suffered serious losses. By the time the capital moved from Ch'ang-an to Lo-yang, its holdings had been reduced to ten thousand *chüan*. But under the Sung, who came to power in the latter half of the 10th century, literature and scholarship revived. The introduction of woodblock printing multiplied the copies of the Confucian Classics and other books, contributing to the growth of official libraries and private collections. (Many professional woodblock carvers were illiterate, but they could faithfully reproduce the distinct calligraphy of individual writers even without understanding the words they carved. The resulting woodblocks might be stored for many years and used for repeated reprintings.) As a skilled printer could produce well over a thousand copies in a day, the production of printed books was much cheaper than manuscript copies or stone rubbings. Thus it was possible to distribute a 130-volume edition of the Classics widely across China.

The world's earliest surviving book on the craft of librarianship was *Lin-t'ai ku-shih* (A tale of the national library), written by Ch'eng Chü (1078–144). Based on a study of earlier Chinese libraries, it was written to encourage the reestablishment of an imperial library after the destruction unleashed by the invasion of the Jurched hordes from Manchuria. Ch'eng argued that such a library was essential to good government. It offered aspirants to the civil service the books they must read to prepare for selective examinations, and allowed the experiences of earlier rulers and the wisdom of former sages to be applied to contemporary issues. Ch'eng Chü also emphasized that the library would be an invaluable resource for scholarly editors, historians, and encyclopedists. In addition to listing the purposes served by a national library, *Lin-t'ai ku-shih* explained the technical aspects of library work—the processes of acquisitions, cataloging, classification, and circulation—as well as the selection and management of library staff and the design of a building fit to house the national library.

Ch'eng succeeded in persuading the government to reconstitute the Imperial Library. Losses were made good by private collectors, who donated books or lent them to be copied. Their participation was not entirely altruistic: donors were rewarded with bounties of money and silk, and the more generous were afforded the opportunity of nominating candidates for the civil service examinations.

The celebrated scholar Cheng Ch'iao (1103–62) was deeply concerned with the preservation of China's literary heritage. "I do not worry about the book sources for the library collections," he wrote. "I am really distressed that there are no rules and regulations for collation. I have now written the book *Jiao chou luo* in order that there are no people who hold posts without qualification in the national library, that there are no books that are eaten by silverfish, and that there are thousands of books that are circulated through the national library." *Jiao chou luo* (The theory of library science and bibliography) set forth "eight methods for collecting and purchasing books" which have been cited and praised ever since by Chinese bibliophiles and librarians. To ensure competence in cataloging the collection, Cheng urged that catalogers be given long-term appointments. Comparing a poorly organized library to "an undisciplined army that made soldiers scattered and lost," he urged the need for careful subject classification based on a thorough examination of each book. All this preparatory work being completed, the books were now ready for circulation—and it was this purpose, Cheng felt, that justified the expense and effort of building a library.[11]

Ch'eng Chü and Cheng Ch'iao were not original theorists; rather, their work embodied contemporary Chinese thinking about the purpose, arrangement, and management of libraries. Although their work had no impact outside of China, it influenced Chinese practice for centuries. It was a good five hundred years before anything like it was published in the West.

Under the Sung, the primary purpose of the Imperial Library was the preservation of literature and the establishment and maintenance of authentic texts of the Classics. While government officials were encouraged to consult the library—where they might read such works as Ssu-ma Kuang's (1018–86) *Tzu-chih t'ung chien*, a comprehensive history whose title (chosen by the emperor himself) meant "The Comprehensive Mirror for Aid in Government"—borrowing privileges were restricted. To prevent the loss of Imperial Library books, they were copied onto special paper, making stolen copies readily identifiable and thus unsalable.

Determining a definitive text of the Confucian Classics became more important as the system of recruiting government officials by competitive examination became established. The Imperial Library had collected rubbings of texts from the surviving Han stone engravings. Based on these and on the texts collected therein, Imperial Library officials worked to compile a definitive edition of the Classics, an effort that culminated in the *K'ai-ch'eng shih ching*. This stone engraving of the Nine Canons—the Five Classics and four later works associated with Confucius and his followers—was intended "to display a model for ten thousand ages."[12]

DURING THE 15TH-CENTURY flowering of Chinese culture and economy under the Ming dynasty, the Imperial Library was enriched and numerous private collections were established. The *Yung-lo ta tien*, an immense encyclopedia drawn from over seven thousand titles in various arts and sciences, was compiled and copied by a corps of three thousand scholars between 1403 and 1408. Written by hand, it extended to 22,937 *chüan* bound in 11,095 volumes. Only one additional set was made; the compilation was never printed, and fewer than 400 *chüan* survive today.

A love of literature and a desire to get ahead in the world have both contributed to the development of private libraries throughout Chinese history. The "burning of the books" was directed largely at private collections, some of whose owners risked death hiding their books in hollow walls instead of surrendering them to the emperor's police. Many an emperor solicited or extorted books from his bibliophilic subjects; and the many restorations of the imperial libraries after catastrophes depended upon copying manuscripts from private collections.

A Chinese gentleman was expected to be an aesthete and a scholar, or at least to affect these roles. Many high officials, and some members of the imperial family, had a genuine love for literature and sought out the company of poets and scholars; some achieved a reputation for literary accomplishment that has come down to our own time. Several of these amateur scholars accumulated substantial libraries and shared them with others. The Chin dynasty (+4th century) bibliophile Fan Wei not only opened his library but provided meals and lodging to the readers from across China who came to consult his books; over one hundred scholars accepted his hospitality. In the middle of the +9th century Su Pien, an official in the revenue department, owned the third largest library in the empire: only the Imperial Library and that of the Chi-hsien Yüan were greater.

During the Ming period, many local princes were amateurs of the book. This taste was adopted by merchants, especially those who had been enriched by franchises from the imperial salt monopoly. They collected rarities, undertook literary scholarship and belles lettres, printed fine editions, and built private libraries. The scion of one merchant family, an official named Yang Hsun-chi, described the bibliophilic urge in a poem called "Inscribed on the Doors of My Bookshelves":

> Mine was a trading family
> Living in Nan-hao district for a hundred years.
> I was the first to become a scholar,
> Our house being without a single book.
> Applying myself for a full decade,
> I set my heart on building a collection.
> Though not fully stocked with minor writings,
> Of major works, I have nearly everything:
> Classics, history, philosophy, belles-lettres—
> Nothing lacking from the heritage of the past.
> Binding up the volumes one by one in red covers,
> I painstakingly sew them by hand.
> When angry, I read and become happy;
> When sick, I read and am cured.
> Piled helter-skelter in front of me,
> Books have become my life.
> The people of the past who wrote these tomes,
> If not sages, were certainly men of great wisdom.
> Even without opening their pages,
> Joy comes to me just fondling them.
> As for my foolish family, they can't be helped;
> Their hearts are set on money alone.
> If a book falls on the floor, they don't pick it up;
> What do they care if they get dirty or tattered?
> I'll do my best by these books all my days,
> And die not leaving a single one behind.
> There are some readers among my friends—
> To them I'll give them all away.
> Better that than have my unworthy sons
> Haul them off to turn into cash.[13]

In their libraries, books on silk or paper rolls were marked with paper labels attached to the end of the roller. These identified the work on the roll. The ribbon used to tighten and fasten the roll was often color-coded, to indicate the class of literature into which the roll's contents belonged.

THE CH'ING EMPEROR Ch'ien-lung (1736–95) appointed a group of eminent scholars to compile the *Ssu-k'u ch'uan-shu*. This "Complete Library of the Four Treasures" followed Hsün Hsü's +3rd-century division of all literature into the categories of classics, history, philosophy, and literary collections. Books in the Imperial Library and other collections were examined, and selected works were transcribed into uniform volumes. The project took nearly twenty years and employed fifteen thousand copyists; it produced seven hand-written copies, each containing more than thirty-six thousand volumes, each housed in a dedicated building. Copies have survived to our day in Beijing and Taipei.

The compilation of the *Ssu-k'u ch'uan-shu* was not entirely a matter of literary preservation. The same process of searching libraries that identified and collected those books to be preserved also served to identify those writings that met with imperial disfavor. "None may remain to after generations," the emperor decreed, "in order to cleanse our speech and make straight the hearts of man."[14] Such works were destroyed, with such thoroughness that hundreds of books known to have existed before Ch'ienlung's time have perished completely. On one day in 1781 it was reported that 52,840 woodblocks for printing "seditious works" had been broken up to use for firewood. As with the "burning of the books" two thousand years before, this "inquisition of Ch'ien-lung" demonstrated that the Chinese well knew the power of the written word.

THE WRITTEN WORD was slower to make its mark on Indian life.

The Harappan civilization that flourished in the Indus valley (in what is now Pakistan) from -2300 to -1750 was a literate one. The Harappans used a logo-alphabetic script, in which some signs represented concepts and others sounds—the same principle that governed the hieroglyphics of Egypt and the earliest Sumerian cuneiform. What we know of it derives from the study of four thousand inscribed seals. Though neither literary texts nor bilingual records have been found, anthropologists have been able to establish that the Harappans spoke a Dravidian language, kin to those spoken today across the south of India.

When the Aryans invaded India (between -1500 and -1200) their Indo–European languages supplanted the Dravidian across northern India. Their religious literature—the hymns of the Vedas, the ritual laws of the Brahmanas, and the philosophical speculations of the Upanishads—was an oral one. An elaborate system of mnemonic procedures formed the basis of their educational system, assuring the accurate transmission of even the longest texts across the generations. Religious knowledge was the exclusive province of a small priestly caste: there was little incentive for reducing it to writing, and none for the creation of libraries.

Two sects arising in the -6th century did not share this reluctance to write down their sacred texts. To both Jains and Buddhists the path to salvation—to escape from the eternal cycle of birth, death, and rebirth—lay through spiritual discipline rather than the performance of ritual. Jainism and Buddhism were proselytizing faiths, and both developed canons of scripture over the following centuries. Both maintained monasteries as religious and educational centers.

Both Vardhamana Mahavira, whom the Jains revere as their inspired teacher, and Siddhartha Gautama, whose followers call him the Buddha, flourished during an era of great teachers. They were contemporaries (or nearly so) of the Greek cosmologists and the prophets of Israel, of K'ung fu-tzu in China and Zoroaster in Persia. Whatever the social and economic factors that brought about this worldwide awakening of philosophy and ethics, it had at least one common consequence: the production of a body of literature whose preservation and transmission were held to be of great importance.

Jain annals record that a terrible famine in the +5th century killed many of the monks who had memorized and transmitted the Jain scriptures. These were reconstructed from the memories of survivors and committed to writing. The Jain way of life emphasized asceticism and nonviolence; but Jains came to see daily reading as a religious duty and the commissioning of manuscripts as a way of earning merit. Over the centuries a great body of commentary was added to the basic works of the Jain canon, and Jain monks often composed secular texts on politics, mathematics, and poetics. These were deposited in the libraries maintained by Jain abbots in conjunction with the temples they supervised. The Jains were merchants rather than farmers, so it was natural for them to be interested in secular as well as religious literature. Their libraries preserved many manuscripts that would otherwise have been destroyed during the Muslim invasions of India.

The Buddhist canon (the *Tripitaka*) consists of three sections: Conduct (*Vinaya*), Discourses of the Buddha (*Sutta*), and Supplementary Doctrines (*Abhidhamma*). These together with their commentaries form a voluminous body of literature; and each of the numerous Buddhist sects had its own version. These were expounded at monasteries, some of which attracted students from all over India. That is no wonder, if this account of the Jetavana monastery in its prime (the +5th century) bears any resemblance to reality: it had "chapels for preaching and halls for meditation, messrooms and chambers for the monks, bathhouses, a hospital, libraries and reading rooms with pleasant shady tank [pond] and a great wall encompassing all." (Although Jetavana owed its fame to the fact that the Buddha lived there for twenty-five years, it was not narrowly sectarian. "The libraries were richly furnished not only with orthodox literature but also with Vedic and other non-Buddhistic works, and with treatises on the arts and sciences taught in India at the time.")[15]

As Buddhism spread across Asia, devotees from other lands made pilgrimages to the Indian monasteries. The most famous was Nalanda, in the north central region of Bihar, whose collection of Buddhist manuscripts attracted scholars and pilgrims from as far away as China. Hsuan-Tsang, a monk from the capital city Ch'ang-an, set off in +629 on a sixteen-year tour of the "western world"—central Asia and India.

When he arrived in Nalanda, he found an immense institution combining six earlier foundations. As has often been the case in India, the search for wisdom was not too narrowly limited by doctrinal considerations: the Nalanda course of studies included not only the varieties of Buddhist thought but a wide range of other subjects. "Always present were 10,000 monks, including hosts and guests, who studied both the Mahayana teachings and the doctrines of the eighteen Hinayana schools, as well as the worldly books, such as the Vedas and the other classics. They also studied logic, grammar, medicine and mathematics. . . . As all the monks were men of virtue, the atmosphere in the monastery was naturally grave and dignified."[16]

Tibetan accounts tell us that Nalanda's library, the Dharmaganja (Piety Mart), was housed in three large buildings. One of them, the Ratnadadhi (Ocean of Gems), was nine stories high; here were housed sutras and tantric literature. The books were placed flat on wooden shelves divided into compartments, with the most valuable manuscripts stored in heavy wooden chests. Tradition holds that a huge inkpot provided the means for many students to copy books simultaneously from dictation. When the monastery was destroyed by Muslim raiders in the 12th century, many of its manuscripts were brought to Nepal and Tibet, where some are still preserved. Hsuan-Tsang copied many manuscripts at Nalanda and brought them back to his native China.

Returning to Ch'ang-an in +645, Hsuan-Tsang deposited his treasures in the Hung-fu monastery, and spent the rest of his life translating the books he had brought back from India. His achievements had earned him the high regard of the emperor, though perhaps not quite as high a regard as he thought justified. For in +652, when he suggested that the state build a stone pagoda to house his texts and protect them from fire, all that the emperor would provide was a tower of brick, and that only 130 feet high rather than the 300 that Hsuan-Tsang had requested. Hsuan-Tsang was not the only traveler to return from India laden with books. The monk Yi-tsing returned to China in +695 with four hundred Sanskrit manuscripts that he had copied at Nalanda. These texts so interested his compatriots that Yi-tsing compiled a short Sanskrit–Chinese dictionary for their use.

Whether all these books were brought back in Chinese or in Indian form is uncertain. Indian books certainly differed in form from Chinese scrolls. They were usually written on palm leaves: leaf buds from young talipot palms were cut open and the leaflets separated, then boiled for several hours. (Tender pineapple leaves might be thrown into the pot to make the palm leaves brighter and more durable.) Then the leaves were dried in the sun for several days, cooled by moonlight, and smoothed and trimmed. This offered a writing surface of perhaps four by twelve inches, allowing ten lines of text—though this varied from book to book. In southern India and Sri Lanka, the letters were inscribed with a stylus and then filled in with soot or charcoal; northerners used reed pens and ink made from lampblack or charcoal, and sometimes wrote on birch bark instead of palm leaves. The pages were pierced in the center and held together with string, then covered with wooden boards, which were often lacquered and brightly painted. Leather bindings were not used, as animal skin was not considered a suitable material for religious literature; instead the books were wrapped in cloth.

The Buddhist love of books and their eclectic taste left behind a substantial monument that was discovered by Western explorers in 1907. Near Tun-Huang, in the desert of Chinese Turkestan, lie the Caves of the Thousand Buddhas. In one of these caves a chamber was sealed up almost a thousand years ago (1035), probably to protect its contents from the impious hands of Mongol raiders. The dry Turkestan climate has preserved over fifteen thousand paper rolls, some dated as early as +400. Most are in Chinese, but among them are texts in Tibetan, Sanskrit, Iranian, Turkic—and even an anthology of selections from Scripture, in Hebrew. Did the Tun-Huang hoard constitute a monastic library, or was it merely a scrap-heap of manuscripts discarded by the neighboring monasteries (there were nearly twenty in the immediate vicinity) when they were replaced by printed copies? There is no agreement among the scholars who have studied them.

THROUGHOUT THEIR EARLY history, both Korea and Japan looked to China for cultural leadership. The Confucian philosophy and the Buddhist religion were widely adopted in both countries. Though neither Korean nor Japanese had any linguistic relationship to Chinese, the writing systems of both countries were heavily influenced by that of China. Japanese and Korean writers took Chinese literature as a model, writing their own works in Chinese in preference to their own tongues, and both countries imported books as well as ideas from China.

Among the ideas imported into Japan from China was that of an imperial university. Toward the end of the +7th century, the emperor Tenji established a training school to prepare selected sons of the nobility for careers in government service. The curriculum consisted primarily of the Confucian Classics and Chinese history, though instruction was also provided in medicine, astronomy, mathematics, and music. Like his Chinese counterpart, the emperor of Japan instituted an agency for the compilation of historical works. The Zushoryo (Office of Books and Charts) produced chronicles and housed historical records.

The Buddhist faith had come to Japan in +552, and Buddhist books soon followed. At the Mountain School founded by the monk Saicho, students followed a twelve-year course of study: "During the first six years the study of the sutras under a master will be their major occupation, with meditation and the observance of discipline their secondary pursuits. Two-thirds of their time will be devoted to Buddhism, and the remaining third to the Chinese classics."[17]

For neither of these schools have we any surviving evidence of a library, save for the necessity of some provision for housing the books from which instructors taught. We know more about the Horyuji Temple, which was built at Ikaruga (seven miles southwest of the ancient capital of Nara) at the beginninng of the +7th century. It had attached to it an octagonal chapel called the Yumedono. This "Dream Hall," which housed copies of the sutras and other Buddhist scriptures, has been called "the earliest trace of libraries in Japan."[18]

After the capital was moved from Nara to Kyoto in +794, the imperial family established a university and also sponsored libraries of Buddhist scriptures attached to the temples they erected. Founded by emperor Saga early in the +9th century, the Goshodokoru (palace library) collected copies of books from other court collections; among the duties of its staff was the provision of reading services for the emperor and his family.

Some aristocrats assembled private libraries (*kuge bunko*) to preserve their collections of religious books, literary works, and family documents. Access to *bunko* was usually limited to family members, but some were opened to the public—though this "public" was limited to the small number of literate people with free time for reading, almost all of whom would be members of the nobility. The first of these was established by Isonokami no Yakatsugu during the +770s. He converted his residence to a temple, and on its grounds stored his books in a house called the Untei. (This "Pavilion of Fragrant Herbs" got its name from the plants used to discourage destructive insects.) Yakatsugu collected non-Buddhist literature, with an emphasis on Confucian writings; the Untei was one of the few places in Japan where one might find a copy of the *Analects*. It was open to "all who loved learning," and was used by the leading scholars of the day. But the Untei did not long survive its founder, who died in +781.

Toward the end of the 12th century, Japan entered a period comparable to the European middle ages. Under the feudal society of the shoguns—the military dictators who controlled Japan for seven centuries—power was concentrated in a warrior class, the samurai. Influenced by Zen Buddhism, the samurai class began to esteem aesthetic as well as military accomplishment. Samurai families established schools and libraries to preserve and transmit the Japanese literary heritage: Chinese classics, Buddhist scriptures, and native writings. Their *buke bunko* (warrior libraries) often contained closely guarded family secrets: historical documents, military strategems, and scientific and technological writings. One of these, the Kanazawa Bunko, was one of medieval Japan's most important centers of learning. Founded in 1275 by Hojo Sanetoki at his villa in Kanazawa (near present-day Yokohama), it set out to collect every existing book in Chinese or Japanese. Although it fell short of this ambitious goal, it housed Japan's finest collection of literary, historical, and scientific texts. Its reading room was open to scholars and priests as well as family members, though the twenty thousand books in its stackroom did not circulate. (Although it entered a decline in the 14th century, the Kanazawa Bunko still exists today. It is maintained as a rare book library by the Kanazawa prefectural government.)

The Ashikaga Gakko, which had been founded in the ninth century as a classical academy, was revived in 1432. Medicine and military science were added to its curriculum. But it was the collection of Chinese classics and other rare books in its library that attracted thousands of students, who could find few other places to study during those unsettled years. Located in Ashikaga, its library was supported by the Tokugawa shoguns after they established their rule in Edo (Tokyo) in 1603.

None of these libraries ever reached the size of Chinese or Korean collections, and their holdings consisted mostly of books in Chinese. (Like Latin in western Europe, Chinese was the universal language of the educated, and was used in preference to the vernacular.) They emphasized preservation of their treasures over public access, forbidding loans and restricting visitors to the use of a single volume at a time. Readers had to do without the comforts of fire, even during the cold Japanese winter; and careful inventories were taken whenever a new librarian was appointed.

During the Edo (or Tokugawa) period (1603–1868), feudal lords and wealthy merchants set up private libraries. Toward the end of the period rental libraries came into existence to serve members of the urban middle class. The opening of Japan to Western trade in 1868 led to the restoration of imperial power. Under this Meiji Restoration, Japan determined to catch up with European technology. Educational institutions were established on a Western pattern, and the library infrastructure of Japan came to resemble that of continental Europe.

5
LIBRARIES OF THE ISLAMIC WORLD

WHEN THE ARABS, inspired by the teachings of Muhammad, swept forth out of the desert in the 7th century, they had no literature save the Koran. Within three hundred years, Muslim libraries spread from Spain to India, across lands that had been parts of the Roman, Byzantine, and Persian empires. Unlike many conquering peoples, the Arabs held a great respect for the civilizations that they conquered. They found in the learning of the Greeks, the Persians, and the Jews a source of awe and inspiration. When the 'Abbasid poet al-Mutannabi proclaimed that "The most honourable seat in this world is in the saddle of a horse," he added that "the best companion will always be a book."[1]

The prophet Muhammad brought letters to the Arabs, and the Arabs brought Islam to three continents. Before Muhammad the Arabs had their poets, and a vigorous oral literature, but books were found only among the few tribes who had adopted Judaism or Christianity. In the Koran, the word of God was delivered to Muhammad by the angel Gabriel. The embodiment of revelation, the Koran was perfect, its every word, every letter, every dot precious and deserving of study. As befitted the most important book in the world, it became the object of an entire scholarly and devotional culture.

To interpret the teachings of Muhammad, his words and deeds and those of his companions (the *hadith*) were collected and studied. Variant readings of the Koran, and explanations of its more complex passages, were produced by a multitude of commentators. Legal opinions, sermons, and accounts of disputations recorded the lively jurisprudence of Islam.

Underlying this literature of the specifically religious sciences was the need for literary studies. Grammar and etymology aided in the understanding of the Koran. Genealogy and history were needed to establish the succession of temporal and religious authority. And the study of philology and geography were essential to the administration of the ever-widening Islamic realm.

Influenced by the ancient literary traditions of Byzantium and Persia, the Arabs studied the philosophical sciences: medicine, astronomy, geometry, philosophy. At first they translated the older works; but the Muslims, who held knowledge sacred, soon became prolific contributors to the scientific literature. It was through their work that Christian Europe received the inspiration for the Renaissance.

The earliest Arab books were written on papyrus, parchment, or poplar bark; like those of their Christian neighbors, the sheets were gathered and bound into codices, rather than pasted together into scrolls. In 751, the art of papermaking was introduced from China into Samarkand, whence it soon spread across the Islamic world. A paper mill existed in Baghdad by 794, but it was in Egypt that the paper industry most flourished, its raw material the linen from that country's extensive flax culture. The resulting abundance of paper lowered the price of books throughout Islam, and the bookshops that arose in every Arab city served as the nuclei for a lively literary culture. With its emphasis on the importance of reading the Koran, and the reverence for learning in general that the veneration of the Koran inspired, Islamic culture ensured a high degree of literacy. The Muslim proscription of graven images directed the artistic impulse away from painting and sculpture toward architecture and calligraphy. The written word and the art of the book were greatly enriched by this emphasis. The book trade became a lucrative one, embracing not only booksellers but also copyists, correctors, and collators of texts. Unlike their counterparts in the monasteries of Europe, Islamic scribes endeavored to reproduce the calligraphy and page layout of their exemplars.

> The caliphs and kings of ancient times had a great interest in the large libraries and bestowed much care about them to get the most beautiful numerous collections. It is said that the greatest libraries in Islam were the following three: First, the Library of the Abbasid Caliphs in Baghdad (The House of Wisdom) . . . Second, the Library of the Fatimide Caliphs at Cairo (The House of Science) . . . the third was the library of the Umayyad Caliphs in Spain.
> —Al-Kalkashandi, 15th-century Arab encyclopedist [2]

TWO HUNDRED FIFTEEN years after the Hegira, the 'Abbasid caliph al-Mamun (r. 813–33) founded the Bayt al-hikma (House of Wisdom) in his capital city, Baghdad. Modeled after the Museum of Alexandria, it was a center of scholarly activity. There books were translated from Greek, Syriac, and Persian by a corps of subject specialists whose work was revised by expert Arabists. Under his father, the Harun al-Rashid celebrated in the *Arabian Nights*, raids into the Byzantine empire had brought back Greek manuscripts from Amorium and Ancyra. Al-Mamun obtained books in more peaceable fashion, dispatching emissaries to Emperor Leo the Armenian, who sent him texts on music, philosophy, mathematics, science, and medicine. (Al-Mamun's translators did not concern themselves with drama, poetry, or history; it was Persian rather than Greek influence that dominated Arabic imaginative literature.) New works were commissioned from Arab historians and scientists, some of whom worked at the institution's astronomical observatory.

Members of the staff, whether astrologer, translator, or conservator, lived in the Bayt al-hikma, where they were on call day and night to serve the caliph's needs. A group of Islamic scholars was maintained to conduct disputations before the caliph. But its library was the most important of its activities.

> Many people from all countries traveled to it in order to study various sciences. In it the books were completely at the disposal of students. . . . This library was known in the whole world and attracted students in such manner that the astronomer Abu-Ma'shar, coming from Khorasan with the intention of going to Mecca to perform the pilgrimage, decided to go and see it. He was so enthusiastic about it that he remained there and did not continue his journey.[3]

The Bayt al-hikma was emulated on a smaller scale by other libraries, not only in Baghdad but also in the other major cities of the caliphate. Many individual scholars had their own libraries, and the funds with which to maintain them: they collected "rare and curious books" in such fields as philosophy, logic, geometry, arithmetic, music, medicine, and astrology, and paid translators well for rendering sought-after works into Arabic.

Though they were privately owned, many of these libraries were made available for the use of the learned community. Scholars, translators, commentators, compilers, and writers used them, as did courtiers who might well have found it useful to read up on the caliph's favorite topics of learned conversation.

BY THE BEGINNING of the 10th century, true public libraries began to appear. Islamic law had by then evolved the concept of the *waqf*, or charitable endowment, and extended it to the establishment of libraries. These institutions, called *dar al-'ilm* (hall of science), were founded to serve as public libraries and to propagate the tenets of a specific Islamic sect. To this end, scholars were maintained in the *dar al-'ilm* for the instruction of students. There was a definite need for these institutions. This was the peak period of scientific activity in Islam, and as the frontiers of the caliphate touched almost every civilization of the known world, there was ample opportunity to collect the literature and the knowledge of the world's peoples. And this was the period of the rise of sects—the orthodox Sunni, the rationalist Mutazilites, the messianic Shi'a and Isma'ili, the mystic Sufi—each of which had its own literature to be collected, taught, and disseminated throughout Islam.

The first *dar al-'ilm* was founded by Ibn Hamdan in Mosul, at the very beginning of the 10th century. Its collection included books on all subjects, with an emphasis on philosophy and astrology, two fields especially dear to its founder. All were welcome there. Lectures were given on the premises. Just as some of today's research libraries provide fellowships in support of visiting scholars, so impecunious foreign scholars were provided not only with ink and paper but also with food and drink.

A similar institution was founded by Sabur ibn Ardasir in Baghdad, around 996. Housed in a building of marble and limestone, it contained 10,400 volumes, including a hundred Korans copied by the Banu-Muqla, an eminent family of calligraphers. Even though religious books dominated, the library included grammar and philology, medicine and philosophy, astronomy and geology. Sabur's dar al-'ilm was one of Baghdad's primary cultural centers, frequented by scholars, poets, and musicians. A visiting Syrian poet recalled how "in the house of Sabur a sprightly songstress enlivened our evenings with a voice as melodious as a dove's."[4] Many scholars donated books and money to Sabur's dar al-'ilm, but not every gift was accepted: only definitive texts of significant works were allowed onto its shelves. Although a definitely Shi'ite institution, it was open to scholars of all Muslim persuasions.

The Muslims first invaded Spain in 710; 250 years later the Umayyad capital of Córdoba was the most cultured city in Europe and, after Constantinople, the continent's second largest. Córdoba's book bazaar and the seventy libraries of Andalusia attracted scholars from all over the Islamic world as well as travelers from the countries of Christian Europe. In the university of Córdoba, the greatest center of learning of Islam, mathematics, astronomy, and medicine were studied. The royal library, founded by Muhammad I (reigned 852–86), was greatly augmented by the caliph al-Hakim II (reigned 961–76). He sent agents to Alexandria, Baghdad, and Damascus, with orders to buy or copy scholarly manuscripts, and in Córdoba he employed copyists, illuminators, and bookbinders. With as many as five hundred people on its payroll, the library grew to four hundred thousand volumes; it took forty-four substantial books just to list them, and six months to move them when the library occupied new quarters. The caliph's love of books spawned public libraries and private collections across Andalusia, as those who sought royal favor strove to demonstrate their patronage of learning. Al-Hakim was not only a collector; his scholarship was so respected that the presence of his marginal notes added great value to his books in the eyes of later scholars. His son Hisham II, who inherited the throne as a child, ruled in name only. Real power lay in the hands of his vizir, Muhammad ibn-abi-'Amir, who sought to win the favor of the clergy by burning the scientific and philosophical books in the royal library. He found an easier way to deal with poets, muzzling them with generous pensions.

In 1004 another al-Hakim, the caliph of Cairo and a zealous Sunni, founded the Dar al-hikma (Hall of Wisdom) in Cairo. It was open to all:

> Whoever wanted was at liberty to copy any book he wished to copy, or whoever required to read a certain book found in the library could do so. Scholars studied the Koran, astronomy, grammar, lexicography, and medicine. The building was, moreover, adorned by carpets, and all doors and corridors had

curtains, and managers, servants, porters, and other menials were appointed to maintain the establishment. Out of the library of the Caliph al-Hakim those books were brought, which he had granted—books in all sciences and literatures and of exquisite calligraphy such as no other king had ever been able to bring together. Al-Hakim permitted admittance to everyone, without distinction of rank, who wished to read or consult any of the books.[5]

But after 1020, it became a center for anti-Sunni activity, as the caliphate embraced the Ismai'lite sect. A center of religious controversy and polemic, it was closed in 1119 for religious nonconformity. Reopened four years later under the directorship of men selected for their piety and Ismai'lite orthodoxy, it existed tranquilly as an Ismai'li institution for its remaining forty-eight years.

The Dar al-hikma was located near the Western Palace, the caliph's residence. It contained a superb library covering every category of science and letters, with books written out by the finest calligraphers of Egypt. In addition to a generous endowment, Al-Hakim provided, from his personal funds and from the state treasury, salaries for librarians and caretakers, and paper, pens, and ink for library users. He had an ulterior motive. By thus facilitating the copying of books from the Dar al-hikma, the caliph helped to ensure the widespread dissemination of Ismai'lite literature.

As the Sunni doctrine, whose adherents today form the most numerous body of Muslims, came into ascendancy, a new form of educational institution arose to spread its teachings. The *madrasa* was foremost a teaching center, specializing in Islamic law; the collection of books and maintenance of a library was secondary to this function. It housed teachers and students, and though administered autonomously was under state control; for its students were destined for the service of the caliphate, and one of the *madrasa*'s purposes was to oppose the Shi'a and Isma'ili sects, now considered heretical.

One of the great *madrasas* was the Nizamiyya of Baghdad, founded in 1064 by Nizam-al-Mulk, who ruled the caliphate in fact though not in name. He enjoyed the company of scholars and liked to visit scientific institutions; he also engaged in the study of *hadith*. One building within the Nizamiyya was designated *dar al-kutub* (hall of books); many of its librarians were literary men, and some served as professors at the *madrasa*. In 1193 the caliph al-Nasir built a new library (al-Nasiriyya) at the *madrasa*, endowing it with thousands of books from his personal collection. This donation was imitated by those of his subjects who shared the caliph's concern for learning—or who wished to be seen as sharing it.

Whether from a love of learning or from a conviction that a great library was a sign of a glorious empire, succeeding caliphs continued to found and maintain libraries. Before the Mongol invasion of the mid-13th century there were thirty-six collections in Baghdad that were open to scholars, of which at least twenty were genuine public libraries.

Other libraries existed in mosques, which had always played a significant role in Muslim education. Many collectors, while not in a position to endow public libraries, desired to place their books at the disposal of those who would learn from them. Many of these men left their books to the great mosques of Aleppo, Damascus, and Cairo. The Grand Mosque of Damascus contained several separate collections, totaling five thousand volumes which were housed in twenty glass cases. Some medical schools and hospitals had small medical and scientific libraries. These libraries were seldom as grand in scope as the *dar al-'ilm* that had preceded them. Like those of the European monasteries, they were instructional rather than research libraries, intended to serve the members of the parent establishment rather than the world of Islamic scholarship. A scholar would often need to visit several libraries to consult the books he wanted for a particular subject.

But there were some great *madrasa* libraries, which came to outshine their parent institutions. Located in the major cities of the Arab world, their librarians were eminent scholars, and their collections were enriched with donations from bibliophiles and collectors. Al-Fadil of Cairo, vizier to the Muslim war-leader Saladin, was "a great bibliophile, loving the book for its exterior beauty as well as for the richness of its learning."[6] When the royal library of the Fatimid caliphs (al-Hakim's Dar al-hikma) was dispersed after Saladin's conquest of Egypt, he seized the opportunity to add its finest treasures to his personal collection. Saladin rewarded his faithful service with choice books from the cities he added to his empire. Al-Fadil also enlarged his collection through the labors of his retinue of copyists, and sent agents across the Islamic world to search out new titles. In all he collected at least thirty thousand books. In 1184 he founded a *madrasa*, called after him al-Fadiliyya, and gave much of his personal collection to establish its library.

Famine struck Cairo in 1251, and the starving students of the *madrasa* sold off al-Fadiliyya's library, offering a book for a mouthful of coarse bread. Other books were lost when the students who had borrowed them neglected to return them, and the library staff was negligent about pursuing them. Thus perished the richest university library of the Arab world.

THE ARAB BOOK collector was typically a member of the royal family or a high government official. Unless he had a scholarly interest in a particular field, his library would be an eclectic one, emphasizing philology, literature, and history, while attempting to represent all areas of knowledge. What made a book really valuable was not its rarity or subject matter, but the beauty of its calligraphy. The Arab bibliophile collected not only fine books but also fine copyists, men renowned for accuracy and beautiful work. Many copyists were employed by collectors, while others were independent craftsmen, producing books to order for collectors.

Bibliophiles insisted on complete and accurate texts, retaining noted scholars to collate and correct them. They especially treasured works in the handwriting of their original authors (just as today's great research libraries collect the manuscripts of contemporary writers) and often extended their patronage to living writers, who repaid their support by dedicating their works to their patrons. Some collectors would commission a major work from a writer and insure its uniqueness by not allowing anyone to copy it.

Scholars built their collections by copying and by purchase. As students, they copied scientific works from the dictation of their professors. (One *madrasa*, the Mustansiriyya in Baghdad, encouraged its students to copy books from its extensive library by providing them with free paper, pens, ink, and lamps.) In later life, they copied books in public libraries and in private collections made available to them. Even when they bought books—there was a flourishing book trade throughout the Islamic world—they would collate, correct, and annotate them. Given the cost and effort of acquiring books, most scholars limited their collecting to books in their specialties or containing knowledge needed in their work. Religious scholars collected only books conforming to the doctrines that they espoused; a Shi'a book would never be found on the shelves of a Sunni collector.

By the 5th Islamic century (the 11th of our era) the religious sciences had come to dominate Islamic thought, almost to the suppression of secular studies. Calligrapher and collector alike turned their attention to religious subjects. In the Islamic heartland, jurists prohibited the inclusion of secular works in religious endowments; but these rules were sometimes broken, and had little impact in Spain and Sicily, the new homes of Arab science.

Collectors were careful to ensure that their books would be well used after their deaths. Passing sometimes through a chain of heirs, their collections would be deposited in public or institutional libraries, there to remind future generations of the taste and wisdom of those who had assembled them. Writers, too, donated their books to libraries, to ensure that their scholarship—and their reputations—would outlast their lives.

The *waqf* (endowment) was defined by an extensive body of Islamic law, which set forth three principal requirements: the presentation to a religious tribunal of a list of the books given, to be recorded in its register; an attestation of qualified witnesses; and the inscription in each book of a formula consecrating it to the endowment.

These lists constituted the first Arab library catalogs, and would name the book, its subject, and its calligraphic style. Seals attached to the pages prevented tampering with their content. They were arranged by subject, though no particular order governed the arrangement of titles within a subject. Because of their status as legal documents, these lists did not name books twice, even if they dealt with more than one subject. (A volume made up of several different works would be classified with the subject of the first book it contained.)

The richness of the great Arab libraries required better finding aids than these legal inventories could provide. But the compilation of unified catalogs was hampered by the requirement that each individual donation be inventoried separately. These records were usually in the form of a roll rather than the more convenient codex, or they might consist of a sheet of paper hanging from each pigeon-hole in an armoire, listing the books contained therein.

The basic principle of classification was that "the book whose subject was the noblest should precede the others."[7] As this nobility was assessed in religious terms, a bibliographical compilation or library catalog proceeded from the sacred to the profane. Three divisions emerged: religious sciences (Koran, theology, and law), those sciences required to support religious studies (literature, philology, and history), and philosophical sciences (medicine, astronomy, and mathematics). When several books dealt with the same subject, the one containing the most verses of the Koran should be placed first; next the one which cited the most *hadith* (sayings of the Prophet and his companions); after that the book whose author is the most highly estemed; then the most useful book; and finally the most authentic.

WHAT DID A great Islamic library look like?

Entering through an oblong portico, the visitor would pass through a second doorway leading into an ornamented room. Its marble floor would be covered with straw mats in summer and with felt rugs and woolen cushions in winter. Curtains covered the windows and doors, offering both books and readers protection from the sun. In winter, they kept out the cold. Running water was piped into the building where a fountain provided for both washing and drinking.

A separate room served as the copyists' workshop. Some scribes worked individually; others might work in groups, copying to dictation so as to produce several copies of the same book. At the library of Banu Ammar in Syrian Tripoli "there were 180 copyists employed . . . , and thirty worked day and night, and all were well paid for their services," if the historian Ibn al-Furat does not exaggerate.[8]

Al-Mukaddasi gives this description of the library at Shiraz:

> 'Adad ad-Daulah founded in Shiraz a residence which had not its equal East to West; no ignorant person entered it but was enchanted, nor any learned person but his imagination was filled with the delights and perfumes of Paradise. He made it intersected with water-courses, the buildings were crowned with domes and surrounded by gardens and parks, lakes were excavated and every kind of comfort that could be thought of. I have heard the servants say that there were 360 rooms and pavilions, in each of which he resided one day of the year, some were on the ground-floor and some above.

The library constituted a gallery by itself; there was a superintendent, a librarian, and an inspector chosen from the most trustworthy people of the country. There is no book written up to this time in whatever branch of science but the prince has acquired a copy of it. The library consists of one long vaulted room, annexed to which are store-rooms. The prince had made along the large room and the storechambers scaffoldings about the height of a man, three yards wide, of decorated wood, which have shelves from top to bottom; the books are arranged on the shelves and for every branch of learning there are separate scaffolds. There are also catalogues in which all the titles of the books are entered. Only persons of standing are admitted to this library. I myself inspected this library, downstairs and upstairs, when all was still in order. I observed in each room carpets and curtains, I also saw the ventilation chamber, to which the water is carried by pipes which surrounded it every side in circulation.[9]

A smaller library would present a more modest appearance. Whether housed in a room of its own, or in a glass-fronted cabinet in a hallway, its location would be in the most prominent part of the building. Books were considered useful as well as ornamental; in *madrasas*, classes would be held nearby so that the books could be referred to as needed.

In any case the books would be housed in wooden cabinets, often ornamented with calligraphic carvings. These cabinets contained several shelves, each divided vertically to form a series of pigeon-holes, in which the books lay on their sides in stacks. The books were arranged in the same order in which they were listed in the library's inventory. (Copies of the Koran were often shelved separately, or on a higher level than other books.) Thus a subject classification was maintained, although with a separate sequence for each collection donated to the library. A locked glass door simultaneously protected and displayed the books; but the protection it offered from theft and dust was offset by the encouragement such an environment offered to the growth of insects. Books were kept away from the floor to avoid damage from humidity.

A visitor entering the library might request a specific book of the librarian, or request that the library's catalog be brought to him. Paper and ink would be provided for him to make notes, but if he intended to copy the entire book he would have to furnish his own supplies and obtain the librarian's permission. (While this might be denied in a private collection, to maintain the rarity or indeed uniqueness of its holdings, it was almost always permitted in public libraries. Some poor scholars earned their living by visiting the great libraries and making copies for sale of their most important books.) He would sit on the floor or on a cushion, his back leaning against a wall. The book would rest atop his crossed legs, or on a small wooden table in front of him. In the palm of his left hand he would hold the paper on which his right hand wrote with a reed pen. Readers were warned not to place books on the ground, nor to hold an ink-filled pen over a book from which one might be copying or making notes. When he was finished, the visitor would hand the book back to the librarian and request another, or leave the library.

The *dar al-'ilm* in Baghdad was open every day, as were the *madrasa* libraries, but in provincial cities public libraries might be open only a few days each week. Hours of operation were generally limited to daylight hours, and those libraries that lent books for outside use kept shorter hours than those whose books were restricted to use on the premises.

Many libraries did lend books, considering it a religious obligation to facilitate copying and study. Some libraries were generous indeed in their lending policies. When the geographer Yakut al-Himawi visited the Persian city of Merv in 1228, he found there ten libraries open to the public. From one of these, the Damiriyya library, he was able to borrow more than two hundred books at a time. The 13th-century Spanish Arab historian Ibn Hayyan cited the generosity of libraries to explain why he never bought books: "Whatever book I want to have I can get on loan from any library, while if I wanted to borrow money to buy these books I should find no-one who would lend it to me."[10]

To prevent loss or damage to the books, they were lent only to readers who could be trusted to respect the books and not to allow them to become lost, soiled, or damaged. When this could not be taken for granted, a prospective borrower might be obliged to leave a sum of money or an item of equal value to ensure the book's return. Typically the period of a loan was one day for each leaf of text; this was considered ample time for the borrower to copy the entire book. In some cases, rather than lend a book to a powerful official who might not choose to return it, its owner would have a copy made to give to the would-be borrower.

Most libraries were open to all Muslims, rich and poor alike. Even those *madrasa* libraries that were open only to affiliates of their parent institutions rarely followed those restrictions rigidly. And although some endowment charters specified that only Orthodox Muslims, or those adhering to a particular sect, were to be admitted, in practice even those restrictions were often ignored by administrators and librarians.

THE FIRST GREAT Arab libraries were were run by eminent men of letters, generalists conversant in both religious and secular sciences. Some were renowned as teachers as well as scholars. But after the triumph of religion over philosophy in the 13th century, religious scholarship and piety rather than a broad knowledge of literature became the qualification for a librarian. The position tended to become hereditary, and as time went on it diminished in responsibility, in reward, and in prestige.

The principal duties of the librarian were the conservation, safeguarding, and preservation of the books in his care. In addition, he often distributed paper and ink to library users, arranged for the binding of books and the pay of the binders, supervised the collation and correction of books in the collection, and provided the administrator of the library's endowment with suggestions for new acquisitions. He was also expected to determine which of the library's potential users were worthy of admittance, and to determine which should have priority in receiving books. One of his qualifications was excellent penmanship, for he had to write the library's catalog, and often served as a copyist as well.

His pay was about half that of a professor, and twice that of a repeater (the assistant who relayed the professor's lectures in the *madrasa*). But as libraries increased in number and decreased in size, the pay and status of librarians decreased. At the Ahmadiyya in Aleppo the librarian received the same pay as did the porter and the sweeper; but unlike these he might earn additional pay for teaching or preaching.

The real power lay, not in the hands of the librarian, but in those of the *nazir* (administrator) of the foundation. He it was who hired and fired the librarian, and gave him his orders. And it was he who held the purse-strings, disbursing money on the advice of the librarian, when he chose to follow it.

The library's funding came from rents on land designated for its support in the endowment that created it. Cloth mills, mints, and wool markets all supported libraries in the Arab east. The library's expenses included the construction and maintenance of its home; furnishing, lighting, and providing water for its quarters; purchasing, copying, and repairing books; purchasing writing materials for the use of staff and readers; and, of course, paying the salaries of its staff.

WHAT BECAME OF the great Islamic libraries?

Not every caliph was a scholar, and many rulers found better use for their funds than the maintenance of libraries. To some of them, libraries were storehouses from which to bestow gifts on their favorites; to others, mere collections of waste paper.

When Saladin conquered Egypt in 1175, he allowed his followers to help themselves to the treasures of al-Hakim's Dar al-hikma. When the Umayyad dynasty ended in Spain (1031) and the caliphate was divided among smaller kings, the royal library was dispersed. After the *reconquista*, Cardinal Francesco Ximenez de Cisneros, confessor to Queen Isabella, organized a purge of Muslim books. At the Plaza de Bibarrambla in Granada, eighty thousand books were burnt in 1499. Fewer than two thousand survived the cardinal's bonfires; these were collected by later Spanish kings and housed in the Escorial palace outside Madrid, where they remain today.

Other Islamic libraries were destroyed by the Crusaders as they swept through Syria and Palestine in the 12th century:

> When the Franks entered Tripoli and conquered it they burned the Academy down to the ground. The cause of the burning was that a priest (may God

curse him) when he saw all those books became beside himself. It happened that he entered the rooms where the Korans were stored and he picked up a volume and behold! it was a Koran. Then he took a second book and it was again a Koran like the first; so he went on till he had picked up about twenty Korans. Then he exclaimed: "All that is to be found in this library are Korans of the Muslims!" After this they burned it . . .[11]

But Christians were not the only ones whose bigotry drove them to despoil Islamic libraries. Many were destroyed by orthodox Muslims intent upon suppressing heretical books. The libraries established by Mutazilites and Isma'ilis were especially vulnerable as Sunni traditionalists came to dominate Islam in the 12th century. Along with "heretical" theological works, these sectarian libraries contained many scientific and philosophical books. Their destruction had a chilling effect on the development of Islamic thought, one that in the opinion of many historians has lasted into our own century.

When the Mongols swept across the Muslim lands in the 13th century, they destroyed the great cities of central Asia and, in 1258, Baghdad itself. In one week most of that city's thirty-six public libraries were destroyed. Al-Nadim's *Fihrist al'ulum* (Index of the sciences) lists the books known to a 10th-century Baghdad scholar; fewer than one in a thousand survives today because of the Mongol raids. Illuminated manuscripts and exquisite examples of calligraphy were burned as fuel, while finely decorated leather bindings went to shoe Mongol feet. Scholars and students were massacred, and the Mongol hordes rode westward across Syria until they were stopped in Egypt. The destruction was not total; the Nizamiyya of Baghdad survived for another century, probably meeting its end during Tamurlane's invasion in the 15th century.

Did the Mongols despise learning entirely? The year after he destroyed Baghdad, the Mongol leader Hulagu built an astronomical observatory at Maraghah, near Lake Urmiyah in Azerbaijan. A neighboring library housed (if we may believe the chroniclers) four hundred thousand volumes, the spoils of conquest from Syria, Mesopotamia, and Persia. What use did he make of these riches? Here the chronicles are silent.

6
THE HIGH MIDDLE AGES

As THE MONASTERIES of western Europe grew richer, they drew away from the old Benedictine ideal of manual labor and from the more recent Benedictine tradition of scholarship. Their new role was to intercede with God through prayer and ritual on behalf of lay society, and to serve that society through education and administration.

Enriched by pious gifts, the monasteries had gained charters freeing them from kings and bishops. They were responsible only to a papacy too weak to supervise them. But as their wealth grew, they became tempting targets for rulers in need of money. Abbots were increasingly chosen for their willingness to serve the needs of the state rather than for piety or scholarship. Some were laymen, and some illiterate: Rumo von Ramstein, who ruled St. Gall from 1274 to 1281, could not write. To such men monastic libraries represented treasures to be exploited rather than repositories of holy wisdom. Many an abbot pawned his cloister's manuscripts to raise revenue.

During the 10th and 11th centuries, a new spirituality swept across Catholic Europe. As urban life revived, wealth increased—and in reaction an ascetic impulse arose among monks and laymen dismayed by the conspicuous wealth of the established monasteries. At Cluny and Citeaux, new foundations arose to restore the true monastic spirit; these spawned many daughter-houses. Located mostly in rural areas, their communal life emphasized liturgy rather than learning. Although the Cluniac and Cistercian monks continued to read and to copy service books and theological works, they disdained secular literature. Prayer, purity, and poverty dominated the new monasticism, to the detriment of study—and of libraries.

But more than ever society still needed an educational system. European economies and governments were growing more complex, and capable men were needed to run them. The Civil Law of the Roman empire, as set forth in the newly rediscovered Justinian Code, provided the administrative basis for governing the monarchies of Europe. Schools to teach it arose in Parma, Bologna, and other Italian cities. The cathedral schools, where theology, music, and canon law were studied by aspiring priests and Church functionaries, developed rapidly in the new urban environment. As European education shifted from rural monastery to urban school, so too did European libraries.

The revival of trade was only one cause of an increasing traffic of people, ideas, and books across and beyond Europe. The same increase in personal piety that changed monastic life led a growing number of men and women to undertake the pilgrimage to Canterbury or Campostela, to Rome or Jerusalem. The Crusades placed the Holy Land for a while in Catholic hands, and placed oriental ideas in Catholic heads for centuries. And when the daughters of kings and barons left the lands of their birth to advance their parents' interests through dynastic marriages, they were often accompanied by courtiers and churchmen from home, and the books they brought with them.

By the middle of the 12th century much of the literary legacy of Rome had become familiar across Catholic Europe, and some of the Greek learning had passed through Arab and Jewish hands in polyglot Spain and Sicily to emerge in the Latin that was common to every literate person in the West. This shared language facilitated travel, and made it possible for an ambitious scholar to find a situation far from his homeland. The Church offered many paths to advancement, but there were others: foreign scholars found a ready welcome at the courts of England and Germany.

Another intellectual influence on Catholic Europe was produced by peaceful contact with the alien cultures of Byzantium and Islam. When Venice established trade relations with Constantinople, books and ideas were among the exports that flowed westward. Many of these in turn had their origins in the libraries of Baghdad and other Muslim cities. In Sicily and Spain the courts of Arab rulers offered a hospitable home for Jewish and Christian as well as Muslim scholars. These environments encouraged the translation of old books and the compilation of new ones. In this way many classics of Greek philosophy, natural science, and medicine, preserved in Arabic editions by Islamic libraries, found their way into Latin and thus into the libraries of western Europe. In addition to ancient Greek writings, the works and commentaries of Jewish and Muslim scholars were translated into Latin. Avicenna, Averroes, and Maimonides joined Peter Lombard and Abelard in influencing the development of scholastic theology, the attempt by Catholic theologians to reconcile Aristotle's philosophy with Christian revelation. Like the attempt of today's physicists to erect a Grand Unified Theory that would account for all of the forces governing the universe and its constituents, the schoolmen attempted to construct an intellectual edifice that would explain the nature of God and of his Creation.

A SIDE EFFECT of increasing piety among laymen was the growth of heretical ideas. Opposition to clerical wealth and corruption led to the rise of anticlerical sects. One of these, the Cathari (Albigensians), spread so rapidly across southern France during the 12th century that it threatened the primacy of the Catholic Church. To combat this required a corps of men equipped to preach sound doctrine and extirpate heresy. This was not a task for ill-trained parish priests or cloistered monks. New orders of priests arose, called mendicants because they relied upon charity rather than landed revenues for their sustenance. These were the friars: Dominicans, Franciscans, Carmelites, Augustinians.

Their founders had differing visions for their orders. St. Dominic de Guzman established the Order of Preachers to spread the faith and refute its opponents, a task that required rigorous theological training. The Order of Friars Minor followed the example of St. Francis of Assisi in returning to the simplicity and humility of the earliest Christians, originally emphasizing personal salvation over education or preaching. The Carmelites and Augustinians began as groups of hermits, but like the Franciscans the spirit of the times made preachers and teachers of them.

The mendicant orders cherished poverty and obedience, but not ignorance. In order to protect the true faith and spread the gospel, a friar needed to know not only theology but also the arts of persuasion that underlay the art of preaching. To train their members for this work, the friars established schools across Europe. (The Dominican *studium generale* in Cologne, where Thomas Aquinas studied under Albertus Magnus, was the intellectual equal of any university in Europe.) In these colleges novices learned grammar and rhetoric, and received a solid grounding in Scripture and theology. Friars sent to preach the faith in foreign lands were taught to understand and speak their languages. The education provided by their colleges was recognized as the equivalent of a university arts degree, and qualified the friars for admission into the university faculties of theology.

Their vows of poverty prohibited the friars from owning personal posessions, including books. So they necessarily relied upon libraries to supply what they needed for their studies, their writing, and their preaching. The mendicants' libraries were working libraries, their books chosen for utility rather than ornament. The occasional sumptuous manuscript was most likely a gift; most such extravagances would be sold and the proceeds used to buy more suitable books. Funds were usually available to provide the books a friar might require for his work, and the territorial organization of the mendicant orders facilitated the borrowing of needed books from other convents. Kenneth Humphreys, who has studied their libraries extensively, concluded that "there is no doubt that between 1250 and 1400 the orders of friars were better equipped than any other religious or secular body."[1]

The splendid libraries that the friars established in their convents served as models for the universities. In many cases the mendicants established libraries at their colleges in the university towns, so that their members studying at the universities could enjoy the access to books that they had become accustomed to in their monasteries.

• • •

THE UNIVERSITIES AROSE to fill the void left when the Benedictine monasteries began to confine their educational activities to their own members, closing the "exterior schools" which had educated both secular clergy (those who were not governed by the Rule of a monastic or mendicant order) and laymen. At first this task was inherited by the cathedral schools. Some of these had existed since Roman days, and others had been founded at the instigation of Charlemagne, to train parish priests and diocesian administrators. Many more came into existence in the newly emerging cities of a Europe that had rediscovered urban life. Both the reviving commercial life and the expansion of central governments required lawyers and administrators; these functionaries required an education beyond that provided monks or parish priests.

As students and teachers gathered—whether in major cities or isolated provincial towns—they organized to regulate their activities and secure recognition of their rights and privileges. The resulting corporate bodies were called "universities," from the Latin legal term for collective entities. The first of these arose in Bologna and Paris. Bologna's specialty was law, while Paris was renowned for theology. It soon dominated the intellectual life of Christendom, and attracted students from all over Europe.

The University of Paris arose from the consolidation of the various schools that flourished near the Cathedral of Notre Dame. In 1200, the masters who gave instruction at these schools obtained a royal patent from the French king Philip II, which gave them a corporate identity and exempted them from the jurisdiction of the civil authorities. Their students lived in colleges endowed by pious benefactors or maintained by religious orders for their members.

It did not take long for monarchs and bishops to see the advantages of keeping their talented youth at home. During the 13th and 14th centuries universities were founded across western Europe. There were twenty-three in existence by 1300, and twenty-two more were founded before the end of the 14th century. Cities vied for the honor—and the profit—of playing host to a university.

The university undergraduate began his studies with the seven liberal arts. The *trivium* of grammar, rhetoric, and logic provided training in reasoning and argumentation: how can the truth be known, and how can it be conveyed to others? The *quadrivium* of arithmetic, geometry, music, and astronomy explained the natural laws governing the universe. (Classical literature, whether Greek or Roman, formed no part of the curriculum.) The instructors were masters in the Faculty of Arts, who read the works of prescribed writers aloud to their students and amplified the text with their comments. Both students and faculty participated in debates which attempted to resolve difficult points.

Many of the students in the arts faculties were very young: some had not reached the age of twelve. Few of those who enrolled ever completed the six years of study required for graduation. The medieval arts student was more like a schoolboy than a modern university student. He was expected merely to listen to his masters' lectures and remember their content. He compiled no research papers and wrote no expository essays. He had no need to use a library; indeed, at most universities he was forbidden to enter it.

The more ambitious young men remained at the university to study for higher degrees. The masters who lectured to the arts students were often themselves students in the higher faculty of theology. In many universities, faculties of medicine, civil law, and canon law prepared arts graduates for professional careers. In these higher faculties, as in the arts faculty, instruction consisted of masters reading to their students from prescribed texts and commenting upon them.

University teaching required books not only for reading aloud to students but also for preparation of disputations. At these public performances, a lecturer would state a question and then present both negative and positive answers to it, supporting both with extensive quotations from the Bible and the Church Fathers. These sources were consulted in the university libraries.

The exorbitant costs of books in an age before printing made it impossible for any but the wealthiest students to purchase their own copies. Mendicants studying theology might receive essential books from their orders. The General Chapter of the Dominicans decreed in 1228 that "each province shall provide for its brothers sent to the university at least three books of theology,"[2] which were usually a copy of the Bible, the *Book of Sentences*, and Peter Comestor's *Historia scholastica*. Secular students relied upon lending libraries maintained by stationers, who rented out textbooks section by section so that students might make their own copies. This practice was closely supervised by the university authorities, who regulated both the fees charged and the soundness of the texts offered for rental.

At many universities in southern Europe law rather than theology was the dominant study. The aspiring lawyer, for whom the basic legal texts would be his lifelong professional tools, began acquiring them while a student. To facilitate this, Bologna's statutes provided that "any doctor or scholar may be required to supply his own copy" to serve as an exemplar, with refusal punishable by a severe fine.[3] Once an authoritative text was obtained, measures were taken to protect it. At Montpellier, the faculty of law decreed that "a *pecia* [section] shall never be given out except with a pledge of gold or silver worth double the price of the said *pecia*," though an exception was made for the poor.[4] The reliance upon stationers made libraries comparatively unimportant. Significant growth of university libraries did not occur until the 15th century in Spain, Italy, and southern France.

• • •

UNLIKE THE BENEDICTINE monks, whose Rule required them to borrow and read a single volume each year, the friars and their secular colleagues in the universities needed access to substantial book collections. A newly founded library would have only a small collection of books, housed in a locked chest or cupboard. The same room might contain a few desks for readers. In some monasteries and cathedrals, partially enclosed spaces were created next to windows, to provide both light and privacy for readers. As book collections grew larger, rooms were designed especially for their accommodation. The principal considerations were the maximization of natural light and the safe housing of large numbers of books.

And libraries were beginning to accumulate books in large numbers. The Sorbonne was founded in 1257 as a theological college independent of the mendicant orders who dominated the teaching of theology at the University of Paris. By the end of the 13th century it possessed one of the finest libraries in Europe, the result of decades of gifts and bequests from secular theologians and their supporters. More than 170 donors from all over Europe were listed in the college records; one of them, Gerard of Abbeville, left three hundred books to the Sorbonne when he died in 1271. By 1290 its library contained over a thousand manuscripts. These included not only theological and philosophical works but also books on science, law, and medicine.

Such large collections were usually divided into two parts. The "public" library or *magna libraria* was a reading room in which scholars and teachers could consult a reference collection of important books. Both its design and its contents were meant to facilitate study. A communal library or *parva libraria* (sometimes called the "private" or "secret" library) was open on a regular basis to lend duplicate books or highly specialized works to members of the parent institution and to allow others to consult the books on the premises. A storeroom rather than a reading room, it fulfilled the function of the "stacks" in a modern library. There were often multiple copies of popular books, so that they could be lent to individual friars or fellows for extended periods of time—even for life. At Merton College, Oxford, as at the Sorbonne, the best copy of each book was kept, chained for reference, in a reading room. Duplicates were locked in chests kept with other valuables in the college treasury. Echoing the traditional monastic practice, they were lent out to students annually. A college officer planned the distribution so as to ensure each student access to the books he needed for his course of study. Each student had the use of between eight and forty books.

The typical scholarly library of the later Middle Ages was housed in an oblong room, three or four times longer than its width, with high vaulted ceilings. Its location on the upper floor of the monastery or college offered protection against floods and damp, and reduced the collection's vulnerability to burglars. Walls, floor, and ceiling were of stone or masonry as a protection from fire. The walls were usually painted green, a color which the 7th-century bishop and encyclopedist Isidore of Seville thought to be restful to the eyes. Large, high windows provided sunlight for the reader. There was no artificial light, and very seldom was there any provision for heating the library.

Library historians trace a succession of arrangements for housing the collections. At first the books—which were mostly large folio volumes, written in a clear hand— were kept on lecterns, sloping surfaces on which a reader could rest the book he was using. These occupied the spaces between the windows, and were arranged perpendicular to the side walls of the library, on either side of a wide central aisle. The reader stood (or sat, if benches were provided) at the place where his book was chained.

To protect them from theft, a chain attached to the fore-edge of each book's cover was attached to a rod running alongside the desktop (or, later, along a shelf). This rod was secured, so that only by means of a key could a book be added to or removed from the collection. The administrator who kept the key was often made personally responsible for the safety of the collection.

To use space more efficiently, libraries began to replace lecterns with a new type of furniture. These stalls (as they are called by historians of library architecture) consisted of double-faced bookcases, from which projected broad shelves at desktop height. The desktops were often hinged to provide access to chests stored beneath them or to additional shelves. The benches placed between the stalls were often double-sided, accommodating readers seated back-to-back with a longitudinal divider between; but some spartan libraries provided only backless benches.

At the aisle end of each bookcase, a frame held a slip of paper on which were inscribed the titles of the books there shelved. The books were placed on the shelves with their spines inward and fore-edges exposed, so that they might easily be brought down to the desktop. The fore-edges of each book were often marked with the shelf number and a short title. Each individual press (bookcase) was designated by a letter, and each shelf within the press by a Roman numeral. These designations, combined into "pressmarks," were inscribed on the inside covers of the books and in catalogs. In some libraries, additional shelving was provided along the walls at the ends of the room. Books were laid flat on these shelves. Some of the larger libraries kept smaller books (octavos) unchained on gallery shelves, accessible only to the library staff, who would deliver them to readers who required them.

This was a precursor of the "wall system," which came into use at the end of the Middle Ages. Books were housed on shelves built into the walls of the library, or in bookcases placed against the walls. This accommodated a larger number of books than did lecterns or stalls, and lent itself to ostentatious display, both of the books themselves and of the decorations of the room in which they were housed. Reading tables were often provided in the center of the room. This precluded the use of chains to safeguard the collection, but as printing came into use it became easier and cheaper to replace missing books. And the wall system alleviated one major problem encountered in libraries with lecterns or stalls. In 1444 an Oxford petition complained that "Should any student be poring over a single volume, as often happens, he keeps three or four others away on account of the books being chained so closely together."[5]

Chaining was not the only evidence of the considerable care taken by medieval libraries to protect their books. The rules of the Sorbonne forbade the carrying of a light into the room, for fear of fire. The observances of an Augustinian priory in England required that the books "be ranged so as to be separated from one another; for fear they may be packed so close as to injure each other or delay those who want them."[6] Hubert of Romans, Prior General of the Dominicans, decreed that:

> The cupboard in which the books are stored should be made of wood, so that they may be better preserved from decay or excessive dampness; and it should have many shelves and sections in which books and works are kept according to the branches of study; that is to say, different books and postils and treatises and the like which belong to the same subject should be kept separately and not intermingled, by means of signs made in writing which ought to be affixed to each section, so that one will know where to find what one seeks.[7]

In some convents the most valuable books were placed in the sacristy for safekeeping, along with the convent archives.

Deliberate abuse of the books posed another danger to the collection. This was recognized in the library regulations adopted at Oxford in 1412:

> Also, for safer custody of the books the university has ordained and decreed that all graduates now in the university and any others permitted to enter the library by the terms of the statute, shall take personal oath before commissioners deputed to this by the chancellor before Christmas that, when they enter the common library of the university to study, they will treat in decent fashion the books which they inspect, doing no damage by erasures or removing leaves or quires. . . .[8]

At Heidelberg no one was allowed to use the library unless he had taken an oath before the rector to "take and have diligent care" for the books, nor to lend his key to anyone who had not taken that oath.[9]

Books were valuable property, often considered by their owners as too valuable to lend. "Because books are singularly opportune for the progress of students," the Dominican Chapter General declared in 1323,

> we will and ordain that books in chains or in the common chest for use may not be pledged, sold, loaned or otherwise alienated by the priors or their vicars or the convent. But if they do otherwise, they shall be compelled by the

provincial priors to make good the value of the book or books from their own goods for the common chest.[10]

Even though it was customary to pledge another book or item of equal value against its return, many monasteries threatened to excommunicate anyone who lent a book. Church councils encouraged leniency, and annulled these penalties, in order that poor scholars might have access to the books they needed, and other libraries might be able to make copies:

> We forbid those who belong to a religious order, to formulate any vow against lending their books to those who are in need of them; seeing that to lend is enumerated among the principal works of mercy . . .[11]

Some lenders drove a hard bargain. Nicholas, who served as secretary to the Cistercian abbot Bernard of Clairvaux in the 12th century, required borrowers to return a new copy of each book he lent along with the original. He would then exchange these duplicates for books that Clairvaux did not own, or sell them and use the proceeds to purchase new books for the collection. At the Sorbonne, books would be lent to nonmembers only upon payment of a deposit sufficiently large to guarantee their return.

Another precaution against book theft relied upon spiritual rather than mechanical safeguards. Curses threatening excommunication, or worse, to anyone stealing or mutilating books were posted. The Cistercians of Vaux-de-Cernay inscribed this anathema in their catalog:

> If anyone attempts to carry away one of these books by theft, by fraud, or in any other manner, let his name be struck from the book of the living, that he not be inscribed with the just but instead, delivered to the fire of hell, be tormented endlessly.[12]

Though there are no surviving measures of their effectiveness, many libraries today display copies of such curses—perhaps not entirely out of antiquarian sentiment.

THE BOOKS THEMSELVES differed from those of the earlier monastic collections. The Benedictine scriptorium had produced a manuscript clearly written in a large, round hand, the text laid out generously on the page, often embellished with rubrics (initial capitals painted in red) and illuminations (illustrations or decorations, often painted in inks of many colors). Pages were large, the most common size being the folio (approximately 8 by 12 inches or 20 by 30 cm). Thick parchment and stout binding—often leather-covered oak—contributed to the magnificence of the book. The leisurely pace of monastic reading allowed such luxury, and the work of making so elaborate a vehicle for the word of God was an act of holiness in itself.

But the mendicants considered this elaboration an impious extravagance, and in the colleges and universities the need was for mass production of texts, as cheaply as possible. Thinner parchment, smaller pages, cramped writing, frequent use of abbreviations, more modest (and more portable) bindings—all were employed in the interest of practicality. The availability of a new writing substrate—paper, which was much cheaper than parchment—made the production of cheap books and multiple copies possible. While these books were produced for the personal use of scholars and students, many found their way into the university libraries, often in bequests from grateful graduates.

It was during this period that many of the features we now expect to find in books came into being. The student or master in a hurry was well served by the tables of contents and subject indexes that began to appear in their books. Texts were subdivided, and chapters and verses established for the Bible. The underlining of quotations in red made the appeal to authority easier to sustain. (These reference tools were especially useful to preachers composing their sermons.) But many a reader had to rely on his memory rather than on any finding aids supplied with the book to find a once-read passage again.

Hugh of St. Victor, director of one of the great schools of 12th-century Paris, realized this:

> It is, therefore, of great value for strengthening the memory, when we are reading books, to take pains to impress on our memory not only the number and order of the verses or the sentences, but also their very colour and form, and at the same time the place and position of the letters—where we saw this or that written, in what part, in what section (at the top, middle or bottom) we have seen it arranged, in what colour we have seen the forming of the letter or the decorated appearance of the parchment.[13]

THE CONTENTS OF their libraries reflected the purpose of the mendicant orders, and varied more from order to order than from country to country. The greater part of the mendicants' libraries consisted of liturgical books, basic theological texts, and preaching aids. Those of the Dominicans emphasized biblical studies, while the Franciscans were more inclined to moral theology.

All of the friars' libraries contained both complete Latin texts of the Bible and individual books. These were usually accompanied by glosses— brief notes, written between the lines of the text or in the margins, that clarified grammatical questions, suggested alternate translations, or interpreted points of doctrine. Glosses had become so numerous over the centuries that scholars began compiling them in separate books, called *postillae*. Another aid to scriptural study was provided by concordances, alphabetical lists of important words occurring in the Bible giving their locations in the text. This material provided the basic tools of biblical study.

More extensive commentary on Scripture was contained in the writings of the "Fathers of the Church"—the early writers, many of them now regarded as saints, who defined the essential doctrines of the Roman Church. The Western Fathers, who originally wrote in Latin, were better represented in the friars' libraries than the Eastern Fathers, whose Greek writings were read by western Europeans only in Latin translation. (Of the Church Fathers, St. Augustine, who wrote in the 4th century, was the most influential; but his Neoplatonism was increasingly being questioned by the scholastic theologians.)

Though the treatises of the Fathers were still widely read, a new style of theological writing was coming into fashion: an encyclopedic approach, in which the various arguments for and against a specific proposition were mustered and a decision rendered. In an age in which books were scarce and library resources very limited, these compilations vastly increased access to the essential writings of Christian doctrine. The most influential of these was the *Sententiarum liber quattuor* (Book of sentences) of Peter Lombard. It could be found—often in multiple copies—in every medieval library. The *Historia scholastica* of Peter Comestor was a collection of biblical narratives, supplemented with commentary from the Church Fathers and the accounts of secular historians. It, too, was widely distributed in medieval libraries.

The selection of commentators in the libraries of mendicant convents and colleges reflected their affiliation. By the end of the 13th century, Franciscans had come to identify with the Augustinian position that reason must be guided by faith, while the Dominicans upheld the Aristotelian view that human reason was sufficient to prove the existence of God and the truth of His revelation. Thus it was natural for the interest in Aristotelean philosophy of Albertus Magnus and Thomas Aquinas—both eminent Preachers—to be reflected in Dominican libraries, while the Franciscans were more interested in the writings of Augustine and the other Church Fathers and in the commentaries of Franciscan writers such as Duns Scotus, Bonaventure, and William of Occam.

While scriptural study was an integral part of their training, it was for a lifetime of preaching that the friars prepared. The works of the Fathers and the lives of the saints supplied arguments and anecdotes for sermons. But it was their own predecessors and colleagues whose writings were most useful, and most numerously represented, in the friars' libraries. Collections of sermons accounted for many of the books lent from conventual libraries.

Canon law—the body of law that governed the Catholic Church—had its sources in the writings of the Church Fathers and the decrees of popes and church councils over the centuries. It was codified during the 12th century by Gratian, a monk who lived in the legal study center of Bologna. The *Concordantia discordantium decretum* (Concordance of discordant canons), usually known as the *Decretum Gratiani*, became the standard compilation of canon law, and spawned a voluminous literature of glosses and commentaries. A later compilation, the *Decretales* of Pope Gregory IX, updated Gratian's work and enjoyed similarly high regard. As it intimately affected the rights and duties of the mendicants, canon law was naturally well represented on the shelves of their libraries.

Though none of the mendicant orders had much interest in secular literature, books on such practical subjects as civil law and medicine were often found in limited numbers. Scientific writings and imaginative literature were seldom included, but there were occasional eccentricities: one Franciscan monastery in Italy had the *Travels of Marco Polo* on its shelves.

While theology, canon law, and homiletics dominated the libraries of the mendicant orders, the universities' collections were by no means exclusively religious in nature. In addition to Scripture and commentary, theology and liturgy, their shelves contained books on logic and grammar, science and law. Summaries and indexes were produced in abundance, to serve those without the leisure or desire to read the Fathers at their original length.

As scholastic theology came to dominate the universities, the importance of the Church Fathers declined in their libraries. Augustine's writings increased in popularity; Origen, Hilary of Poitiers, Ambrose, Jerome, Gregory I, and Isidore of Seville were still collected; but later works in the patristic tradition were ignored. Latin grammar and the classics also went into decline; but Aristotle and his commentators, commentaries on Peter Lombard, and collections of sermons were popular.

Although classical literature was not part of the university curriculum, the Latin writers were read by scholars and collected by university libraries. Vergil was the most popular of the classical poets, with Ovid and Horace also well represented. Latin translations of Aesop's fables and those of Avianus provided lighter reading. Roman historians and their Christian successors as well as local writers and chroniclers contributed to library collections. Scientific collections were spotty, at best. Most common were elementary books on arithmetic and *computus* (the all-important art of calculating the dates of Easter and other movable feasts). Euclid's *Elements* and some books on astronomy and astrology were sometimes found. Medical literature consisted of Hippocrates and Galen, as well as Muslim and Jewish books translated from Arabic into Latin. These formed the course of study in the university faculties of medicine. Universities where law was studied would have the Justinian Code and Gratian's *Decretum* as well as some of the extensive literature of legal commentary.

Almost all the books in a medieval library were in Latin, though there might be some devotional works, romances, or chronicles in the local vernacular or that of a neighboring country. Rarely, a Greek or Hebrew psalter might be found, furnishing the only example of Scripture in its original languages.

• • •

THE FRIARS AND the universities were not the only collectors of books. The Benedictine monasteries never entirely abandoned their literary activities, and in some these were carried out with great distinction. Several abbots were scholars who prided themselves on building fine libraries. In those dioceses whose bishops were interested in literature and learning, monastic collections often reflected these concerns. Robert Grosseteste, bishop of Lincoln from 1235 to 1253, studied Greek and Hebrew. The library of Ramsey Abbey, which was in his diocese, contained several Hebrew books purchased from synagogues suppressed when the Jews were expelled from England in 1290.

Cathedrals and churches maintained libraries, to serve the needs of their clergy and to make available the word of God to their parishoners. The typical church library might contain a Bible and a few theological books, chained to a desk in the choir or locked up in a chest or cupboard. But some cathedral collections approached university libraries in size and scope: Christ Church, Canterbury, had 1850 volumes in the 14th century. At Bamberg, favorite city of the German emperors, the cathedral library was enriched with splendid manuscripts by Henry II and his successors. Chartres Cathedral in France had an eclectic library rich in classical literature, philosophy, and astronomy and astrology.

Libraries were not limited to institutions. As cities flourished, an urban middle class began to amass private libraries. Merchants and other laymen bought religious books such as psalters and saints' lives, but they also read Cicero, Seneca, Livy, and Ovid. They—and their wives—were the primary audience for the new vernacular literature, books such as Dante's *Divine Comedy*, the *Romance of the Rose*, and Chaucer's *Canterbury Tales*.

There were distinguished private collections throughout the High Middle Ages. In Italy, where universities did not possess extensive libraries, professors had to provide their own books. The Bolognese legal scholar Franciscus Accursius, whose *Glossa ordinaria* was one of the most influential commentaries on the civil law, owned two hundred manuscripts. Many men of affairs collected books, sometimes with an ardor bordering on fanaticism.

In his *Biblionomia*, Richard de Fournival (1201–60), the chancellor of Amiens cathedral, used the metaphor of a garden to describe his library. Three plots represented philosophy, the "lucrative arts" of medicine and law, and theology. The detailed classification scheme that Fournival devised for his collection—which has been estimated at over three hundred books—followed the progression of studies in the university. It began with philosophy and its allied subjects from the *trivium* and *quadrivium*, proceeded through medicine, canon law, and civil law, and ended with the most sublime of subjects, theology. (After Richard's death his collection became part of the library of the Sorbonne.)

Richard Aungerville de Bury, who was bishop of Durham from 1333 to 1345, enjoyed the company of scholars and the society of books. He owned books by the wagon-load; they so crowded his house that he had to step over them to reach his bed. As an emissary of King Edward III he traveled widely, purchasing books in England and on the continent. He found the libraries of Paris irresistible:

> O Holy God of Gods in Sion, what a mighty stream of pleasure made glad our hearts whenever we had leisure to visit Paris, the Paradise of the world, and to linger there; where the days seemed ever few for the greatness of our love! There are delightful libraries, more aromatic than stores of spicery; there are luxuriant parks of all manner of volumes, there are Academic meads shaken by the tramp of scholars; there are lounges of Athens; walks of the Peripatetics; peaks of Parnassus; and porches of the Stoics.[14]

A confidant of the king was in a position to do favors for many people, and de Bury was not above accepting bribes. Thus "there flowed in, instead of presents and guerdons, and instead of gifts and jewels, soiled tracts and battered codices, gladsome alike to our eye and heart." Where did these books come from? "The aumbries of the most famous monasteries were thrown open, cases were unlocked and caskets were undone . . ."[15] De Bury justified his raids upon cathedral and monastic libraries by claiming that he was rescuing books from neglect and ignorance, but these were resented bitterly by monks who set more store by scholarship than by politics.

What became of de Bury's library? He intended to leave his books to Durham College at Oxford, and indeed provided for this in his will. But he died a debtor, and many of his books were resold to the abbeys from which they had been acquired. The only permanent monument that de Bury left behind is his *Philobiblon*, a celebration of the importance of books and a memoir of his collecting activities—and there are doubts as to his authorship of it.

The German physician and theologian Amplonius Ratinck de Berka (1364–1435) was more successful at ensuring the preservation of his collection. He owned 635 manuscripts that he had bought, acquired by exchange, or copied in his own hand; over 100 of these were medical books. In 1412, shortly after cataloging them, he gave the collection to the college that he had founded at the University of Erfurt. It remained there until the university was dissolved; 435 of the books survive today in Erfurt's Wissenschaftliche Allgemeinbibliothek, as does the catalog that Amplonius compiled.

> Hidden wisdom and hidden treasure—of what use is either?
> —Ecclesiasticus 20:30

THE FIRST LIBRARY catalogs were simple shelf-lists compiled, not to facilitate intellectual access to the contents of the collection, but rather to inventory and identify a highly portable species of valuable property and to record donations. Charlemagne's son Louis the Pious, who reigned from 814 to 840, required monasteries and cathedrals to make lists of the books they owned. A brief note of a book's contents might be provided as an aid to the description of the physical object, along with its author and title, its opening and closing words (or those of the second and next-to-last leaves, which were less exposed to wear and damage), and the readily apparent physical features: the script in which the text was written, any illustrations, the format and binding. (Unlike their Muslim counterparts, Christian scribes did not attempt to duplicate the page layout of their originals. Thus, while the first leaf of a particular text would always begin with the same words, the second leaf would vary from one copy to another, allowing its initial words to be used as a way of identifying a particular copy.)

Many book-lists failed to identify the individual works within a composite volume, and there were many composite volumes in medieval libraries. The true key to a library's collection was its librarian: it was the rare library whose holdings were so extensive that one man's memory could not serve as a guide. For such extensive collections the Benedictine librarian Peter of Arbon had this advice:

> If there is so great an abundance of books that the memory is not able to comprehend their number or retain their names, let [the librarian] make a brief booklet for himself . . . in which he will record every single book by name with certain distinctions, that is, so that he assigns a page to each author sufficient for his books, a page for Augustine, for Ambrose, for Jerome, and likewise for each of the others. If you do this you will have an enduring record of books; you will be able to know what you have and what you do not have, and the monastery will have a sure testimony.[16]

This sort of systematic arrangement was an early form of cataloging as we know it today.

The first form of subject cataloging was undertaken for purely utilitarian purposes. By listing the library's collection of saints' lives in calendar order together with their locations, the appropriate book could easily be located for reading aloud during meals on their feast days. (This was done at St. Gall as early as the 9th century.)

Most medieval catalogs listed books in this order: the Bible; writings of the Church Fathers; theological works; homilies; saints' lives; and secular literature. As in Islamic libraries the hierarchy of value proceeded from the most sacred—the word of God—down to the profane. This replicated the grouping of books by subject on the shelves. At the Cistercian monastery of Altenzelle in Saxony, colored labels distinguished the books by subject matter: red for theology, green for medicine, black for law. A more complex scheme was devised by the 13th-century French bibliophile Richard de Fournival, who described an ideal library in his *Biblionomia*. He used both colors and letters to identify the subjects of books, and by differentiating among various forms of the letters (such as capital, minuscule, and uncial) was able to provide for many distinctions. A century later the library of the Sorbonne was arranged on similar principles.

The theologian of the Sorbonne needed access to a large collection: scriptural works and commentaries, the writings of the Church fathers, and the harvest of the liberal arts. He needed intellectual as well as physical access to these resources, which meant that the library catalog must go beyond its earlier role as a mere inventory of one species of movable property. No longer was it sufficient to list each book briefly by author and title. An analytic subject catalog recorded each text in the library, even those that formed part of a composite volume. Unlike today's catalogs, subjects were not listed alphabetically. Instead, the subject arrangement of the Sorbonne library catalog followed a hierarchy of authority, in which texts of Holy Scripture had precedence. Next came Peter Lombard's *Sentences*—the basic encyclopedia of theology in the medieval university— with its voluminous train of commentaries, questions, and summaries. Complete writings of saints and of doctors of the Church came next, followed by selections and anthologies. Then came the writings of the ancient philosophers, who could be viewed as forerunners of Christian thought. Medicine, the liberal arts of the *quadrivium*, and jurisprudence brought up the rear. Obviously this classification reflected the theologian's view of the world.

Union catalogs—that is, lists including the holdings of several libraries—emerged in France, England, and Germany. The Sorbonne's library contained a listing of the books held by four other Parisian libraries. In the early 13th century, the Cistercian abbey of Savigny produced a list of its holdings together with those of four neighboring Benedictine abbeys in Normandy, and in the 14th century a similar catalog in Regensburg combined the holdings of three Benedictine monasteries with those of several mendicant orders. The most ambitious of these projects was the *Registrum librorum angliae*, which listed the works of 85 writers in 160 English Franciscan monasteries. Under each author's name was a list of his works, each marked with code numbers identifying the libraries holding them. This was expanded in the early 15th century when John Boston, a monk of Bury St. Edmunds, increased its coverage to nearly seven hundred writers and added twenty new libraries. This helped the monastic librarian or master of the scriptorium to locate books that might be borrowed for copying, and was a boon to the itinerant friar. But the impact of these projects was limited. It was not until the age of printing that scholars and students could reasonably hope to have access to books whose manuscripts were not available locally.

7
GUTENBERG'S LEGACY

JOHANN GENSFLEISCH ZUM Gutenberg was not the inventor of printing. For several decades woodblocks had been used in Europe to print playing-cards, religious illustrations, and chapbooks. This art probably reached Europe through a chain of transmission from the Chinese, who had been using it to reproduce definitive editions of the Confucian Classics since at least the 9th century, an outgrowth of the even earlier process of carving them into stone. Even the use of movable type had been anticipated, not only by Gutenberg's fellow goldsmiths, who used metal punches to mark their work with distinctive symbols, but by oriental inventors. Beginning in the 11th century, Chinese printers made movable type from baked clay, wood, tin, and bronze; but it was in Korea, whose writing system was syllabic rather than ideographic, that movable type made from metal was most widely used. Contemporary Korean sources record the printing of books from cast metal type as early as the 1230s. The Bibliothèque Nationale in Paris owns a Buddhist book printed from movable metal type in 1377.

Some of his contemporaries were seeking ways of producing "artificial script," but it was Gutenberg who combined the technology of the goldsmith's punch with that of the winepress. The result was the printing press—a machine that combined flexibility, rapidity, and economy to allow the production of books that the increasingly literate, increasingly numerous European city dwellers could afford to buy and read.

Printing did not at first revolutionize the appearance of the book. Gutenberg's forty-two-line Bible (1452–76), which is generally held to be the first printed book in Europe, looked very much like a fine manuscript. It was intended to. The prospective purchasers of an expensive book knew very well what one should look like. Solid, heavy letters, hand-colored decorations, contractions and ligatures to ensure that lines of text were even in length—all these were deliberate imitations of scribal practice. As with any new technology, it took years of experimentation, and new generations who had grown up with printing as a part of their intellectual environment, before the possibilities of the new medium were realized.

By mechanizing the mass production of books and pamphlets, which had previously required the efforts of workshops full of scribes, the printing press facilitated the spread of new discoveries, techniques, and ideas, and of criticism and censure of old ones. It proved a powerful force for creating and destroying institutions. It allowed the rise of a flourishing trade in papal indulgences, printed forms commuting the pains of Purgatory for the purchaser or his relatives. It allowed the rapid dissemination of Martin Luther's condemnations of the corruption within the Roman Church that permitted this traffic. And it allowed the dissemination of Scripture that encouraged the literate layman to judge the controversy for himself. It even played a role in the very survival of languages: when two contending tongues were spoken in one land, the first in which the Bible was printed tended to flourish while its rival declined.

Printing itself was too good a secret to keep. It spread rapidly across Europe, especially after Gutenberg's city of Mainz was pillaged in 1462. By 1500 there were 260 places where the art was practiced. Tens of thousands of titles had been published, and at least ten million volumes had come off the presses. Almost half of these were bibles, prayer books, and other standard Christian texts. But more than half were not.

THE HUMANIST MOVEMENT of the 14th century had sought inspiration from the Greeks and Romans. The Italian poet Francesco Petrarch (1334–74) and his contemporaries sought to revive in their work the classical literary tradition. They also very consciously set out to create a literature in the spoken language of their day. Throughout the 14th century, Dante, Petrarch, Froissart, and Chaucer were establishing the vernaculars of Europe as literary languages. The invention of the printing press strengthened both these movements.

Manuscripts were not only expensive to produce. Their value depended upon the fidelity of their copyists, who were not always as accurate in their work as a scholar might like. Petrarch lamented:

> Who will discover a cure for the ignorance and vile sloth of these copyists, who spoil everything and turn it to nonsense? If Cicero, Livy, and other illustrious ancients were to return to life, do you think they would understand their own works? There is no check upon these copyists, selected without examination or test of their capacity. Workmen, husbandmen, weavers, artisans are not indulged in the same liberty.[1]

To ensure that the Greek and Latin classics were published in complete, accurate editions, editors and printers searched the libraries of Europe for the best available manuscripts. These were purchased, exchanged, borrowed, or sometimes stolen, and turned over to the printers to serve as copy.

The Venetian scholar and printer Aldus Manutius (1449–1515) produced a series of carefully edited texts of Greek classics. Many of these were based on manuscripts from the Biblioteca Marciana, which had been established in 1468 with the donation of Cardinal Johannes Bessarion's library of 745 manuscripts, 482 of them in Greek. In Basel, Johann Amerbach (1443–1513) and his partner and successor Johann Froben

(1460–1527) issued scholarly editions of the Greek and Latin classics and the Church Fathers. With the eminent humanist Desiderius Erasmus of Rotterdam as their editorial advisor, their publications were acclaimed throughout Europe. They stimulated scholarship as much by their uniformity as by their authenticity: having the same words on the same page in every copy made it possible for scholars to compare and discuss texts.

Even before Gutenberg the enthusiasm of the Italian humanists for the ancient writers led them to collect and compare manuscripts of classical texts, laboriously compiling authoritative editions. The Florentine humanist Coluccio Salutati (1330–1406) had called for the establishment of official repositories for carefully edited copies of important texts, from which authentic copies could be made for wider distribution. The same concern had led the Chinese emperors to order the Confucian Classics carved in stone, and the Parisian authorities to supervise closely the copies supplied to students by university stationers.

The humanists' travels in the service of Church or prince gave them the opportunity to visit libraries across Christian Europe. In the 15th century, Church councils proceeded at a leisurely pace. The Council of Constance lasted from 1414 to 1418, and the Council of Basel from 1431 to 1439. Council business often required the borrowing of documents from monastic collections, while lengthy recesses in the proceedings afforded prelates and secretaries ample opportunity to visit nearby monasteries in search of literary manuscripts.

When Poggio Bracciolini (1380–1459), who served for many years as papal secretary, visited St. Gall in 1416, he was appalled at the way the monks treated their treasures. "O ye men who love the Latin language," he heard the books calling, "do not allow me through neglect to be entirely destroyed here; save me from these chains!"[2] Obeying their summons, he copied manuscripts of works that had been lost for centuries, and dispatched the results to his friends in Florence.

Poggio prospected for manuscripts across much of western Europe, visiting the renowned monasteries of Reichenau and Fulda, and wandering as far afield as Cologne, London, Paris, and Rome. He did not always confine himself to making copies of the treasures that he unearthed. Germany was to him "a prison where Roman classics were held captive by Teutonic barbarians,"[3] and he felt justified in liberating these captives and sending them to Italy. His efforts might have violated the Eighth Commandment, but they preserved many a text from disappearing during the upheavals of succeeding centuries.

Similarly, Giovanni Aurispa (1370–1459), who had brought 238 manuscripts to Italy from Greece, found important manuscripts at Basel and Mainz; and several of his compatriots made major discoveries in the monastery and cathedral libraries of Italy. By the end of the 15th century, when Angelo Politian made a systematic tour of Italian libraries, there were few texts left to be discovered. And the work of Manutius, Froben, and other scholar–printers ensured that the classical heritage would be disseminated widely across the libraries of Europe.

The resulting books found their way into a wide range of environments. Cathedrals and monasteries still maintained libraries, at least in those countries that remained Catholic. In the Protestant lands of the north, monasteries were dissolved. Their book collections, purged of papist publications, were distributed to royal, princely, civic, or scholastic libraries. Both Catholic and Protestant leaders saw in the printing press a valuable resource in the struggle for ideological supremacy within Christendom; and both sides viewed libraries as arsenals of intellectual weaponry. Without libraries, said the Dutch Jesuit Peter Canisius, "we are like soldiers who march into battle without any weapons."[4] A good library, said the Lutheran jurist and mathematician Gottfried Wilhelm Leibniz, "would contain material to defend the true religion against its adversaries."[5]

The same sense of national pride that expressed itself in the creation of vernacular literatures led to the collection and compilation of historical records. In 1517 the dukes of Bavaria appointed Johannes Aventinus their historiographer and instructed him to prepare an official history of their realm. "Day and night without rest," Aventinus reports, he went "across the entire land of Bavaria, pounding at the door of every convent and monastery, sifting every box of papers, perusing and copying word for word every pertinent manuscript, charter, privilege, letter, chronicle, verse, saying, adventure story, missal, prayer book, inventory, calendar, obituary, saint's life . . ." in fulfillment of his ducal commission "to discover, inspect, and transcribe the old documents, antiquities, and records stored in our Bavarian monasteries."[6] When Richard Hakluyt set out to compile the *Principall Navigations, Voiages and Discoveries of the English Nation,* he consulted not only seamen and geographers but also writers ancient and modern. "How many famous libraries I have searched into," he exclaimed in his preface, recounting his labors in the colleges of Oxford and in the stately homes of the Elizabethan nobility.[7]

A similar impulse motivated Church historians. Franciscan Peter Crabbe, who published in 1528 a collection of the acts of Church councils, boasted that he had searched for sources in more than five hundred libraries. The Dutch Jesuit priest Heribert Rosweyde began at the start of the 17th century to collect, examine, catalog, and edit the lives of saints, in order to publish an authoritative collection in the order in which they appear in the Church calendar. His work was continued by another Dutch Jesuit, John van Bolland, who edited the first volume of the *Acta sanctorum* for publication in 1643. (The work has continued over the centuries, and under the auspices of the Bollandist Society the sixty-seventh volume was issued in 1940. Another seven or eight volumes, covering the last fifty days of the liturgical year, remain to be produced as of 1998.)

IT WAS IN private collections that the greatest progress was made in the establishment and administration of libraries, and in their use. While kings and princes, motivated by ostentation or piety, had collected books since the days of the Sumerians, it was under the influence of humanism that monarchs and nobles began to build serious libraries.

Petrarch had been an avid collector of Latin literature, a passion that he transmitted to his literary descendants. By the end of the 14th century, the upper classes in northern Italy had eagerly taken up the search for classical books. Flushed with the treasures discovered at Constance and Basel, they expanded their horizons to all of northern Europe. They abstracted or copied the Latin texts they found and exchanged books with their fellow collectors. Some also visited Greece, or sent emissaries there; and after the Turks took Constantinople in 1453, they eagerly embraced the Greek manuscripts that the Byzantine refugees brought with them to Italy.

Niccolo de' Nicoli (1363–1447), a Florentine bookseller, was so enthusiastic a collector that, though originally a wealthy man, he died heavily in debt. His enthusiasm was that of a missionary, not a miser: he made his books available to those who would read or copy them, and he lent them freely to his friends. Although he knew almost no Greek, he collected Greek books so that scholars might be able to consult them. Niccolo's will had provided for a self-perpetuating board of trustees to maintain his collection. Because no endowment was provided, they had to turn over the supervision of the trust to Niccolo's friend and patron Cosimo de' Medici (1389–1464), who directed not only an international business empire but also the political life of Florence. Cosimo divided Niccolo's books between his private collection, housed in a splendid room in the Medici palace, and the public collection that he had established in the Franciscan monastery of San Marco in Florence.

The library housing this collection was designed by Michelozzo Michelozzi, the Medicis' favorite architect. It was a long, narrow, vaulted room, divided into three parts by rows of columns. The books were distributed among sixty-four lecterns fashioned from cypress wood. They were not crowded together: none of the lecterns held more than six volumes. As the collection grew in size, a "Greek library" was added. In this room were placed all the non-Latin books, Greek as well as the few in Arabic, Armenian, and Hebrew.

Cosimo hired Tommaso Parentucelli (1398–1455) as his librarian. In addition to cataloging the collection, Tommaso drew up a list of books needed to ensure that Cosimo's library represented the best of classical and sacred literature. This canon was used by other bibliophiles to guide their collecting; it is an early manifestation of that dedication to books that led Tommaso to refound the Vatican library when he ascended the papal throne as Nicholas V.

Cosimo de' Medici was a business man with a taste for literature; his grandson Lorenzo "the Magnificent" (1448–92) was the uncrowned prince of Florence. As befit his eminent position, he surrounded himself with artists and scholars, and enlarged Cosimo's library to well over one thousand manuscripts. Almost half of these were in the Greek language. Lorenzo sent the scholar John Lascaris to Constantinople for Greek manuscripts, where he acquired several hundred. Many of them contained texts previously unavailable in Italy. Lorenzo also collected Italian literature. Florentine humanists borrowed liberally from his collection, often transcribing books so that they might have their own copies. Between 1480 and 1494 the library lent 155 works, both Latin and Greek; there were times when a single borrower had ten of them in his possession. Lorenzo's books, together with those Cosimo had placed in San Marco, were moved in 1571 to the Bibliotheca Laurentiana in Florence, a marble palace designed by Michelangelo.

Federigo de Montefelto (1422–82), Duke of Urbino, was a rival to the Medicis at book collecting. He put thirty or forty copyists to work, a contemporary biographer tells us, and sought the catalogs of other libraries in order to ensure that his collection surpassed theirs. In this library "all books were superlatively good, and written with the pen, and had there been one printed book it would have been ashamed in such company."[8] Vespasiano de Bisticci (a bookseller who helped Cosimo de' Medici, Duke Federigo, and Pope Nicholas V to build their libraries) goes on to claim that this library contained the complete works of all known writers, ancient and modern, sacred and profane, whether composed in the classic languages or written in Italian. No doubt he exaggerates; but a contemporary inventory of the Urbino library lists 1,104 manuscripts, including many in Greek and Hebrew. Among Latin books, there were many examples of classical, patristic, and humanist texts, beautifully decorated by the miniaturists of Ferrara and Florence. Every book in his collection was written on vellum, bound in crimson, ornamented with silver.

The collection occupied a room twenty-two feet by forty-five feet. Clear north light came through windows set high in the twenty-three-foot walls, which were lined with bookshelves. Latin verses in praise of books and libraries were inscribed on the cornices. A large bronze eagle served as a lectern; in the small study adjacent, carved armchairs surrounded a reading table. But the Duke's books served him for recreation as well as study: he maintained at his court five men to read aloud during meals. Except during Lent, when spiritual works were read, the Duke listened to the Roman historian Livy—in Latin.

Federigo Veterano served the dukes of Urbino as librarian for forty years. His duties were spelled out in the court regulations:

> The librarian should be learned, of good presence, temper, and manners; correct and ready of speech. He must get from the gardrobe an inventory of the books, and keep them arranged and easily accessible, whether Latin, Greek, Hebrew, or others, maintaining also the rooms in good condition. He must preserve the books from damp and vermin, as well as from the hands of trifling, ignorant, dirty, and tasteless persons. To those of authority and learning, he ought himself to exhibit them with all facility, courteously explaining their beauty and remarkable characteristics, the handwriting and miniatures, but observant that such abstract no leaves. When ignorant or merely curious persons wish to see them, a glance is sufficient, if it be not some one of considerable influence. When any lock or other requisite is needed, he must take care that it be promptly provided. He must let no book be taken away but by the Duke's orders, and if lent must get a written receipt, and see to its being returned. When a number of visitors come in, he must be specially watchful that none be stolen.[9]

Federigo de Montefelto's descendant, Duke Francis Mary II, bequeathed the collection to the citizens of Urbino to be maintained as a public library. But Pope Alexander VII, who claimed that he wished to ensure "their preservation and proper treatment,"[10] had the books taken to Rome, overcoming the resistance of Urbino's citizens with a promise of exemption from taxes. In 1658 they were incorporated into the Vatican Library, "for the increase of the splendor of the Holy See, and the benefit of Christendom."[11]

Although the popes had collected books for centuries, no permanent papal library had survived the tumults of medieval life and the removal of the papacy to Avignon in 1309. The Bibliotheca Vaticana, today one of the world's great treasure houses, traces its founding to 1450. Pope Nicholas V, who as a young man had been librarian to Cosimo de' Medici, used money collected during that jubilee year—when one hundred thousand pilgrims, bearing contributions to Church coffers, flocked to Rome—to augment the surviving papal collection. He donated 340 manuscripts from his own collection, and purchased additional books with Church funds. He sent agents across Europe in search of books, and bought manuscripts from the Imperial Library when Constantinople fell to the Turks in 1453. He employed Byzantine scholars to translate Greek manuscripts into Latin, and hired copyists from Florence and Bologna to produce new copies of Latin classics. At his death in 1455, the Vatican Library had grown to 1,209 volumes.

Nicholas's successors maintained the library and opened it to scholars outside the Vatican. Sixtus IV declared in 1475 that the library's purpose was "to serve the dignity of the serving church, to further the faith, [and] for the use and honor of scholars and all those who are devoted to the study of sciences."[12] He had a large suite of rooms in the Vatican Palace outfitted for the purpose, and employed some of the finest artists and craftsmen in Italy in their construction and decoration. Great artists and writers sought inspiration in the Vatican Library: the architect Donato Bramante, the writer Baldassare Castiglione, and the painter Raphael. Scholars of the Church also used its treasures. Cardinal Francesco Ximenez de Cisneros—the man who had burned the books of Muslim Spain—compiled the Complutensian Bible, a polyglot collection of texts in Hebrew, Aramaic, Greek, and Latin. Some of the library's Greek manuscripts were sent to him in Spain. It took the pope's personal intercession to get them back.

The Vatican Library grew by gift and bequest, by copying and purchase, and sometimes by outright theft. In 1508, Pope Leo X sent the monastery of Corvey a newly printed edition of the *Annals* of Tacitus in involuntary exchange for their manuscript. "We have sent a copy of the revised and printed book in a beautiful binding to the Abbot and his monks, that they may place it in their library as a substitute for the one taken from it," he explained. "But in order that they may understand that the purloining has done them far more good than harm, we have granted them for their church a plenary indulgence."[13]

ELSEWHERE IN EUROPE, princely and private collectors showed less interest in ancient manuscripts. Devotional and moralistic works, historical chronicles, and courtly epics and romances were favored in France, Germany, Spain, and England. And a generation of bibliophiles arose for whom the printed book was as worthy of a place in their collections as the manuscript.

Jean Grolier de Servin (1479–1565) was educated in Paris by the Italian humanist Gaspar d'Argile, a useful preparation for his career in the service of a French state that was in the process of conquering northern Italy. His literary tastes and scholarly interests were shaped by his years in Milan, where he served as treasurer of the French army and the government that ruled northern Italy under French supervision.

His library contained about three thousand volumes, including both manuscripts and printed books. He was a friend of the Venetian printer Aldus Manutius, and an early patron of the Aldine Press. In addition to Greek and Roman classics, Grolier owned many historical and religious works. But more than its content, Grolier's library was renowned for the magnificence of its bindings. At first he replaced plain leather with rich fabric, a material more opulent than durable. In 1536 a treaty between the king of France and the sultan of Morocco made fine Moroccan goatskin leather in many colors available in Europe, and Grolier retained the best binders in France to produce the geometrically tooled covers that have delighted bibliophiles for more than four centuries. These books were not kept solely for display; they were meant to be read by "Io.

Grolierii et amicorum," Jean Grolier and his friends, a phrase incised into each book's cover.

Grolier's collection was sold after his death. His books are today the prized possessions of individuals and institutions across Europe and America. But a century after his death tastes had changed: a satirist speaks dismissingly of a collector of splendidly bound books and of "the tannery which he calls a library."[14] The 17th-century bibliophile needed guidance in assembling a library that would bring him respect rather than ridicule, and a young Frenchman offered to provide it. Henri de Mesmes appointed Gabriel Naudé his librarian in 1622, when Naudé was a twenty-two-year-old medical student in Paris. Five years later, Naudé wrote *Advis pour dresser une bibliothèque* (Instructions concerning erecting of a library), which circulated in manuscript for several years before its publication in 1644. Naudé took as his topic "the choice of books, the means of procuring them, and how they should be disposed of, that they might appear with profit and honour in a fair and sumptuous bibliotheque." His intended audience was the wealthy aristocrat who desired to assemble a library; in 17th-century Paris there were many such whose wealth exceeded their knowledge of literature. And not only in Paris: John Evelyn's English translation was published in 1661. Naudé urged the beginning bibliophile to seek the advice of more experienced collectors and to read the *Philobiblon* and other books on collecting. He should also obtain copies of every available library catalog, ancient or modern. And he should collect as many books as possible: every book, no matter how bad, will someday be wanted by somebody. "For certainly there is nothing which renders a Library more recommendable, than when every man findes in it that which he is in search of, and could no where else encounter . . ."[15]

Gottfried Wilhelm Leibniz did not agree. He advised Duke John Frederick of Brunswick–Lüneburg, whom he served as librarian from 1676 to 1680, that a library should contain

> as much as is needed to furnish basic information on all important subjects— theology, public or private law, medicine, mathematics, philosophy, literature, and history. Selection rather than size determines what is necessary, and, for my own use, I would often prefer a small, well-chosen library, belonging to an individual, to a great mass of books belonging to a noble lord or a community, which is only for show and which does not contain books which are useful.[16]

Naudé urged collectors to open their libraries to the public. There is no point in collecting books, he asserted, unless they are made available to any who can make use of their contents. Books should be lent for limited periods of time to "persons of merit and knowledge"; but careful records should be kept. A good librarian should be hired to make this possible, and to produce two catalogs: one by subject, and one by author. The latter would help to identify books needed to complete the collection, as well as to avoid purchasing the same book twice; it would also assist those who wished to read all the works of a particular writer.

One did not need to be an aristocrat to be a book collector. Many a churchman, lawyer, and physician owned a working library of a few dozen or a few hundred professional books, leavened perhaps with a few volumes of classical or vernacular literature. Practical men rather than aesthetes, they had no prejudice against printed books, often using them to replace manuscript copies in their collections. (Even university libraries discarded manuscripts when printed copies became available. The discarded books were often sold to bookbinders, who used them as book covers or backing-strips.) They often bequeathed their books to universities, or to the public libraries that were established in churches and monasteries in northern Europe.

Merchants, though usually literate, were not renowned for reading. A prayer-book to pray from and an almanac to tell the feast days were library enough for the bourgeois Frenchman, according to a 17th-century account. His Spanish counterpart made do with devotional books, commercial manuals, and a travel book or two; he was not in the habit of reading fiction.

The printed book was much cheaper than the manuscript: an octavo volume cost an educated man only a day's pay or two. The printed octavo was portable as well as affordable, a boon to the diplomat or secretary who spent much of his time traveling—or waiting.

IN 1524, MARTIN Luther addressed a pamphlet "To the Councilmen of All the Cities in Germany, That They Establish and Maintain Christian Schools." These were to educate Protestant Germany's political, commercial, and religious leaders; and they would need libraries. "No effort or expense should be spared to provide good libraries or book repositories, especially in the larger cities which can well afford it," he proclaimed, citing Paul's Epistles in support of the importance of reading.[17] He blamed the sorry state of German education on the fact that "men failed to found libraries but let the good books perish and kept the poor ones."[18]

Luther had no interest in catering to popular literary tastes; his intention was to gather together and make available the books needed to guide a Christian community:

> My advice is not to heap together all manner of books indiscriminately and think only of the number and size of the collection. I would make a judicious selection, for it is not necessary to have all the commentaries of the jurists, all the sentences of the theologians, all the *quaestiones* of the philosophers, and all the sermons of the monks. Indeed, I would discard all such dung, and furnish my library with the right sort of books, consulting with scholars as to my choice.[19]

He would stock libraries with the Holy Scriptures ("in Latin, Greek, Hebrew, and German, and any other languages in which they might be found") and the best commentaries on them; books useful for learning the languages of the Bible; chronicles and histories ("a wonderful help in understanding and guiding the course of events, and especially for observing the marvelous works of God"); and books on law and medicine.

Other Evangelical reformers offered similar advice. Caspar Hedio urged the Palatine Count Ottheinrich "to build a library of books of the holy scriptures, jurisprudence, medicine, and all kinds of histories," which would contain not only books in Latin, Greek, and Hebrew but also "a German library in a publicly accessible area for pious God-fearing citizens and laymen."[20] This would encourage young people to improve their souls during time they might otherwise spend in taverns or bowling greens. But the count chose instead to subsidize the printing of Evangelical pamphlets, reserving his library for fine books and manuscripts; most of these were left to the University of Heidelberg.

Despite the enthusiasm with which German cities established public libraries, Luther's dream was only partially realized, doomed by the lack of resources on the part of city governments and lack of interest among the clergy. The libraries became treasuries in which rare books and manuscripts were preserved, treated as valuable properties rather than sources of guidance for the people. The dissolution of the monasteries by Protestant princes enriched many municipal collections with yet more manuscripts and incunabula; but except for historical and legal documents, the public libraries had little to offer. Used mostly by teachers and pastors, their contents reached the general public only indirectly, as reflected in classroom lectures and Sunday sermons.

Luther had never intended his words to lead to the destruction of libraries, but his attack on the authority of the Church had unforeseen consequences. Inflamed by his proclamation of the "freedom of the Christian man"—and by the radical pamphlets that poured forth from the printing presses—workers across Germany took up arms against their political and ecclesiastical masters. In 1525 the German lands were torn asunder by the Peasants' War, a rebellion against the power and property of Church and nobility. Peasant mobs looted and burned palaces, churches, and monasteries. Archives of written and printed records were a special target, for there were kept records of debts and obligations. Books, seen as symbols of oppression, shared their fate. At Auhausen, its abbot complained, "A valuable library of twelve hundred books in all disciplines, which have cost the blessed Dean of Eichstätt and me over fifteen hundred gulden, the Devil's children have torn into several parts, have spoiled and cut to pieces, and burned and thrown into the wells."[21]

THE PRINTING PRESS had at first only a limited impact on university libraries. Neither the curriculum nor the composition of the student body changed to any great extent. The role of the university was to defend orthodoxy in religion and philosophy and to educate administrators for the needs of church and state, not to contribute new discoveries to the store of human knowledge. That function was assumed by the academies and learned societies that came into being across western Europe in the 16th century.

At first these were concerned with the recovery of ancient learning and its application to contemporary questions. Their members examined Greek and Latin texts and discussed them in detail, studying not only their literary content but also the historical, geographical, and biographical knowledge they revealed. The goal of their endeavors was to understand the classical world, and to recreate its glories in their own time.

Under the influence of Francis Bacon, they increasingly turned their attention to scientific discovery. This work depended less on the recorded wisdom contained in libraries than upon the truths revealed by observation and experiment. Rather than consulting the wisdom of the ancients, they read a new form of literature: the learned journal. These printed the proceedings of learned academies and transactions of scientific societies. University libraries rarely bothered to collect this material. Library acquisition budgets—where these existed at all—were minuscule, and universities depended upon gifts and legacies for the increase of their collections.

But to the extent that the invention of printing was responsible for the Protestant Reformation, it eventually did come to have a major effect on universities and on their libraries. In northern Europe existing universities were reformed, and new ones established, to train a Protestant clergy and to educate physicians, lawyers, and public officials for the service of the Protestant state. In those countries that remained Catholic, Jesuits and other teaching orders maintained their dominance not only over faculties of theology but also over university life as a whole.

In German universities, the arts faculties that had prepared young teenagers for higher studies were transformed into faculties of philosophy that claimed status equal to other parts of the academic community. Their students were older, their teachers increasingly secular, and their scholarly activity more evident. In most of these universities, the library was administered by the faculty of philosophy, and reflected in its contents the religious loyalty of the parent institution. More often than not the library was more ornamental than useful: a storehouse for valuable gifts, a repository of learned manuscripts, but not at all an essential part of the students' educational experience. They were rarely accessible to students. Typically they were open only a few hours a week. Such lending as they did was to professors only.

Their fortunes ebbed and flowed with the tides of war and politics. Some were burned or plundered by invading armies or appropriated by powerful nobles. Thousands of manuscripts and printed books from the University of Heidelberg library were sent to Rome in 1623, as repayment by the victorious Duke Maximilian I of Bavaria for papal support during the

Thirty Years' War. A decade later, invading Swedes looted the Würzburg University library, many of whose treasures found their way into the university library at Uppsala and the court library in Stockholm. A sadder fate befell the libraries of the University of Mainz and the Jesuit college. Carried off by Gustavus Adolphus, they were lost in the Baltic Sea en route to Sweden.

Others found their collections enhanced by the holdings of dissolved monasteries. In Protestant countries, where monasteries were routinely suppressed, the fates of their libraries varied with the piety or cupidity of the secular powers. While the books often found their way into princely libraries or private collections, in many cases universities were the ultimate beneficiaries. Even in Catholic lands many monasteries were secularized, and their books transferred to nearby universities. This too was the fate of the libraries of Jesuit colleges when Pope Clement XIV suppressed the Society of Jesus in 1773.

During the English Reformation, royal commissioners visited Oxford, removing from the university painted windows, religious ornaments, and other "popish" elements, and pillaging the university and college libraries. Books were taken from the shelves ". . . some to serve their jakes [latrines], some to scour their candlesticks, and some to rub their boots." John Bale reported this as a "detestable fact,"[22] but not everyone shared his disgust. Richard Layton, one of Henry VIII's "Visitors" to Oxford, reported gleefully that the schoolman Duns Scotus "is now made a common servant to every man," with his works "fast nailed up upon posts in all common houses of easement."[23]

The library that Duke Humfrey, youngest brother of King Henry V, had provided in the middle of the 15th century was totally destroyed. It was not restored until 1598, when Thomas Bodley undertook to reestablish a "public library" for the university. Bodley's first librarian, Thomas James, was an ardent Protestant who considered the Inquisition's *Index librorum prohibitorum* (Index of forbidden books) the best guide to choosing books for the university library. But in fact most of the printed books were acquired through the services of leading London booksellers, one of whom traveled across Europe, even visiting Catholic Spain, and sent back large consignments of continental publications. Many manuscripts were contributed by collectors who had acquired them during the dissolution of the monasteries; both Catholics and Protestants saw Oxford as a safe haven for these historical documents. By Bodley's death (1613) his library contained fifteen thousand works in seven thousand volumes, at least one-tenth in manuscript. Almost all the books were in Latin. English was not considered a scholarly language, and Bodley thought English literature too frivolous and transitory for a university library. But Bodley was ahead of his time in his enthusiasm for oriental languages. He arranged for the acquisition of books in Greek, Hebrew, Arabic, Turkish, and Persian, and even added titles in Chinese, though there was nobody in Oxford who could read them.

1. Cuneiform clay tablet of the Epic of Gilgamesh. This relic from King Assurbanipal's library in -7th-century Nineveh is now in the British Museum. (Department of Western Asiatic Antiquities, no. K 3375) © The British Museum.

2. The Library of Alexandria in Ptolemaic Times In this drawing by Roy G. Krenkel, Hellenic scholars are shown examining scrolls and discussing their contents. By comparing manuscripts and assessing their authority, the scholars of Alexandria put together definitive texts of Homer and the other great writers of ancient Greece. (Used by permission of Barry Klugerman, literary executor for the Krenkel estate.)

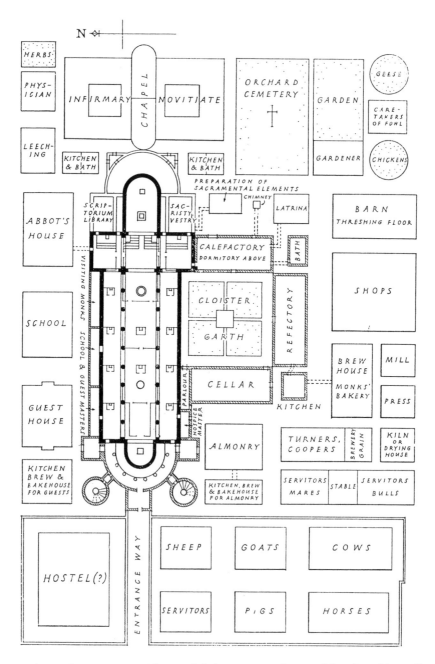

3. The Perfect Monastery. This English-language rendering of the Plan of St. Gall (circa 820) shows the ideal arrangement for a self-contained community devoted to the service of God. The monastery of St. Gall, in today's Switzerland, was built to an approximation of this plan. The library and scriptorium were located at the north end of the chapel, to secure the best light for reading and copying manuscripts. Cattle and sheep provided parchment and leather (for bookbinding), and geese furnished quills to make pens. (From Kenneth John Conant, *Carolingian and Romanesque Architecture, 800-1200,* Penguin, 1966)

4. The Big Wild Goose Pagoda, Ch'ang-an (present-day Xi'an), China. It was here that Hsuan-Tsang deposited the Buddhist manuscripts that he brought back from his pilgrimage to India. Though often restored over the intervening centuries, this is substantially the same building that the Emperor Kao-tsung built. (Photograph by Dr. Glen Dudbridge, in Sally Hovey Wriggins, *Xuanzang: A Buddhist Pilgrim on the Silk Road,* © Westview Press 1996. Reprinted by permission of Westview Press.)

5. House of Wisdom, Baghdad. In this drawing by Trevor Newton, a scholar consults a book, perhaps in preparation for a disputation before the library's founder, the 'Abbasid caliph al-Mamun. (From *Aramco World,* March-April 1987, by permission of the publishers)

6. Interior of the Biblioteca Malatestiana, Cesena, Italy. This photograph by Alinari shows a fifteenth-century monastic library arranged on the "lectern" system. The books were chained in place on bookshelves below the sloping tables on which they rested while in use.

7. Chained Library, Hereford Cathedral, England. This sixteenth-century library (restored in 1930) was arranged on the "stall" system. To prevent theft, books were chained to rods above the shelves. The chains were long enough to allow the books to be laid flat on the tabletop that protruded from each press (bookcase). The label at the end of each press lists the books it contains. (Photograph from Streeter, *The Chained Library*)

8. Manuscript from the Urbino Library. This page from an illuminated manuscript of the Bible illustrates both Duke Federigo's exquisite taste and the sublime craftsmanship of the Florentine artisans who produced it. Little wonder that the Popes coveted Federigo's books—and brought them to the Vatican Library, where they remain today. (Ms. Urbinate Lat. 1, f.27.r., Biblioteca Apostolica Vaticana, Rome. Foto Biblioteca Vaticana.)

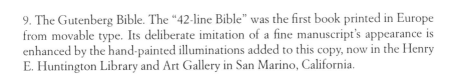

9. The Gutenberg Bible. The "42-line Bible" was the first book printed in Europe from movable type. Its deliberate imitation of a fine manuscript's appearance is enhanced by the hand-painted illuminations added to this copy, now in the Henry E. Huntington Library and Art Gallery in San Marino, California.

10. Circular Reading Room of the British Museum Library. Soon after it opened in 1857, the *Illustrated London News* printed this drawing of Antonio Panizzi's magnificent reading room. Although the British Library has recently moved to new quarters next door to the St. Pancras railway station, the Circular Reading Room will continue to serve visitors to the British Museum in Bloomsbury.

11. Gottingen University Library in the Nineteenth Century. This engraving by I. Poppel (after a drawing by O. Eberlein) shows Europe's greatest academic library in the era when it made such a strong impression on visiting American scholar George Ticknor, later one of the founders of the Boston Public Library.

12. "The Rivals, Which Shall It Be?" This cartoon by J. Williams Benn, portraying the social reformer's hope for the public library, appeared as the frontispiece to the first edition of English library pioner Thomas Greenwood's *Free Public Libraries* in 1886.

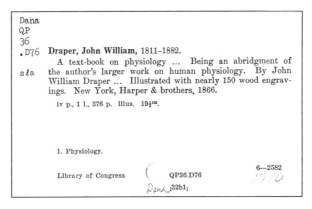

13. Catalog Card for John William Draper's *A Text-Book on Physiology,* one of millions of cards published by the Library of Congress Cataloging Distribution Service. The availability of printed cards such as this relieved libraries of the necessity of cataloging and classifying every book in their collections. Today this cooperative cataloging is produced and distributed through electronic databases.

14. MEDLINE on the Web. The World Wide Web offers access to an immense array of information resources, many of them available free of charge to anyone with access to a computer and an Internet connection. "Internet Grateful Med" is an easy-to-use version of the world's largest biomedical bibliography, designed to let physicians and nurses do their own literature searches. It is produced by the National Library of Medicine.

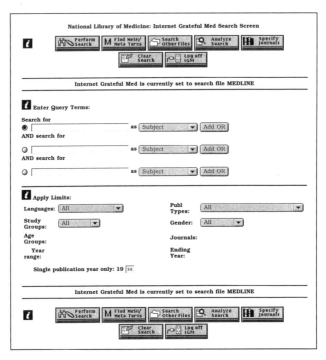

8
TREASURIES OF THE BOOK

FOR AS LONG as the book has been in existence, there have been book lovers and book collectors. In the age of the manuscript book, only the wealthy could afford private book collections. As the printing press cut the cost of books, the working library became a common aspect of professional life. The printed book was utilitarian and affordable, and many a middle-class doctor, lawyer, pastor, and merchant owned a collection of the books that were becoming increasingly tools of his trade.

But this did not diminish the appeal of the fine book to the writer, the printer, or the collector. The idea that beautiful thoughts, beautifully expressed, should be beautifully recorded, was not abolished by the hand of Gutenberg; indeed, his printed Bible was designed in emulation of a fine manuscript. As the art of printing evolved, printers developed their own aesthetic of book production, informed as much by the technological possibilities of movable type as by the heritage of calligraphy and illumination. The binder, and later the illustrator, the engraver, and the lithographer added their skills to the design and realization of the fine book. And the collector, whether motivated by love of literature or delight in ostentation, eagerly sought out a physical artifact appropriate to the housing of the literary craftsmanship he treasured.

The first prerequisite of book collecting was the possession of substantial disposable wealth, and so the first book collectors were the princes temporal and spiritual—a distinction that, through much of European history, was seldom a firm one. To pope or bishop or pious king, a fine library of sacred books was not only a source of pleasure and enlightenment: it was a shrine to the word of God. And to king or duke or worldly prelate, the splendor and wealth embodied in a fine library was a display of majesty that served political as well as intellectual interests.

Popes and princes were institutions as well as people, and their book collections often came to have an institutional as well as a personal character. The popes' collections were incorporated into the Bibliotheca Vaticana, and kings' libraries often evolved into national libraries. Over the centuries these were transformed from personal collections of fine books to multifaceted institutions serving the highest purposes of state and society. Many of the libraries assembled by doctors, lawyers, bankers, and merchant princes in emulation of royal and ducal collections underwent the same transformation.

The great private collections did not inevitably become public upon the demise of their founders. Many went to auction, to settle estate taxes, to provide for the material needs of the collector's heirs, or, as one collector's will put it, to afford fellow bibliophiles the pleasure of the chase. The catalogs of some of these sales, compiled by expert bibliographers and subject specialists at the great auction houses of Europe and America, are treasured as works of substantial scholarship: many are used as checklists by collectors and dealers.

These collectors, whether expert or novice, relied heavily upon the advice and expertise of their booksellers. The antiquarian book trade embraces an extensive variety of dealers: some whose elegant showrooms display illuminated manuscripts, incunabula, fine bindings, and modern first editions to wealthy collectors and librarians with large acquisition budgets; others in shabby storerooms whose creaky wooden shelves, laden with dusty volumes, attract the impecunious academic and the bargain-seeking browser. Dealers have long worked together to ensure that a collector's desiderata can be circulated worldwide, and supplied from any available source, be it attic or monastery. (In the aftermath of World War I, many an impoverished European monastery sold its treasures to American collectors or universities. Yale University and the Library of Congress acquired their Gutenberg Bibles at this time.)

Subject specialists, who routinely buy and sell individual books and entire collections within their areas of interest, have played a large role in building libraries. Their specialized bibliographical knowledge has often allowed them to bring to the attention of their clients desirable titles previously unknown to them. In many cases they acted as agents for collectors, representing them at auctions or negotiating for the purchase of major treasures, and discreetly selling on their behalf books no longer wanted.

Although the merchandise they deal in is often centuries old, antiquarian booksellers have kept up with the times. The trade at first depended upon printed auction catalogs to know what books were available. More recently, dealers advertised their wants and offerings in weekly magazines whose listings were routinely checked against their stock by subscribers. This is giving way to computerized databases. But the concept is the same. The antiquarian book trade is based on the principle that for every book there is a customer—and for every dealer there is a profit to be made in uniting them.

THE ANCIENT ARISTOCRACY of Europe, and many of the families who rose to wealth in banking and commerce, had been collecting books for generations. Even when the current head of the dynasty lacked interest in books, dynastic pride or sheer inertia often kept the books within the family. When a bibliophile inherited the collection, he might add to its existing strengths, or supplement its riches with material peculiar to his own taste. If he needed guidance, he could turn to the dealers his forbears had patronized, or seek the counsel of fellow collectors within his social circle. If he were serious about its development, he might hire a scholar to serve as his personal librarian.

The dukes of Brunswick–Wolfenbüttel began collecting books in the 16th century, when Duke Julius purchased several private collections and added to them books from dissolved monasteries. His descendants in the 17th and 18th centuries built up the family collection, which included libraries at Hannover, Braunschweig, and Wolfenbüttel. It was at Wolfenbüttel that the heart of the collection was located, and there the dukes themselves cataloged their books. They soon turned over this task to eminent scholars. Gottfried Wilhelm Leibniz, philosopher and mathematician, added the supervision of the library to his work as privy councilor at the end of the 17th century, and the writer Gotthold Ephraim Lessing served as Wolfenbüttel librarian during the 1770s. The Wolfenbüttel catalog served as the model for other great European libraries, and today the Herzog August Bibliothek remains a major resource for the scholarly study of the cultural history of the early modern period. (With the demise of the last reigning duke in 1954, it became the property of the state of Lower Saxony.)

The Spencers got a later start. In the 18th century the first earl Spencer collected Elizabethan literature and passed on his taste for book collecting to his son. The second earl purchased the Hungarian count Reviczky's fine library of early printed editions of the Greek and Roman classics, which also included specimens of the most important European printers. After his retirement from public life in 1807, Lord Spencer devoted his time to literature and book collecting, becoming well known in the bookshops and auction houses of Britain and continental Europe. By 1818 Spencer was only eight books away from his goal of assembling a complete collection of classical first editions. He sent the young clergyman and bibliographer Thomas Frognall Dibdin on a "bibliographical, antiquarian, and picturesque tour," the better to find hidden treasures in the obscure monastic and municipal libraries of France and Germany, and succeeded in acquiring desired volumes even from the Royal Library at Stuttgart. At his death the forty thousand volumes at Althorp, the family home in Northamptonshire, were widely acknowledged to be "the finest private library in Europe."[1]

The industrial revolution and the expansive opportunities of 19th-century North America created a new set of rich men and women who were determined to enjoy their wealth. Some engaged in lavish displays of ostentation, some in philanthropy—and some, combining both impulses, began to collect paintings, sculpture, and fine books. Some became collectors out of a genuine love for the objects they collected; others for the prestige of owning the finest creations of the most gifted artists and writers. Whatever their motives, the collections they amassed had a profound effect upon libraries.

Many collectors, with sentimental ties to the universities they had attended, took pleasure in building up the libraries of their alma maters. Often they collaborated with university librarians, with the goal of turning over to the institution, through gift or bequest, a resource for scholarship as well as a monument to munificence. Rather than submerge their collections into an existing library, some chose to erect institutions that would preserve and continue both their endeavors and their reputations. William Clements and John Carter Brown, builders of large collections of Americana, affiliated their libraries with those of major universities (Michigan and Brown, respectively) and housed them in their own buildings on campus.

Those whose education was self-imposed, or for whom feelings of civic pride or patriotism outweighed the memories of youth, often placed their collections within the great public or national libraries. Other collectors created entirely independent foundations. John Pierpont Morgan (1837–1913) became the foremost financier in America. Investment banking, railroads, and steel interests brought him the resources with which he assembled extraordinary collections of art and literature. His collecting was inspired by his aesthetic sensibilities rather than any bent for scholarship; his twenty-five-thousand-volume library emphasized beauty and rarity over intellectual importance. Scholars were admitted to the marble edifice that Morgan erected next to his midtown Manhattan home, but the books and manuscripts were primarily for his own pleasure. He bequeathed them to his son, who established the Morgan Library as "a public reference library for the use of scholars as a memorial to his father."[2] As one of many resources for bibliographical and literary research in New York City, it has proven more valuable to scholarship than its origins might have suggested.

The Huntington Library might well have become another of those resources, but its founder Henry Edwards Huntington (1850–1927) fell in love with California, where he had extensive real estate and electric railway interests. He amassed a significant collection of English and American historical and literary documents. With the aid of such leading booksellers as George D. Smith and A. S. W. Rosenbach, he purchased many entire collections, and secured the highlights of several others at auction sales. "The ownership of a fine library is the surest and swiftest way to immortality," he believed; and to ensure that immortality Huntington endowed an institution to maintain his library and art collection in perpetuity. The Huntington Library and Art Gallery opened its grounds in San Marino as a botanical garden and displayed its pictorial and literary treasures to the public. But its primary purpose was to provide the means for research into "the origin and progress of the civilization of the English-speaking peoples with special reference to their intellectual development."[3] To this end, the library not only preserved its books and made them available for consultation by scholars, it maintained a research staff of distinguished scholars, provided grants to invited visitors, sponsored conferences, and published both documents from its collection and research studies of its materials. Henry Huntington, once a "collector of rare and unique objects" had become—as one of the library's first trustees remarked—a "patron of research."[4]

This form of philanthropy was not unique to America. The Manchester manufacturer and merchant John Rylands had subsidised the preparation and distribution of Bibles and hymnals in England and on the Continent. He left an enormous fortune, which his widow used to establish a public library for theological students. To ensure that they would find the books they needed in their research, she began to assemble a reference collection of standard works in history, religion, and general literature. When in 1892 the Althorp library was put up for sale, Mrs Rylands purchased it to prevent its removal to the New York Public Library. The purchase of the Haigh Hall library assembled by the earls of Crawford and Balcarres brought an equally valuable collection of oriental manuscripts to Manchester. These additions transformed the John Rylands Library into one of the world's finest collections of fine books, and a center for literary and bibliographical scholarship. (In 1972 it became part of the University of Manchester.)

EVEN IN THE Renaissance period some royal libraries served the needs of statecraft as well as the pleasures of princes. Legal deposit laws, introduced in the 16th century, were intended to ensure that all books printed in the realm were represented in the royal collection. These laws not only ensured that the intellectual output of the kingdom or duchy was gathered in a central location: they also simplified the process of keeping a watchful eye on what was being written and printed.

The Ordonnance de Montpellier of 1537, the earliest such law, required that a copy of every book printed in France be sent to the royal library at Blois, and that a copy of every book imported into France be offered for sale to the library. Three centuries later, Napoleon decreed that multiple copies of all publications be submitted to the police; duplicates were deposited in the national library.

Ever since Charlemagne, the kings of France had maintained personal libraries. Inspired by the Saracen libraries he saw while on crusade in the Holy Land, the saintly Louis IX (r. 1226–70) strove to emulate them upon his return to France. He had the writings of the Church Fathers copied from monastic collections and installed in Saint-Chapelle, his palace chapel, where the learned might consult them. But upon his death the books were divided among his favorite monasteries. It was not until the reign of Charles V (1364–80) that a true royal library came into being, one that was intended as a national treasure rather than a purely personal resource. Though it was established for the king's use, many of his successors allowed students to use the Bibliothèque du Roi, some even opening it to the public on a regular basis. Shortly after 1567 the royal library's 3,650 titles were transferred to Paris, where they might be more easily consulted by literary men and scholars at the university. But it was not until 1735 that the library was permanently opened to the public, who were allowed to use the books twice a week.

The French monarchs had been none too scrupulous in their acquisition programs. Charles VIII (r. 1483–98) was an avid collector; after the seige of Naples he collected most of that city's Royal Library. The Bibliothèque du Roi absorbed three Jesuit libraries when that order was expelled from Paris in 1764. This precedent was maintained after the Revolution. Monasteries were suppressed, the properties of aristocrats and émigrés confiscated, and the libraries of Europe despoiled of their treasures by Napoleon's armies. The great royal libraries of Europe, as well as many university and monastic collections, were plundered. After Napoleon's downfall at Waterloo, most of these treasures were returned to their owners, but many remain still in the Bibliothèque Nationale.

From its medieval beginnings the Bibliothèque du Roi grew steadily through the purchase of eminent private collections and its own acquisition efforts. French diplomats were instructed to procure books from the countries to which they were accredited; as their purchases included publications on those nations' colonial empires, the royal library's collections covered most of the world. Missionaries and traders also brought back to France printed books and manuscripts from the lands they visited. Duplicate books were exchanged with libraries in other countries; the king exchanged books with the emperor of China. Nor was French history neglected: specially trained scholars were sent across the kingdom and assigned to copy monastic charters and other documents. This work proceeded on so grand a scale that in a single year (1670) it took 340 folio volumes to hold the transcripts received from two provinces. The Englishman Martin Lister, who visited the Royal Library in 1698, was favorably impressed with what he saw:

> This library consists of at least 50,000 volumes of printed books, and 15,000 manuscripts in all languages. They work daily and hard at the catalogue which they intend to print. I saw ten thick folios of it, fairly transcribed for the press. . . . They have two indexes; one of the matter and contents of books, and another of authors, wherein are all the works they have, . . . and the titles likewise of all that they know of that are wanting, with an * in the margin, . . . that they may know what they have to buy . . .[5]

As the Bibliothèque du Roi increasingly assumed the character of a national library, it attracted donations and bequests. During the 18th century, as its collections grew, the library's physical plant and its administrative structure were expanded to accommodate the books and the increasing number of scholars and writers who came to consult them. A catalog of the collections was begun, though only a portion of it was published.

By the time of the French Revolution, the Bibliothèque du Roi had amassed nearly two hundred thousand printed books and more than twenty-five thousand manuscripts. It was decreed a public library in the aftermath of the Revolution. Despite an initial hostility to all things that might "offend the eyes of Republicans by shameful marks of servitude,"[6] a decree requiring the effacement of royal symbols and the armorial bearings of the nobility as well as the removal of prefaces and dedications addressed to kings or nobles was never enforced. Instead the Revolutionary authorities emphasized the need for greater public access to the collection. They ordered that the library be open to students for four hours daily (on nine days out of every ten, the "decade" having temporarily replaced the week in the Revolutionary calendar) and to casual visitors on three out of every ten days. The collections were augmented with books confiscated from aristocrats executed or exiled, and from the resources of churches and monasteries. So many books were acquired in this way that fifty years later many remained "uncatalogued, unclassed, and even unstamped."[7]

LIKE MANY OTHER British institutions, the British Museum evolved more accidentally than purposefully. Neither king nor Parliament assumed the task of preserving the nation's heritage, nor did any part of the British government undertake to build up a collection of learned literature to serve the needs of scientists and scholars. A handful of wealthy individuals collected historical documents, literary manuscripts, and scientific specimens, which were later given or sold to the nation. Sir Robert Cotton's (1571–1631) collection contained many books that had been monastic property before the Reformation. Robert (1661–1724) and Edward Harley (1689–1741), first and second earls of Oxford, were avid collectors of political history. Sir Hans Sloane (1660–1753), a wealthy London physician, acquired botanical and zoological specimens as well as scientific books and drawings.

Sloane's will offered his collections to the nation at a bargain price. To raise the required twenty thousand pounds, the impoverished Parliament ordered a lottery. Its proceeds were used to buy the Sloane collections, and to endow a British Museum to house them along with the Cottonian and Harleian collections. Just before the museum opened to the public in 1759, King George II presented it with the Royal Library. Its books and manuscripts had been collected by his predecessors since the reign of Edward IV, many of them (like Cotton's collection) from monasteries suppressed during the Reformation.

In its early days, the British Museum was not a very lively place. Its meager finances did not allow for any systematic expansion of the collection, so its growth depended almost entirely upon gifts. The superannuated physicians and clergymen who comprised its staff were seldom troubled by visitors; they regarded readers more as a nuisance than a constituency. But the museum soon outgrew its quarters in Montagu House. Its library was doubled in size by the donation of George III's books—his heir George IV, the "Prince of Pleasure," preferred mistresses to manuscripts. And the Elgin Marbles and other treasures brought home by globe-trotting Britons required more suitable accommodation. So a new building was designed in Bloomsbury, the home of the British Museum to this day.

When the Italian political exile Antonio Panizzi (1797–1879) was appointed Keeper of Printed Books in 1837, he set forth an ambitious statement of the library's role:

> This emphatically *British* library ought to be directed most particularly to British works and to works relating to the British Empire, its religious, political and literary as well as scientific history, its laws, institutions, commerce, arts, etc. The rarer and more expensive a work of this description is the more . . . efforts ought to be made to secure it for the library.[8]

To fulfill this plan, Panizzi insisted upon the rigorous enforcement of mandatory deposit laws, which publishers had got into the habit of ignoring. He secured an appropriation of ten thousand pounds a year from Parliament for the purchase of books. The young Vermonter Henry Stevens, who had traveled to London to purchase books for American libraries, was hired to return home and "sweep America for us, as you have done London for America."[9] (By 1865, Stevens had acquired one hundred thousand books for the British Museum.) And Panizzi improved both the physical facilities of the library and its staff, so that they might be adequate for the collection he meant to build: one that would not only possess "every book that was printed either by Englishmen or in English or relating to England,"[10] but would also own "the best library of each language outside the native country of that language."[11]

By the end of Panizzi's tenure at the British Museum, it was impossible to write authoritatively on any aspect of British history or culture without resorting to the magnificent circular reading room that he had built. ("Certainly I have never seen any room so completely adapted to its grand purpose of intellectual labor for a large number of persons," wrote George Ticknor.)[12] The library's influence spread far beyond London. American researchers used it regularly. "In the London library," one student reported, "I can learn more about American financial history in a day than I can learn in New York in a week."[13] Karl Marx based his scientific interpretation of history on the economic tracts and historical essays he read there while preparing *Das Kapital,* and Vladimir Ilyich Lenin found in the British Museum's collections not only revolutionary literature from Russia unavailable in his native land, but also documents from the English and French revolutions. "The economics section is particularly full," Lenin observed, because "they are merchants, you see. They have to trade with Russia and they have to know her."[14]

Thomas Carlyle called the British Museum "a really excellent Library, where one *can read.*"[15] Other national libraries received less favorable notices from their users. William Thackeray wrote to Antonio Panizzi from Paris, describing the Bibliothèque Nationale:

> The accommodation is so entirely inferior to that which the British Museum gives us: that comparisons are quite out of the question. The catalogue you consult is the librarian of whom however learned one cannot ask too many questions and on whom there is a constant pressure of applicants. If I had to write on a French subject, the French Revolution for example, I would go to London for the books . . . rather than apply here, where instead of a catalogue at my orders, I must trust to the good memory and complaisance (both of which are very great) of the librarian.[16]

He had an easier time of it than did J. G. Kohl, a German writer who had visited the Imperial Library in St. Petersburg a few years earlier:

> To get a book to read in the library itself is utterly impossible, though you can point out where it stands. You must first write down the title in a large register, and then, if it is not lent and can be found, you are supplied with it on the next library day. But on the days appointed for reading [three days each week] you may many a time knock in vain, because it may happen to be one of the numberless festivals of the Russian church. . . . It happens sometimes that you may wait for weeks in vain for a single book. The first time, the entry of the book has perhaps been overlooked, and you must write down the title again; next time you are told it is not to be found, or the librarian, to whose department it belongs, is not in the way. Sometimes you are yourself prevented from attending on a library-day, and then you lose your claim to the wished-for book, which has meanwhile been removed from the table; so that you are obliged to go on a fourth or fifth day to enter it again, and at least on a sixth or seventh to read it.[17]

WHAT IS THE role of a national library in a democracy? In 1774, when the Continental Congress assembled delegates from the American colonies in Philadelphia, it secured borrowing privileges from the Library Company of Philadelphia, with whom it shared Carpenter's Hall. After the Revolution, the new American government enjoyed access to the libraries of New York and Philadelphia. But in 1800 the national capital was moved to Washington, a new city whose literary infrastructure was nonexistent. What library could members of the Congress and officers of the government consult for information they might need in the course of their duties?

Elbridge Gerry, a representative from Massachusetts, urged in 1789 that Congress establish a library of its own. But the Boston *Independent Chronicle* argued that congressmen should already know all they need of history, law, and political science to manage the government. "It is supposed that the members are fully competent for these purposes, without being at the expence of furnishing them with Books for their improvement."[18] Despite such opposition, a small library was established for the use of Congress; with its emphasis on law and parliamentary procedure, it was clearly intended to be a working collection for legislators.

When British invaders burned the Capitol during the War of 1812, the three thousand volumes in that congressional library were dispersed or destroyed. Thomas Jefferson, who was deeply in debt, offered to sell his personal collection—one of the finest libraries in North America—for whatever price the Congress saw fit to offer. With over six thousand volumes, its scope went well beyond narrowly defined legislative concerns. But Jefferson claimed that "I do not know that it contains any branch of science which Congress would wish to exclude from their collection; there is, in fact, no subject to which a Member of Congress may not have occasion to refer."[19] Some critics would have liked to exclude one branch of science—"books of an atheistical, irreligious, and immoral tendency,"[20] that is, the writings of Voltaire and other writers of the French Enlightenment— and others complained of the collection's unnecessarily broad scope. But Congress narrowly voted to approve its purchase.

The resulting Library of Congress was just that: at first, not even the president was accorded access to it. (He, and the other members of the executive branch of the national government, relied upon the State Department library, a collection of state legislation, works on international law, and books on history, geography, and political science.) Its permitted clientele was gradually expanded, but with no intention of making it a resource for scientists and scholars. That role was at first assumed by the Smithsonian Institution, which had been founded in 1846 under the terms of the Englishman James Smithson's bequest "to found at Washington . . . an establishment for the increase and diffusion of knowledge among men." As the institution's trustees groped toward a definition of their charge, some observers considered the Smithsonian the ideal home for the nation's central collection of scientific literature. But its director, Joseph Henry, intended the institution to concentrate its efforts and resources on performing scientific research and publishing the resulting discoveries. Its ambitious publication program produced several series of journals and reports that were sent to scientific societies and learned academies around the world; the publications received in exchange were transferred to the Library of Congress.

After the Civil War, the library began to seek out material basic to an understanding of American history, purchasing collections of early printed publications and manuscript material. The library looked outward as well as inward. As immigration and commerce increased America's concerns with events overseas, one librarian with previous ties to the diplomatic service secured the help of American embassies and consulates worldwide in expanding the collection. John Russell Young summed up the library's desiderata in one expansive sentence:

> Public documents, newspapers, serials, pamphlets, manuscripts, broadsides, chapbooks, ballads, records of original research, publications illustrative of the manners, customs, resources and traditions of communities to which our foreign representatives are accredited, the proceedings of learned, scientific or religious bodies, the reports of corporations such as railways, canals, or industrial companies, legislative records and debates, public decrees, church registers, genealogy, family and local histories, chronicles of county and parish life, folklore, fashions, domestic annals, documents illustrative of the history of those various nationalities now coming to our shores, to blend into our national life, and which as a part of our library archives would be inestimable to their descendants—whatever, in a word, would add to the sum of human knowledge, would be gratefully received and have due and permanent acknowledgement.[113]

"There is, in fact, no subject to which a Member of Congress may not have occasion to refer." As the truth of Jefferson's words became ever clearer, the demands on the time and energies of congressmen made it less and less likely that they would actually use their library. In 1911, only 93 of 490 members had made any use of it whatsoever. To bring the library's resources to bear upon the nation's needs, a Legislative Reference Service was created, to provide congressmen and their staffs with information assembled from materials within the library. This was in keeping with the progressive spirit of the times, which advocated the application of scientific information to the solution of societal problems. Like its counterparts in state capitols, the Legislative Reference Service freed lawmakers from dependence upon lobbyists for information on proposed legislation and help in drafting bills.

During the 1940s, Librarian of Congress Archibald MacLeish set forth three Canons of Selection:

> 1. The Library of Congress should possess in some useful form all bibliothecal materials necessary to the Congress and to the officers of government of the United States in the performance of their duties.

> 2. The Library of Congress should possess all books and other materials (whether in original or copy), which express and record the life and achievements of the people of the United States.

> 3. The Library of Congress should possess, in some useful form, the material parts of the records of other societies, past and present, and should accumulate, in original or in copy, full and representative collections of the written records of those societies and peoples whose experience is of most immediate concern to the people of the United States.[22]

Increasingly the Library of Congress was becoming America's *de facto* national library, though its politically astute directors were careful to emphasize its ties to the Congress, from which after all it received its appropriations. It neither sought nor received any such official designation: the only American libraries explicitly designated as "national" are two specialized collections, the National Agricultural Library and the National Library of Medicine. But although it was never officially assigned this role by its congressional masters, the Library of Congress has assumed a leadership position in many aspects of American librarianship. No statute compels American libraries to follow its lead in collection development, cataloging, or preservation of materials; but economics and sheer common sense have induced many libraries to take their direction in these matters from the Library of Congress.

American librarians early realized that there was no need for the same book to be cataloged in detail by every library that owned it. After all, the basic bibliographical details of the ordinary printed book—author, title, imprint, physical aspects—did not vary from one copy to another. Nor did its content. A common list of terms by which to describe its subject matter was worth having for its own sake; and once such a list existed, much time and cost would be saved by applying it only once to each book. So when the Library of Congress, which received more books than almost any other American library, began selling copies of its printed catalog cards in 1901, many other libraries began to purchase them, in effect turning over much of the task of cataloging their collections to the L.C. catalogers. In that same year, the Library of Congress and the New York Public Library began exchanging catalog cards. Over the years additional American libraries began to contribute cataloging information to a National Union Catalog maintained in Washington. By 1955 it contained more than thirteen million cards; eventually it was replaced by multivolume sets of catalog cards photographically reproduced, several cards to a page. In recent years this cataloging information has been produced on magnetic tapes and optical discs to facilitate interactive searching by computer.

As the Library of Congress's collections grew from Thomas Jefferson's six thousand volumes to almost a million by the end of the 19th century, it outgrew the subject arrangement that had been inherited from Jefferson. An expansion of Francis Bacon's three kinds of science—memory, reason, and imagination—into forty-four subject divisions, it was no longer capable of dealing with the proliferation of specialties that had emerged from the expansion and professionalization of learning. Even the Dewey Decimal Classification, admirably suited though it was to public and college library collections, was not detailed enough to reflect the contents of the Library of Congress. So the library devised its own classification, drawing upon Melvil Dewey's Decimal Classification and Charles Ammi Cutter's Expansive

Classification, but based on the patterns in which its collection had evolved. The Library of Congress Classification—twenty large classes, whose printed schedules occupy two meters of shelf space—has been adopted by large libraries across the United States and around the world.

Another area in which the Library of Congress has undertaken a leadership role on behalf of American libraries is that of the conservation and preservation of library materials. Though the invention of wood-pulp paper made possible the production of cheap books and newspapers, it imposed a limited life-span on those publications. The rag paper used by the first printers has lasted for over five hundred years with little or no deterioration, but the chemicals used in wood-pulp paper provoke a gradual disintegration. The pages of a fifty- or hundred-year-old volume may crumble in its reader's hand: dismaying enough in a printed book, and truly disheartening in archival or manuscript material. Librarians have developed several strategies for arresting, reversing, or at least mitigating the decay of their collections. They have microfilmed newspapers, laminated precious documents, and experimented with chemical technology for removing or neutralizing the destructive acids from pulp paper. The Library of Congress has been in the forefront of this work, conducting tests of deacidification technology at an army facility previously devoted to chemical warfare research, and using innovative computer techniques to preserve and distribute rare pictures and documents.

Though the Library of Congress is still, in the letter of the law, an agency designed to serve the legislative branch of the United States government, it has become in fact the American national library, and is becoming one of the cornerstones of the evolving worldwide research library system.

IN COUNTRIES WITH a well-developed educational system and a long tradition of libraries, the national library's role is often defined in terms of preserving the national cultural patrimony, and making it readily accessible to those who would study it. For example, Hungary's National Szechenyi Library undertakes to collect any document

> issued in the country and from abroad (a) that was written in Hungarian on any subject; (b) that was written by a Hungarian author on any subject and in any language; (c) that refers to Hungary or the Hungarian people by subject written by any author in any language.[23]

The work of the national library may include the development of special cataloging rules and classification schemes, such as the expanded version of the Library of Congress schedules for Canadian history and literature produced by the National Library of Canada. Even in developing countries the national library is usually charged with the maintenance of the national bibliography and the provision of relevant information to international bibliographical projects.

In some cases the role of the national library goes well beyond the mere preservation of the national heritage. The Bibliothèque Nationale du Mali is enjoined "to publicize, uphold, and exhibit Malian cultural values,"[24] and similar expectations exist in other newly independent countries. Nor is this exclusively a phenomenon of our era. In the mid-19th century the Imperial Public Library in St. Petersburg assembled a comprehensive collection of foreign-language publications about Russia. This Rossica Collection was part of an imperial strategy to define the Russian national identity. Its geographical scope reflected Russia's claim to rule extensive lands on the borders of the Russian heartland—Finland, the Baltic provinces, Ukraine, the Caucasus, central Asia, and Siberia—and the publication of a catalog in French and German was meant to justify that claim to European scholars. The project was enthusiastically supported by the nationalist intelligentsia.

Even when territorial claims are not involved, national libraries often find themselves enmeshed in politics. By mounting exhibits of important works from their collections, or borrowed from other libraries, they can make strong assertions on cultural matters. When these deal with sensitive periods of history or delicate aspects of interethnic relations, they have often provoked considerable controversy.

Less controversially, national libraries often serve as repositories for books received as gifts from friendly governments, and as sites for ceremonial occasions. The British Library today plays a symbolic role in the swearing-in of members of Parliament. Where once the King James Bible was sufficient for the purpose, in a multiracial Britain that has elected Muslims, Jews, Hindus, and Sikhs to the House of Commons it has become customary for new MPs to take their oath on their own holy books. The British Library lends exemplary copies of sacred texts from its rare book collections for this purpose.

In developing countries, the national library has often been charged with a major role in the creation and dissemination of the national culture. Shortly after it became the first European colony in Black Africa to win its independence, Ghana defined the functions of its National Library Centre:

(i)   To acquire, preserve and make available, all library and related materials concerning Ghana whether they are produced locally or abroad.

(ii) To acquire, preserve and make available library material in all fields of knowledge, for the benefit of scholars, research workers, advanced students and government personnel.

(iii) To serve as a permanent depository for all publications issued in Ghana.

(iv) To compile and publish the national bibliography.

(v)   To compile and maintain a National Union Catalogue of all books owned by the country's libraries (except light fiction and children's books).

(vi) To serve as an interlibrary loan centre on a national and international scale.

(vii) To serve as a national and international exchange centre.

(viii) To publish special bibliographies of important collections.

(ix) To provide bibliographical services for the libraries of Ghana.

(x) To serve as a centre for co-operative activities among the nation's libraries.

(xi) To provide library services to Parliament and Government Departments.[25]

In most Black African nations, as in many other developing countries, the national library has been responsible for providing basic library services to the literate adult population, at least in the capital city. "National libraries in developing countries must play this dual role," explained the director of the Bibliothèque Nationale du Benin. "It is the only way that they will be able to establish and organize a network for the development of libraries in their country."[26]

In many developing countries a good part of the national cultural patrimony is held in repositories thousands of miles away. Archival materials essential for scientific and historical research on Africa are preserved in London, Paris, Brussels, Madrid, and Lisbon. An African librarian remarked that

> Apart from several million people who speak the English language in addition to their own, all that now remains of the British Empire is a cluster of extensive collections of official documents in London: the librarians are the last of the imperialists![27]

This is not a straightforward issue of repatriating artifacts removed from their country of origin: these documents, created under the auspices of colonial governments, are witnesses to their history as well as that of the lands they governed. Fortunately, such technologies as microfilm and computerization allow both former colony and former metropole to preserve these literary remnants of their shared history.

9
THE REPOSITORIES OF KNOWLEDGE

BY 1700 THE universities of Europe had become almost entirely irrelevant to the enhancement of learning and the diffusion of knowledge. They were strongholds of orthodoxy, intended to prepare clergymen for a lifetime of unquestioning propagation of the faith. To anyone other than an aspiring clergyman—and in much of Europe that meant to anyone other than a younger son of the gentry without an aptitude for the military life—the universities had almost nothing to offer. Medical or legal training could be had through apprenticeship to an established practitioner, and neither finance nor commerce nor politics required or rewarded a university education.

University libraries generally reflected the intellectual unimportance of their parent institutions. The scope of their collections had not greatly advanced since the age of the manuscript; and if their size had increased that was largely the result of religious controversies arising from the Reformation. The published accounts of the voyages of the great Age of Discovery; the scientific writings of Copernicus and Galileo, of Harvey and Newton; the imaginative literature of an era that had produced Shakespeare, Molière, and Cervantes—all were ignored by the university curriculum and the libraries that existed to support it.

Despite the flowering of vernacular literature in the 16th and 17th centuries, the contents of university library collections were almost entirely in Latin and (to a much lesser extent) Greek. Humanists like Erasmus who wanted their books accessible to the learned population of Europe wrote and published them in Latin, knowing that everyone whom they might wish to address read that language.

The Enlightenment changed all that. The Reformation had destroyed among both Protestants and Catholics the idea that a single religion would unite Western civilization. The Age of Discovery had revealed the existence of entire new continents and new ways of reaching old ones; no longer was a journey to a different country unthinkable save for conquest, crusade, or pilgrimage. And the rediscovered writings of ancient Greece and Rome led men to think of alternatives to existing social and political arrangements.

Those whose horizons had been expanded by the Renaissance and the Reformation began to rethink the idea of education and of the university. They envisioned an institution that would prepare young men for careers in the new world that was unfolding around them. New universities and other institutions were founded to train men to serve the administrative needs of the state.

These new universities required new libraries. A university that sought to transmit existing knowledge saw its library mainly as a mechanism for the safekeeping of books. But as universities sought to increase the sum of knowledge, a more dynamic sort of library was called for. And as knowledge—and the publications by which it was transmitted—increased rapidly, as it did in the latter half of the 18th century, university professors and other scholars could not hope to collect private libraries sufficient to their needs. The universities had to provide the intellectual resources with which their senior members could sustain themselves.

It was during the 18th century that the university library began the transition from treasure-house to intellectual heart of the university. This process began in Germany, and was most evident at Göttingen.

The University of Göttingen opened in 1737 in a small town a few miles from Hannover, capital of the electorate of Brunswick. Göttingen was conceived as a research university as well as a teaching institution: as a community in which knowledge would be added to the store of humankind as well as transmitted from one generation to another. This would not be possible without a strong, well-developed library, and Göttingen owed much of its reputation—by the end of the century it was esteemed the leading university of the German-speaking world—to the care with which its library was conceived and organized.

Christian Gottlob Heyne, Göttingen's chief librarian from 1763 to 1812, pored over auction catalogs and lists of new books from the semi-annual Leipzig fairs, placing orders with booksellers and despatching bidding instructions to agents across northern Europe. Believing that "the number of books is that which counts least," he held that "the true worth for the university consists in purposeful selection." Heyne called for

an uninterrupted planned acquisition of what is needed . . . for a library which is organized according to a scientific design, not according to predilection for a particular subject; not for ostentation; not for the luster of the superficial; but for the inclusion and embrace of the most important works of all periods and peoples in all sciences and in domestic literature; [a library] in which the fleeting, changeable taste of the day and literary fashion . . . are only of secondary importance.

Heyne's goal was a library that was useful rather than ornamental, in which "luxury editions are not readily acquired if they do not have also intrinsic scientific and artistic merit." The university library should contain books which

illuminate the art and taste, not only of one country, but all educated nations; . . . which represent the learned, the classical, the artistic antiquity of all periods;

which contain, further, the language knowledge and, the foundation of all human knowledge, the history of all peoples and times, and in its support, the inestimable collection of geography and ethnography with the remaining auxiliary sciences and auxiliary studies of history, politics, and political geography.[1]

This philosophy, and the diligence with which it was put into practice, attracted to the Göttingen library gifts from all over Europe. Whether a luxurious edition of Shakespeare from the king of England or a collection of Russian books sent by the Academy of Petersburg, these donations enhanced the library's reputation as well as its holdings. Entire collections were acquired as well; but it was the steady, careful selection of the best new publications that made Göttingen the best university library in Europe. In 1799 an official of the royal library, visiting from Berlin, told Heyne that a published catalog of the Göttingen library would serve every library in Europe: instead of cataloging its own collection, it could simply annotate its copy of the Göttingen catalog to show its own holdings.

Not every university boasted so fine a library as Göttingen's. George Ticknor, who twenty years before had studied in Göttingen, visited Prague in 1836. At the Charles University he noted that "the library contains about ninety-three thousand volumes, a beggarly matter for such an institution; and, what is worse, they looked as if they belonged to the studies of the sixteenth and seventeenth centuries, rather than to those of the nineteenth."[2]

The medieval university library had required its treasures to be used on site. The early modern library—at least in Protestant countries—expected readers to use its books in their homes. Printed books could be more easily and cheaply replaced than manuscripts; and the type of learning prevalent in the modern university required the consultation of privately owned books as well as those from the university collection. The university library was an uninviting place in which to spend any substantial period of time. The damp and cold were seldom allayed by stoves, for fear of fire; and the same consideration kept lamps out of libraries. December's daylight lasts only eight hours in northern Europe, so it is little wonder that many libraries curtailed their hours in winter.

In the sunnier countries of Catholic Europe, university libraries tended to support in-house use rather than circulation. (In several French university libraries, books had remained chained well into the 17th century.) They provided reading rooms separate from the bookshelves, and remained open for longer hours. Their celibate users were not distracted by the demands of family life.

The book rather than the user was still the focus of the 18th-century university library. Librarians were expected to have a wide knowledge of languages and of the literature of learning, but there was no science of librarianship that they were required to master, and no library schools or formal training programs. The librarian was often a poorly paid member of the philosophy faculty, who regarded his work in the library as a supplement to his meager salary rather than as a vocation in its own right. The operation of the library was a nuisance to such a man: at Halle in Germany, one librarian resigned his post rather than undertake to keep the library open four hours a week. And in many universities the librarian was held financially responsible for loss or damage to the collection, hardly an incentive to maintain a liberal lending policy.

BRITISH NORTH AMERICA lacked the abundance of opportunities for professional training that existed in the mother country, and American colleges early diversified from their original purpose of training clergymen. Benjamin Franklin explicitly proposed a modern curriculum for the University of Pennsylvania; even the most traditional of colleges educated physicians, lawyers, and men of business as well as ministers of the gospel. At all of the colleges founded in America before the Revolution, libraries were accorded central importance. Although the Massachusetts General Court granted four hundred pounds for the establishment of a college in 1636, it was not until two years later, when the Rev. John Harvard bequeathed three hundred books and almost eight hundred pounds, that the new college was able to begin operations. It is significant as well as appropriate that the fledgling seminary was named Harvard College. According to Yale legend, ten prominent Connecticut ministers gathered in 1699, each bringing a number of books which he laid on the table saying, "I give these books for the founding of a College in this Colony."[3] And Samuel Davies, president of the College of New Jersey at Princeton, wrote that "a large and well assorted collection of books . . . is the most ornamental and useful furniture of a College, and the most proper and valuable fund with which it can be endowed."[4]

The American college libraries were small. During the colonial period the largest collection, at Harvard, contained fewer than fifteen thousand volumes. Most colleges owned between one and three thousand. Despite their small size, these collections were adequate to support the curriculum, which emphasized theology and the classics, and to provide students with access to the best of English literature. Only a small proportion (less than ten percent) of these books was purchased; most were obtained by gift or bequest. Fortunately, the donation of books to college libraries was a popular benefaction, and both American and European donors gave generously—and sometimes unwillingly: the Harvard College library received many books confiscated from Tories during the Revolution.

Most colleges occupied a single building in their early years, in which the library was most commonly located on the second floor, above the chapel. A large, centrally located room, it was also used as the site of trustees' meetings, dinners for eminent guests, and commencement gatherings. At

Harvard, rules adopted in 1765 provided that the library would be open on Fridays from nine to eleven in the morning "for borrowing and returning Books by Graduates & undergraduates." Students would enter the library one at a time "in their Order"; they might borrow three books, to be returned at the end of six weeks. Valuable books could not be borrowed, but might be consulted in the library on Wednesdays, in May, June, September, and October—and on the "one Day in a Month, from the last of October to the last of April," when the library rules required that a fire be made. These rules also required that "the Librarian or his Substitute shall constantly be present, while there is a Fire, and shall see it thoroughly extinguish'd by Day Light."[5] Candles and lamps were barred. And with good reason: fires frequently destroyed or damaged college libraries, and together with the hazards of war seriously disrupted the growth of library collections.

While library rules permitted only limited access to books, this did not greatly disadvantage students. Well into the 19th century, college instruction in America relied more upon the textbook than upon the library. Students read standard introductory works on philosophy, mathematics, and the classics, demonstrating their absorption of this material through classroom recitation. Neither original thought nor creative synthesis of published opinion was required. Science and modern languages, when added to the curriculum in midcentury, were subordinate to classical studies; and there was very rarely any attempt to teach the application of knowledge. Law and medicine were rarely taught in colleges. Those who did not qualify for these professions through apprenticeship studied at independent, noncollegiate institutions.

In 1816, Bostonian George Ticknor compared Harvard with Göttingen, where he was then studying:

> One very important and principal cause of the difference between our University and the one here is the different value we affix to a good library, and the different ideas we have of what a good library is. . . . We found new professorships and build new colleges in abundance, but we buy no books; and yet it is to me the most obvious thing in the world that it would promote the cause of learning and the reputation of the University ten times more to give six thousand dollars a year to the Library than to found three professorships, and that it would have been wiser to have spent the whole sum that the new chapel had cost on books than on a fine suite of halls. . . . I cannot better explain to you the difference between our University in Cambridge and the one here than by telling you that here I hardly say too much when I say that it *consists* in the Library, and that in Cambridge the Library is one of the last things thought and talked about—that here they have forty professors and more than two hundred thousand volumes to instruct them, and in Cambridge twenty professors and less than twenty thousand volumes . . . we are mortified and exasperated because we have no learned men, and yet make it *physically* impossible for our scholars to become such, and that to escape from this reproach we appoint a multitude of professors, but give them a library from which hardly one and *not* one of them can qualify himself to

execute the duties of his office. You will, perhaps, say that these professors do not complain. I can only answer that you find the blind are often as gay and happy as those who are blessed with sight. . . .[6]

Undergraduates whose intellectual interests were not fulfilled by the classical curriculum joined the literary societies which flourished on nearly every American campus before the Civil War. Devoted to "literary composition, oratory and debate," these societies offered students both an avenue toward self-improvement and a forum for discussing the political and social issues of the day. To support these activities the societies maintained libraries of their own, with reference collections, subscriptions to popular periodicals, and extensive collections of English-language fiction and drama, history and biography, travels and voyages, politics and economics. These provided the intellectual resources needed for formal debates as well as the material of recreational reading. (At Columbia in the 1830s, students borrowed ten books from literary societies for every one from the college library.)

As the curriculum changed, the need for the independent literary societies declined, and their role in campus life was assumed by fraternities and athletic teams. The society libraries were often incorporated into the official college collections, which themselves became more broadly accessible to undergraduates. Whereas the college student in colonial times might be able to borrow books once a week during the hour or two when the library was open for that purpose, by the end of the 19th century most college libraries in America were open six or seven days a week, from morning to night. Large reading rooms and extensive reference collections accommodated students working in the library building, which improvements in heating, lighting, and ventilation made a more attractive place in which to read or study. More liberal circulation policies made it easier for students to borrow books to read at home or in their fraternity houses or dormitories. These changes were instituted not only to benefit the increasing number of undergraduates, whose studies were now embracing a wider range of the natural and social sciences, as well as agriculture, engineering, and other vocations. As American universities, led by new foundations such as Cornell, Johns Hopkins, and Clark, began to follow the German model of increasing as well as transmitting knowledge, the needs of graduate students and research-minded faculty members began to shape the academic library.

In earlier days American scholars had conducted their research, whether historical, philological, or scientific, without recourse to universities. They depended upon their own private libraries and those of friends and colleagues, and also used the resources of learned societies such as the American Philosophical Society in Philadelphia and the American Antiquarian Society at Worcester. And they traveled abroad, as George Ticknor had done, to use the great libraries of Europe.

• • •

WHEN CAMBRIDGE UNIVERSITY'S Trinity College set up a "Scholar's Library" for its undergraduates, it was "provided, that the scholars are to make use of these Books, not in the library, but in their chambers. . . ."[7] At the beginning of each term, one student remembered, "the libraries were again ransacked of their copies of Campbell on the Gospels, Beausobre on the New Testament (most excellent books these), Watt's Scripture History, Valpy's New Testament, . . . Garnier's Algebra and Analyse Algebrique, together with Lacroix's Algebra, and some others. . . ."[8]

In 1823, a Trinity freshman explained his high regard for the Scholar's Library: "Many books, such as Clarendon, are too expensive to buy, and not easily hired. I can procure these for nothing. This is a grand point in which Trinity surpasses . . . all her rivals. . . ."[9] Future clergyman, writer, and university professor Frederick Denison Maurice had access to those books for four hours a day: the library was open daily except Sundays and saints' days from 11 to 3. Undergraduates were required to wear academical dress in the library.

Maurice was not the only library enthusiast. Though some of his fellow undergraduates were "gay men" who spent their time hunting, gaming, and wenching, Oxford and Cambridge had many "reading men" who used their college libraries for extracurricular reading as well as for their formal studies. By the end of the century, undergraduates rather than faculty members were the college libraries' primary users. The college fellows increasingly found it necessary to resort to the larger university library in order to find the materials needed for their research.

The Bodleian Library at Oxford and the University Library at Cambridge had grown considerably since midcentury. Following the lead of Antonio Panizzi at the British Museum, they became more assertive about demanding the copies of new British books to which they were entitled under copyright law. They purchased current foreign literature and subscribed to a wide range of periodical publications. Their concern was research rather than rarity; they were more interested in European doctoral dissertations than in medieval manuscripts, though many of the latter were received from the College libraries.

After the Napoleonic wars, many of Germany's old universities were dissolved and new ones arose. Under the influence of Wilhelm von Humboldt and other educational reformers, the German university was transformed from an institution in which knowledge was transferred from omniscient professor to passive student into a center for the discovery of new knowledge and the development of students' intellectual capabilities. A leading instrument in this process was the seminar. A small group of students, working under the guidance of their professor, solved research problems that required them to work with original source materials and to learn and use the tools of scholarship in their discipline. The traditional closed-stack central library could not support this level of intellectual activity.

The seminar demanded a new sort of library: one in which a wide range of publications was placed in the hands of professor and student alike, without undue administrative or architectural barriers between the book and its reader. An American scholar who had studied in Germany described the seminar library as "a well-lighted, well-equipped comfortable place for study and research," and explained that

> These select libraries are supported by private subscription, special endowment, or definite appropriation from year to year. There is always a professorial director who has authority, within certain specified economic limits, to order the books for his seminary. The room and library are placed in the charge of an advanced and trustworthy student, sometimes the senior member, who is regarded as the professor's deputy, and is a man having authority over the other members, some of whom serve as willing proxies. The library is managed upon principles of comity and general accommodation. Each member has a key to the room and comes and goes as he pleases. He has a private desk or a drawer in the seminary table, where he keeps his notes, papers, and writing materials. The room is accessible at all hours during the day and evening, and is usually an attractive place for quiet, uninterrupted work.[10]

In many cases books in the seminar libraries came from the professors' private collections. Books were not expensive in Germany, and it was not unusual for a scholar to own a working library of ten or twenty thousand volumes. This lessened the dependence of professors upon the central university libraries, and reduced demand for reform of their policies.

The idea of a library profession was emerging in Germany, and with it the idea that there were basic principles of library science that could be applied to the cataloging, physical arrangement, and user services of all university libraries, rather than each developing its own idiosyncratic procedures. The specialist nature of German scholarship, together with the publication of systematic author and subject catalogs of many libraries, made interlibrary loan both a possibility and a necessity—especially when an expanding railway network and a dependable postal system made borrowing and lending among libraries safe, fast, and cheap.

The technical colleges and independent research institutes that evolved during the 19th century did not usually have central libraries. Students learned in the laboratory rather than the library, and professors and research scientists valued journals over books. Small book collections existed within departments or individual professors' offices. Access to these was limited to faculty members and advanced students; even at university-affiliated research institutes, they were not made available to users from the parent institution.

This multiplication of specialized collections, together with the increasing use of closed stacks to house the bulk of university library collections and the lack of coordination of acquisitions and cataloging, frustrated the students and faculty members for whom finding and reading the books that they needed was a cumbersome chore. It also affected the librarians whose budgets, already inadequate to deal with the flood of scholarly publications, were depleted by excessive duplication of books among their splintered constituencies. After World War I, the poverty of German universities forced the curtailment of these independent specialized collections.

At that, they were better off than their counterparts in southern and eastern Europe. University authorities might call the library the most important of the university's faculties, the most important teacher of the students. But in France, Spain, and Italy many university libraries were housed in outmoded buildings, with inadequate seating for readers and insufficient space to house the collections. In the stacks, books often stood two or three deep on the shelves; and bookshelves overflowed into attics, cellars, and corridors. Boxes and packets of uncataloged books, theses, and pamphlets were stored wherever room could be found for them. Catalogs were inadequate, staff insufficient, and library hours limited. "At the beginning of the 20th century," says a French historian, "[their libraries] were, as they remain today, one of the weak points of our universities."[11]

As KNOWLEDGE GREW in size and scope, and as library collections grew likewise, it became increasingly necessary to find some way of identifying and retrieving publications on a particular subject. This was equally important in those libraries where patrons had to choose books from catalogs and in those where they enjoyed direct access to the shelves. It was not sufficient to catalog the collection; it needed also to be classified, so that its contents could be discovered through some rational arrangement either of the books themselves or of their descriptions in a public catalog.

In early libraries, Christian as well as Muslim, books were arranged according to their relationship to the word of God. Scripture itself held the highest rank—literally so in Muslim libraries, where it was considered blasphemous to place secular works on shelves above the Koran—then sacred commentaries, doctrinal writings, and auxiliary materials. In Western libraries, this evolved into the "faculty system," in which books were divided into arts, philosophy, theology, and medicine, without further subject arrangement. As scientific activity expanded and a secular viewpoint became predominant in intellectual life, leading thinkers began to consider the categories into which human knowledge might be divided. Just as Carolus Linnaeus set forth the relationships of plants and animals in his *Systema naturae* (1736), the source of the scientific nomenclature used for living creatures to this day, so philosophers devised taxonomies to cover the entirety of creation, including the works of man.

In the *Advancement of Learning* (1605), Francis Bacon divided all human knowledge into History (memory), Poesy (imagination), and

Philosophy (reason), for each of which he offered further subdivisions. When the French philosopher Jean d'Alembert devised the subject arrangement for Diderot's *Encyclopédie* in 1751, he modeled it upon Bacon's categories. Thomas Jefferson used this adaptation of "Lord Bacon's table of science" as the basis for arranging his own book collection into 44 "chapters." (When his books were sold to the United States government, a modification of his classification scheme was used in the Library of Congress for several decades, and it had some influence on the design of the modern Library of Congress Classification.)

Even those libraries that used some form of subject arrangement assigned to each book a fixed place on the shelves, which was recorded in the library's catalog by means of a pressmark specifying the bookcase (or press), shelf, and position of each volume. This system required the assignment of new call numbers whenever an expansion or rearrangement of the library changed the physical location of its books. Melvil Dewey, a young American librarian, proposed instead that each book be assigned a relative rather than a fixed location, according to a detailed table of numbers that identified the exact subject of each volume.

An earnest young man from rural upstate New York, Dewey had a lifelong passion for rationality and efficiency. As a small child, a cousin later remembered, "it was his delight to arrange his mother's pantry, systematizing and classifying its contents."[12] Appointed assistant librarian of Amherst College while still a student there, Dewey read hundreds of books and pamphlets on library management and visited dozens of other libraries. He decided that the traditional American method of cataloging and arranging books was vastly inefficient: an alphabetical subject index was hard to maintain and harder to use, and the practice of assigning each book a fixed location made it difficult to combine a logical subject arrangement with a sensible use of shelving space. So he devised an elegantly simple plan for cataloging the subject matter of a library collection.

Instead of an alphabetical listing, in which the subdivisions of a single topic might be widely separated by the accident of nomenclature, subjects would be indicated by means of a simple numerical code. This would be based on a logical hierarchical structure, in which each of ten principal topics would be divided into ten subdivisions, each of which would be further divided into as many as ten classes. An alphabetical subject index would guide cataloger and reader alike to the appropriate class number, thus accommodating the variety of terms that users might bring to the search for information. And the system was not limited to the one thousand classes its outline provided; by use of further decimal numbers, an infinite profusion of subdivisions could exist.

Dewey suggested that his Decimal Classification would serve equally well to arrange books on the shelf and entries in a catalog. Whether a library placed its books on open shelves or in closed stacks, it would have to assign each one a call number only once, upon its accession to the collection. As Dewey explained, it made more sense for a library "to assign numbers to its books, which are permanent, and not to its shelves, which are liable to frequent changes."[13] In a period of rapid growth, libraries had enough of a backlog of books to catalog and prepare for use without the added burden of revising the catalog and renumbering the books at frequent intervals. Dewey published his Decimal Classification in 1876, after three years' trial at Amherst. It was rapidly adopted by libraries in America and Europe (96 percent of American public libraries were using it by 1926), and it is still widely used today.

This same principle of flexibility led to the development of the card catalog. By recording each book on a separate card, the catalog could be kept constantly up-to-date. Readers would no longer need to consult printed catalogs that were out-of-date on the day they were issued; and as library hours were extended, the card catalog was more easily accessible to its potential users. The dictionary catalog, in which author, title, and subject entries were combined in a single sequence, was well suited to use with the Dewey system. The adoption of standard rules for the cataloging of books—Charles Ammi Cutter's "Rules for a Dictionary Catalog" were first published in 1876, in the same U.S. Bureau of Education report that contained the first publication of Dewey's Decimal Classification—made it possible for a central agency to provide catalog cards for popular books, thus sparing each library the time and cost of cataloging every book for itself.

The Dewey Decimal Classification was well suited to the academic and public libraries of its time, and with constant revision has served tolerably well in smaller American libraries to the present day. But libraries with very large collections soon found it inadequate. European librarians adapted Dewey's scheme to produce the Universal Decimal Classification, whose elaborate provisions for indicating details of subject, language, form, place, and time were especially well suited to the literature of science and technology. In America, the Library of Congress developed its own classification, which after almost a century is not entirely complete. Unlike the decimal classifications, which adopted a theoretical approach to the assignment of categories and imposed a uniform pattern of ten subdivisions upon every subject, the L.C. classification was based upon "literary warrant"—the actual pattern of subjects represented by the books in a very large collection. By foregoing the easily learned and readily applied decimal building-blocks that Dewey devised, the Library of Congress produced a massively complicated system that can bring order to million-volume libraries. It has been adopted by national and university libraries worldwide, sometimes with locally produced modifications to cover in detail those aspects of national life not completely understood in Washington.

• • •

DURING THE EARLY years of the 20th century, a small number of universities both in America and in Europe trained the bulk of higher degree recipients. As the demand for scientists and professionals trained to the doctoral level increased, more institutions began to offer graduate-level instruction. This led to a vast expansion of academic libraries throughout the Western world, and to a similarly great expansion of the scope of academic library collections. As professional education increasingly took place in the university environment, research and scholarship came to play an important role in the accreditation of degree programs. The practitioners of newly aspiring occupations sought to improve their status by imitating this process, and by the end of the century nearly every occupation that could manage to do so was represented on campus. As the number of professional academics expanded, so did the fields in which they conducted research. In the middle of the 19th century the study of English literature was only beginning to find a place in the Anglo–American curriculum, and in the 1920s and 1930s American writing was beginning to be admitted as a subject worthy of study. By the 1970s the literatures of ethnic minorities, women, and popular culture were being mined for the matter of scholarship. This process was abetted by resistance to the traditional restriction of university study to the high culture, as well as by the willingness of newer institutions and younger scholars to seek new ground on which to build their reputations—and their library collections. Increasingly the academic world was coming to see potential scholarly value in almost every scrap of recorded material. No matter how esoteric, or how unprepossessing, some library somewhere was eager to collect it. A new university in Bowling Green, Ohio, might never hope to rival Harvard's collections in the Greek classics or Yale's treasure-trove of western Americana: but it could reasonably aspire to establish one of the world's best collections in popular culture.

As knowledge accumulated in printed form, and in an increasing number of nonprint media, it was impossible for even the most affluent and ambitious library to collect everything. As this became more widely realized, various schemes were instituted to ensure that scholars might have access to materials that could not be collected by their home institution. Cooperative acquisition agreements divided among the participating institutions the responsibility for developing comprehensive collections of material from specific subject or geographical areas. Such a plan was adopted by German universities in the aftermath of World War I, when there was little money available for library acquisitions. Bonn bought Romance philology and literature; Göttingen, English; and so forth, with nine academic libraries taking part in the scheme.

One of the first of these in America was the Farmington Plan, in which several dozen major academic libraries undertook among them to collect all new foreign books and pamphlets "that might reasonably be expected to interest a research worker in the United States."[14] Similar arrangements were made to ensure that little-used materials would be preserved for future generations of scholars. The Midwest Inter-Library Center, established at the University of Chicago in 1951, housed such materials as old college catalogs, foreign dissertations, and outdated textbooks. These could be consulted by visitors, or mailed to member libraries for use by their readers. Expanding to serve a national constituency, it changed its name to the Center for Research Libraries, and undertook to acquire for American researchers a collection of potentially important material for which there was as yet little scholarly demand.

Resource sharing among libraries also came into vogue. Standards for interlibrary loan were adopted by library associations, with national libraries usually serving as lender of last resort. To facilitate this, union catalogs were established to show the holdings of participating libraries. Most of these were maintained at one central location, as the expense of compiling and maintaining them was considerable; indeed, some in the United States were established as job-creation schemes during the Great Depression of the 1930s. Union catalogs were consulted in person or by postal query, though some were widely distributed in book or card form. The National Union Catalog, maintained by the Library of Congress in Washington, was distributed in card form to over a hundred major American libraries and principal libraries abroad. The *Union List of Serials*, published in five massive volumes, was purchased by most of the major libraries of North America.

In addition, the published catalogs of major libraries and important special collections served as bibliographical resources for identifying and locating books, preventing unnecessary duplication of highly specialized titles among libraries, and verifying the description and location of items sought through interlibrary loan. Improvements in printing technology, together with the expansion of academic and research libraries during the 1960s, led to the publication of photographic reproductions of the card catalogs of many significant collections. These ranged from such basic collections as Columbia University's Avery Architectural Library and the American Geographical Society's research library to such esoteric ones as the J. Lloyd Eaton science fiction collection (University of California, Riverside) and the *Catalog of Folklore and Folksongs* of the Cleveland Public Library.

More recently, the development of online public-access catalogs has made the holdings of libraries worldwide accessible to scholars on distant continents. But this is not the same as providing access to the contents of these collections. Despite claims that anyone with a computer and a modem can "browse through the Library of Congress," very few library resources are actually available for reading online. There is still a tremendous gap between knowing that a particular book exists in a particular library, and being able to see its contents on the computer display screen.

All this pertains to academic libraries in the world's industrial nations. In the developing countries, universities and university libraries are much more limited in resources. All too often, the high price of books and journals from the developed world, together with the difficulties of obtaining hard currencies with which to pay for them, places these publications beyond their reach. Tropical climates are hard on library collections, and frequent warfare and political instability in non-Western countries also threaten the preservation of library materials. A file of reprints obtained gratis from Western researchers, supplemented by photocopies ordered at considerable expense from the Centre Nationale de la Recherche Scientifique or the British Library Document Supply Centre, often constitutes the working library of the Third World researcher. Even the promise of electronic communication is a mirage, as few undeveloped countries possess either the technical or the social infrastructure to make a library service dependent on computers and telecommunications a feasible proposition. Some attempts have been made to surmount this problem, as by distributing collections of key publications in CD-ROM format and providing training in the use of the necessary hardware. But even this is dependent upon the largesse of Western donors.

10
LIBRARIES FOR THE
PEOPLE

THE IDEA OF the public library is, on the face of it, an improbable one. Only recently in human history has there been widespread agreement that people have inherent rights deserving of universal respect. (Remember that the United States enforced chattel slavery until 1865.) The idea that every person should be educated is an even more recent and radical one. And the idea that society should provide its members with the means to continue their education independently was more radical still.

We find in the Protestant Reformation the beginnings of the idea that every member of society must have at least enough education to read the Bible. As theological controversy increased, the ability to read a broader range of religious writings became important. This required not only the knowledge of how to read, but physical access to the books as well. And with the spread of democracy, an educated populace became as much a necessity in the political as in the religious sphere.

The "public" libraries of Renaissance Europe were intended for the use of scholarly gentlemen. If any others had been interested in their contents, it would have occurred neither to them nor to those in charge of the libraries that they should be given access to them. Even after the Reformation, most "public" libraries were meant for the use of clergymen or public officials.

The true public library, in the sense that we use the term today, came into existence as a response to the needs of an evolving democratic society. Originating in the subscription library, an institution established by the upper middle classes for their own use, it became transformed into a vehicle for shaping the thought and behavior of the lower classes of society. Much of its evolution in Great Britain and the United States was as a way of socializing immigrants, whether internal or external, to the needs of an urban industrial society.

More recently, the public library in Western countries has devolved from an instrument of education, intended to uplift the working classes, into a relatively minor cultural and recreational facility for the middle classes. Only in service to children does the old missionary zeal linger with any real success. However, as access to information increasingly replaces the provision of books as the focus of (at least) adult service, the public library may perhaps regain the importance its proponents have always thought it should have—unless computer-literate people learn to live without it.

WHEN GUTENBERG INVENTED the printing press, there were very few in Europe who were able to read, and most of them did their reading in Latin. The Reformation created among Protestant laymen a need to be able to read the Bible in their own tongue; and the increasing size and importance of national governments provided both need and incentive for the development of literacy. By 1800, at least in the Protestant countries of northern Europe, over half the adult population could read simple vernacular texts.

These numbers do not tell the whole story. The audience for books was multiplied by the practice of reading aloud, both within the household and among workmates and neighbors. In fact, reading aloud was common even when individuals were alone. Until the 18th century, readers would peruse their texts closely, reading the Latin slowly and often aloud, so as to extract all of the meaning the author placed there. (This form of reading persists today among orthodox Jews, who learn Talmud in pairs, reading aloud to each other from the ancient Aramaic text.)

As the number of books increased, and national languages began to supplant Latin even in scholarly writing, a different pattern of reading emerged. People read more books, and read them more rapidly and in silence. There was so much more knowledge to be acquired, and with the multiplication of copies a previously read book could more readily be consulted again should the need arise.

The very concept of authorship changed. When books were rare and travel difficult, the gathering of excerpts from existing texts was a valuable service to scholarship. The learned compiler who put his knowledge of the extant literature at the disposal of his fellows was entitled to claim the resulting work as his own. In an age when the appeal to authority conferred more legitimacy than priority of innovation, this was looked on as creativity rather than plagiarism. But as the spread of printing and the efforts of humanist editors made the great works of antiquity and the Middle Ages widely available in reliable editions, the extension rather than the reformulation of knowledge became the goal of the learned.

A growing number of people were reading more for profit than for the joy of learning. The increasing size and complexity of both church and state engendered an increasingly voluminous literature, not only of legal codes and commentaries but also of books on statecraft and administration. The expansion of commerce created a demand for texts on bookkeeping, foreign-language dictionaries, and accounts of the customs, institutions, and products of the many lands with which trade was carried on.

As the number of people with free time increased, reading became popular as a leisure activity. The vernacular prose novel came into existence, and began to displace epic poetry and drama as the chief vehicle for the literary imagination. Travelers' tales and historical narratives attracted many of the same readers who flocked to the novel; and doubtless there were many who did not clearly distinguish fact from fiction.

In England, as in other European countries, there was no unanimity concerning the desirability of mass literacy. Belief in the inevitability of the class system was widespread. Even many of those who supported widespread public education saw as one of its most important purposes that of making the lower orders content with their place in society and prepared to fulfill their heaven-ordained role. There were many who felt that all the education a farm laborer or factory worker needed could be provided by the parish priest during his Sunday sermon.

THE REVEREND THOMAS Bray (1658–1730) combined a strong belief in the importance of libraries with an impressive talent for organization. He founded both the Society for the Promotion of Christian Knowledge, which for nearly three hundred years has played a significant role in the publication and distribution of religious literature, and the Society for the Propagation of the Gospel in Foreign Parts, which provided the means for establishing libraries across the British colonies in America.

Bray proposed that every Anglican priest sent to America be provided with a "sufficient library of well-chosen books" with which to "inform himself and instruct others." In addition, each parish should be equipped with a collection of Bibles, catechisms, prayer books, and devotional works for loan to parishioners. And in each colony a "Library of more Universal Knowledge" would be open to all who wished "to launch out farther in the pursuit of Useful Knowledge, as well Natural as Divine."[1] This practical philosophy, together with the colonists' hunger for books, ensured the popularity of Bray's libraries. Between 1695 and 1704 he established five provincial libraries, thirty-eight parochial libraries, and thirty-seven lending libraries for laymen on the North American continent, as well as libraries in Newfoundland, Bermuda, and the West Indies.

Bray intended his libraries to shape the intellectual life of the American colonies in worldly as well as divine matters. One third of the books in the provincial libraries were devoted to "Human Knowledge": history, geography, medicine, philosophy, poetry. Even the parochial libraries contained secular books, to help the ministers in their duties as tutor and schoolmaster. But their primary function was to advance the teachings of the Church of England and resist the influence of dissenting doctrines. Bray was especially concerned with the challenge posed by the Society of Friends. He provided book collections in several cities to support efforts to convert the Quakers.

Bray's libraries were heavily used until the Revolutionary War, when many of the collections were damaged or destroyed. After the Revolution, practical concerns rather than religious advancement were to dominate the rise of libraries in America.

IN 1727, BENJAMIN Franklin tells us in his autobiography,

> I had formed most of my ingenious acquaintence into a club of mutual improvement, which we called the Junto; we met on Friday evenings. The rules that I drew up required that every member, in his turn, should produce one or more queries on any point of morals, politics, or natural philosophy, to be discussed by the company; and once in three months produce and read an essay of his own writing, on any subject he pleased . . . [It was] the best school of philosophy and politics that then existed in the province; for our queries, which were read the week preceding their discussion, put us on reading with attention upon the several subjects, that we might speak more to the purpose . . .[2]

Three years later, Franklin proposed that Junto members contribute their books to a common library, giving "each of us the advantage of using the books of all the other members, which would be nearly as beneficial as if each owned the whole." But some members found it inconvenient not to have their books at home, and the experiment was abandoned after a year's trial. As a result, Franklin recalled,

> I set on foot my first project of a public nature, that of a subscription library. I drew up the proposals, got them put into form . . . and, by the help of my friends in the Junto, procured fifty subscribers of forty shillings each to begin with, and ten shillings a year for fifty years, the term our company was to continue. We afterwards obtained a charter, the company being increased to one hundred. This was the mother of all the North American subscription libraries,

the Library Company of Philadelphia, which still flourishes today. Its influence extended beyond Philadelphia, Franklin claimed:

> These libraries have improved the general conversation of the Americans, made the common tradesmen and farmers as intelligent as most gentlemen from other countries, and perhaps have contributed in some degree to the stand so generally made throughout the colonies in defence of their privileges.[3]

In March 1732, they sent forty-five pounds and a list of titles to London merchant Peter Collinson; and in October they had their books. The library, housed at first in the Junto's meeting room and later in a room in the State House, was open to any "civil gentleman," but only subscribers could borrow books. Its contents reflected the Junto's combination of literary and practical interests, including titles on mathematics and natural science as well as Homer and Vergil, contemporary magazines like the *Tatler* and the *Spectator*, and practical works such as Daniel Defoe's *Compleat English Tradesman* and Philip Miller's *Gardener's Dictionary*.

This differentiated the Library Company from the libraries generally available in the mother country. Public libraries existed in England, the gift or bequest of public-spirited benefactors. But these were intended for the use of clergymen, and their shelves contained little other than works of divinity. Few of these parish libraries had been endowed with funds sufficient to keep them up to date. They represented more the pious hopes of their long-dead founders than the current intellectual needs of their prospective readers.

AS BOTH THE number of readers and the taste for reading increased, the book trade grew likewise. Booksellers multiplied, and a periodical press devoted to book reviewing emerged. But books were expensive; few could afford to buy all the books they desired to read.

A commercial economy will generally find some way to satisfy a widespread want. Just because books were too dear to buy did not mean that they must be too dear to read. In 15th-century London, John Shirley's customers could rent as well as buy manuscripts of Chaucer's poetry, and in 16th-century Spain aristocratic ladies rented chivalric romances. By the 18th century, French and British booksellers charged a fee for reading books in their shops and rented them for home reading. London coffeehouses provided newspapers and magazines for their customers, as an essential complement to the beverages they served—for those who didn't want coffee or beer, reading privileges were sold by the hour—and the *cabinets de lecture* of Paris and Vienna offered those who paid a small entrance fee the opportunity to read newly published books as well as current periodicals. Subscription reading rooms offered middle-class readers access to published news and comment in more genteel surroundings, while aristocrats enjoyed the reading facilities of their clubs, which often extended to books as well as periodicals.

For those who preferred to read at home—and for the wives and daughters of the middle and upper classes, who had no choice in the matter—circulating libraries began to provide the opportunity. Literary and philosophical societies, and libraries formed expressly for the purpose, circulated books to their upper- and upper-middle-class members. Lower-middle-class readers formed book clubs that used pooled funds to purchase small collections; some were maintained permanently, while others were sold once the books had been read by all the members, and new ones purchased with the proceeds. Whatever class they served, these collections emphasized serious and improving reading. For lighter fare, readers turned to private circulating libraries specializing in fiction. In London, William Lane's Minerva Press offered ten thousand volumes for loan in 1790; in Bath and other spas, novels from the libraries alleviated the tedium of the water cure. And we are told of "twenty men and women gathering in a locksmith's shop to listen to the newest number of the Pickwick Papers, borrowed from a circulating library at 2d. [two pence] a day."[4]

Mudie's Select Library brought respectability to the industry in 1842. Charles Edward Mudie offered his middle-class customers both the convenience of access to an immense collection of current books and the assurance that nothing they might find at Mudie's would cause the slightest embarrassment when read aloud within the family circle. All this was well within the reach of moderately affluent Londoners. For one guinea per annum one could borrow as many books as one wished—one volume at a time. Higher subscription fees allowed more liberal borrowing privileges, extending Mudie's customer base to clubs and literary societies; railways and royal mail ships carried his books throughout Britain and the empire. The three-volume novels of the mid-19th century sold for thirty-one shillings sixpence; for two thirds of the price of a single novel, Mudie's customers could have their choice of current fiction—not to mention a wide range of nonfiction books—for an entire year.

Those English readers who were unable to pay the subscription fees of the private circulating libraries were served, if they were served at all, by the small libraries established by the Society for Promoting Christian Knowledge and the Religious Tract Society. These collections were small— one hundred volumes or so—and were kept in churches, chapels, and schools. Though there were several thousand of them, they had little to offer the working-class reader. Their books were almost entirely religious in nature, as were those of the "itinerating libraries" that served rural regions. As competition to the tavern for the scarce spare time of the tired workingman they were extremely ineffective.

WHILE MUDIE AND his competitors provided leisure reading for the middle classes, public-spirited Britons concerned themselves with the presumed needs of their social inferiors. The Public Libraries Act of 1850 was not enacted because of working-class demands for tax-supported libraries; it was one of many social reforms undertaken as a response to the rapid growth of urban centers after the Industrial Revolution. The political agitation of 1848, when both England and continental Europe were swept by radical movements, alarmed the leaders of British society. Unlike many of their counterparts on the continent, they responded with reform rather than repression.

The 1850 act allowed (but did not require) cities to create public libraries and expend tax money on their maintenance. Few cities did so; in many, proposals to fund public libraries were repeatedly and overwhelmingly defeated. There was considerable opposition to providing libraries out of public funds, and not only because it would increase taxes. Some felt that the provision of libraries should be left to mechanics' institutes and other private organizations; others, distrustful of any increase in the spread of popular education, saw the public library as a catalyst for political agitation.

Even where public libraries were established, the act's penny-in-the-pound did not raise enough money to support them properly. After a building was provided, there was seldom enough left to buy books or pay staff adequate wages. Without attractive, balanced collections, libraries could attract little patronage or public support; and the current fiction that proved most attractive to readers was seldom likely to turn up in collections obtained by gift or bequest. The patrons that the public library was most successful in attracting—cranks and vagrants—drove away middle-class readers and reduced their interest in supporting the institution. Both its supporters and its opponents regarded the British public library as an educational and cultural program for the working classes—and therein lay its essential difference from the public library in America.

BENJAMIN FRANKLIN'S LIBRARY Company was imitated throughout British North America, especially in the New England colonies. The Redwood Library of Newport, Rhode Island, and the New York Society Library each owned nearly a thousand books at the beginning of the Revolution; and by 1780 there were fifty-one "social libraries" in New England alone. These were voluntary associations of artisans, merchants, and farmers, whose subscription fees provided the funds used to buy books and maintain reading rooms. In these they received current journals from Britain and America. Their book collections emphasized history, biography, travel, and literature; science was more popular than theology.

Readers who were not members of social libraries could patronize the circulating libraries maintained by many booksellers, dry-goods merchants, and other entrepreneurs who saw them as a profitable sideline that would increase traffic through their shop doors. Like their British counterparts, the bulk of their collection was fiction, though most attempted to maintain titles covering a wide range of interests. But there was more money in novels than in sermons.

Although New York had taken the lead in finance and commerce, Boston was still the foremost American literary and cultural center. It retained something of its Puritan heritage, but a Unitarian social conscience was increasingly evident in the city. It was in this atmosphere that the Boston Public Library came into being.

It was not the first tax-supported library in America. In 1820, the town of Salisbury, Connecticut, had voted funds for the support of the Bingham Library, which had been established by Caleb Bingham's gift seven years earlier. Peterborough, New Hampshire, established a town library in 1833, the first in America to receive regular support from public funds. And in

1835, New York became the first state to enact a law creating school-district libraries, "intended not so much for the benefit of children attending schools as for those who have completed their common school education."[5] But Boston was the first American city to decide that a public library was an essential aspect of modern urban life, one that should be established and maintained by the municipal government.

The New England states, whose economy increasingly depended upon manufacturing and commerce, were the leaders in the founding of public libraries, just as they were in the establishment of free public education. The abolition of property qualifications in the 1820s had greatly increased the number of eligible voters; without schools and libraries, how could they exercise the franchise intelligently? The region's cities were dominated by a well-educated class of merchants and manufacturers, who held a broad view of the social advantages of public libraries. Not only would they help to keep working people away from the tavern and the brothel; public libraries would also provide mechanics and clerks with the tools to upgrade their skills. The availability of books on agriculture, technology, geography, and commerce would increase the prosperity of the commonwealth, by making its citizens more efficient at their several vocations. And a public library would help to attract migration and investment to its community.

The arguments for establishing public libraries were not all utilitarian. The religious sentiments of New England's business leaders—whether a Calvinistic morality inherited from Puritan forbears, a Quaker tradition of benevolence, or a Unitarian belief in the perfectibility of mankind—inspired the foundation of numerous charitable institutions. A strong sense of civic pride encouraged the formation of public libraries. These were not entirely dependent upon tax support. The philanthropic efforts of successful businessmen and the benefactions of native sons who had achieved affluence in the booming territories to the west often provided the basis on which a town library was erected.

These libraries contained a range of materials combining concessions to popular taste with a confidence in the capacity and desire of the populace for self-improvement. Fiction was by far the most popular category, with James Fenimore Cooper and Captain Marryat the most popular writers. Among nonfiction books, the most frequently consulted or borrowed were history, biography, and travel. Though pious philanthropists might be disappointed at the limited interest in religious books, scientific and technical works were well used by ambitious young readers.

Library users included professional men, artisans, and those in "mercantile callings": clerks, salesmen, merchants, and bookkeepers were heavily represented among those who thronged the reading rooms. Bartenders, wood choppers, and washerwomen were discovered among the Boston Public Library's users. "The assembled crowd is often motley," Boston's

Examining Committee reported in 1870. "But, the more motley, the more various and dissimilar its ingredients, the better the proof of the widespread influence of the library. Rich and poor assemble together and alike in this narrow dispensary, and a great many of them too."[6]

With few other educational opportunities open to them, women were among the most enthusiastic users of public libraries: in 1869, 46 percent of the Boston Public Library's eleven-thousand-odd users were women. They often led the efforts to establish libraries in small towns, and were instrumental in transplanting the public library idea to other regions of the country.

These were slower than the New England states to establish public libraries. While the Boston Public Library opened its doors in 1854, it was not until 1879 that the New York Free Circulating Library came into existence. Privately founded, it did not receive municipal funding for the first seven years of its existence. New York was not used to the idea of tax-supported library service. The legacy of John Jacob Astor and the donation of James Lenox had established great scholarly libraries that were open to the public; but their intimidating atmosphere, restricted hours, and lack of circulating collections rendered them useless to the vast majority of New Yorkers. The presence of these privately endowed institutions convinced many New York leaders that libraries were a charitable enterprise rather than an essential municipal service.

This attitude was vigorously opposed by Andrew Carnegie, who believed that in a democratic society government must assume responsibility for providing education at all levels. Carnegie, born of poor Scottish parents, made a colossal fortune in the steel industry. He gave millions of dollars for the construction of public library buildings in the United States and the British empire, but only on the condition that the municipality receiving the gift guarantee to establish and maintain the library with annual appropriations of public money. Carnegie's offer convinced many cities to institute tax-supported libraries rather than wait for some benefactor to endow one.

IN THE LARGER cities of Great Britain and America, public libraries contained separate reference and circulating collections, both of which were housed in closed stacks. Readers would choose books from a printed catalog; many libraries required that ten or a dozen selections be made in case the first choice was unavailable. Request slips would be handed in at the counter, and library assistants would retrieve the books from the stacks and hand them over the counter to the reader. (To save time and effort, many libraries installed "indicators"—arrays of pigeon-holes displaying whether each book was available or already in use.)

Much of the library's space would be devoted to a capacious reading room. There would often be a separate "ladies' reading room," or at least a section of the main reading room reserved for women; less frequently, there would be a children's room. There might be a newsroom, in which readers could stand before sloping tables and peruse a wide selection of newspapers. (Many librarians felt that these rooms attracted undesirables to the library. Some would black out the racing news in order to discourage the patronage of bookmakers. Others complained of the "verminous old soaks" who resorted to the newsrooms when they had exhausted their drinking-money, and worried that "the smell from tramps and outcasts was keeping readers from our books"[7]—which is still a cause for concern in public libraries today, though usually expressed in more delicate language.)

The emphasis on reference collections was only partly due to concern for the safeguarding of valuable books. Equally important was the need to provide a place for reading to working people who often could not afford the light and heat that would enable them to read books in their dismal living quarters. In an age of cheap gin and cheaper beer, the stifling comfort of the public house or corner saloon was a potent rival to the charms of literature. Librarians knew that they must offer more than the loan of books if they were to entice the working classes. For the same reason, public libraries were open late into the evening (especially as electric lighting came into use) and on Sundays. Many cities established branch libraries to bring books closer to their expanding residential neighborhoods.

With the improvement of working-class educational and housing conditions, the nature of reference collections changed. They increasingly catered to the needs of students and specialists, who resorted to them for detailed information on commerce, industry, or local history. Lending collections accounted for an increasing proportion of library resources; the space devoted to reading rooms shrank as library design came to emphasize open access to the book collection.

As readers gained direct access to books, the nature of the library catalog changed. In a closed-stack collection, users were best served by a classified subject catalog, in which broad headings might be subdivided into smaller topics, with a listing of the library's books in each class. This was done in the largest libraries; many smaller ones simply listed books alphabetically by author under a few broad subject divisions. The books themselves were shelved in broad classes in order of accession, sometimes with separate sequences for books of different heights to save stack space. So long as the catalog indicated clearly where a library assistant might find the book, there was no need for its shelf location to correspond to its content. But as libraries came to offer their readers direct access to their shelves, a better system was needed for finding the books they wanted. This was provided by the card catalog and the Dewey Decimal System.

The mere provision of books and catalogs was not enough. "Where there is leisure for it," a prominent librarian argued, "applicants for books should receive the best assistance the attendants can render in the form of information not furnished by the catalogs, or general aids in making selections."[8] As encyclopedias, indexes, and directories became widely available, libraries increasingly offered their patrons help in finding answers to their questions, where these were contained in books in the library's collection. This "reference service" was facilitated by the practice of dividing large public library collections into subject departments, staffed with librarians whose training and experience qualified them as subject specialists.

IN THE EARLY years of the public library movement, there was considerable controversy over the place of light reading in the collection. While many librarians deplored the popularity of fiction, they harbored the hope that its provision would attract readers whose taste could be improved. "[T]he attention of the readers is being gradually and progressively drawn from light literature to historical and biographical works, general literature, and books of a more practical tendency," a British librarian boasted in 1856.[9]

Public libraries and librarians, like teachers and clergymen, saw themselves as upholders of the established order. Their educational and social mission was to enable men and women to rise within society as currently constituted, not to provide them with the intellectual tools to overthrow it. Radical literature was seldom to be found on library shelves; many critics had opposed the provision of newspapers in libraries because their availability might foster political agitation.

Even as late as 1928, the American Library Association's guide to *Periodicals for the Small Library* warned librarians that "many of the staid old conservative magazines of the past now are distributors of social and political theories of at least doubtful desirability and of fiction of whose desirability there is, unfortunately, little or no doubt."[10] It was decidedly unsympathetic to any minority viewpoints. Recommended religious periodicals were limited to Protestant publications, totally excluding Roman Catholic and Jewish magazines. Political radicalism was anathema.

Like many other Americans dismayed by the Bolshevik Revolution in Russia and the societal changes sweeping the U.S. in the wake of World War I, the guide's compiler overreacted; his 1932 edition displayed more tolerance for minority religious and political views. As the educational and religious leaders who had once been the strongest upholders of established ways evolved into the establishment's most severe critics, librarians also came to cherish diversity of opinion and free access to the widest possible range of viewpoints. Opposition to censorship has become a central part of the librarian's professional ethics, and public libraries have often come under attack for making unpopular publications available. Libraries today are among the strongest defenders of freedom of the press and of intellectual freedom in general.

In 1939 the United States celebrated the 150th anniversary of the Bill of Rights, the ten amendments that enshrined the basic freedoms of American citizens in the newly adopted federal constitution. In that year the American Library Association proclaimed a "Library Bill of Rights":

1. As a responsibility of library service, books and other reading matter selected should be chosen for values of interest, information, and enlightenment of all the people of the community. In no case should any book be excluded because of the race or nationality, or the political or religious views of the writer.

2. There should be the fullest practicable provision of materials presenting all points of view concerning the problems and issues of our times, international, national, and local, and books or other reading matter of sound factual authority should not be proscribed or removed from library shelves because of partisan or doctrinal disapproval.

3. Censorship of books, urged or practiced by volunteer arbiters of morals or political opinion or by organizations that would establish a coercive concept of Americanism, must be challenged by libraries in maintenance of their responsibility to provide public information and enlightenment through the printed word.

4. Libraries should enlist the cooperation of allied groups in the fields of science, of education, and of book publishing in resisting all abridgement of the free access to ideas and full freedom of expression that are the tradition and heritage of Americans.

5. The rights of an individual to the use of a library should not be denied or abridged because of his race, religion, national origin, or political views.

6. As an institution of education for democratic living, the library should welcome the use of its meeting rooms for socially useful and cultural activities and discussion of current public questions. Such meeting places should be available on equal terms to all groups in the community regardless of the beliefs and affiliations of their members.[11]

It has served as the model for similar policy statements in several other countries.

IN CONTINENTAL EUROPE, the establishment of public libraries lagged behind developments in the English-speaking countries. The European educational system emphasized the preparation of young men for their life's work rather than the production of an informed citizenry. The development of a lifetime habit of reading as an essential aspect of self-education did not command the public imagination, nor did it appeal to philanthropists with the means to support public libraries. And readers were accustomed to owning books rather than borrowing them, a practice encouraged by the comparatively low price of books on the Continent.

In many countries of 19th-century Europe, illiteracy was high and educational opportunities limited. The only public libraries were either scholarly collections whose owners had opened them to outside readers or small libraries established to serve the public schools that were beginning to spread across the Continent. In eastern European countries, the educated classes often preferred books in Latin, French, or German to those in the national languages—which in many cases they knew only haltingly if at all. (A census of Hungarian libraries in 1885 revealed that in larger collections Hungarian-language books ranked third in number, after titles in German and Latin.)

Even in western Europe, public libraries served only a small number of people. Despite France's Revolutionary enthusiasm for opening the libraries of aristocrats and monasteries to the masses, the books in those collections were more useful to scholars and theologians than to the general public. Municipal libraries were concerned with preserving the nation's literary heritage, not with accommodating the needs of the reading public. Library positions were frequently bestowed upon deserving but impecunious writers, leading one journal to observe that

> poets appear to the government to have special aptitudes for preserving libraries, where they love the silence and the dust which permits them to evoke the soul of things—when they are not disturbed by the impertinent noise of some indiscreet reader.[12]

Even in those libraries founded specifically for the use of the common people, the book collections reflected the literary standards of intellectuals and cultural bureaucrats rather than the tastes of ordinary readers. Books were chosen more for their conformity to approved political or religious doctrine than for their popular appeal. Serious literature rather than ephemeral fiction was the rule: even as late as 1952 an American visitor observed that "one simply does not find mystery stories and the like in the Parisian public libraries."[13] Subscription fees were often charged, which discouraged poor families from using the public libraries.

Working people turned to newsstands and commercial lending libraries for their reading matter, or to privately operated libraries. Many industrial companies provided "works libraries" for their employees, and religious societies played a major role in bringing library service to small towns and rural areas. Beginning in 1934, Action Catholique Féminine established a network of "libraries for all" that grew to over eighteen thousand by the early 1970s. But these hardly offered the wide range of literary genres and political and religious viewpoints that an English-speaking reader was accustomed to finding on the shelves of a British or American public library.

TWO YEARS AFTER the Russian Revolution, the citizens of Petrograd were encouraged to use public libraries:

> As the proletarian revolution wants you to be sober and clear minded you should not fail to obtain a book at your local library. We are sure that neither a single teacher nor a single school will enlighten you as much as your local

library. And the most important thing, comrade, is that books will help you abolish the most baneful inequality, the inequality of the intellect.[14]

Lenin himself was a strong believer in the value of libraries. In 1913 he wrote admiringly of the New York Public Library,

> In Western countries . . . they hold that great public libraries, with hundreds of thousands and millions of books, ought not to be the property only of scholars . . . they are anxious for readers to read books bought at public expense in their own homes; they see the pride and glory of the public library not in the number of rarities it possesses . . . but in the extent to which books circulate among the people.[15]

Like Karl Marx, who wrote much of *Das Kapital* in the British Museum, Lenin was an avid library user. He had read in the British Museum, the Royal Library in Stockholm, the Swiss National Library in Berne, and the Academy of Sciences in St. Petersburg. His wife, Nadezha Krupskaya, had been a librarian herself, and played a major role in the development of Soviet library policy. Her book, *What Lenin Wrote and Said about Libraries* (1929), was the most popular Russian book on librarianship.

Public libraries, like other aspects of education, were seen as vehicles for the advancement of the Communist Party and the Soviet state. Their role, according to Lenin, was to "educate the public strictly towards a revolutionary outlook and revolutionary action."[16] State entities controlled the publication and distribution of all forms of literature, so there was never any opportunity for the production of books or periodicals that attacked the Soviet system or called into question the principles of communism. But just because the books in public library collections had been acceptable when first published did not mean that they would remain so. When the party leadership changed, or the party's teachings were revised, those books whose contents were now unacceptable were removed from the shelves, or the contents purged by the excision of the offending pages.

Soviet public libraries were located in housing developments, factories, workers' clubs, and cultural centers. (Many were maintained by labor unions.) They provided extensive advisory services to their readers, in support of their role in fighting illiteracy and encouraging worker self-education. This also enabled libraries to steer their readers toward those books that enjoyed the favor of the party. Even the cataloging of the collection "must be based on the Marxist–Leninist outlook" and "subordinated to the principles of the Bolshevik Party."[17] A Russian revision of the Dewey Decimal Classification was prepared to remove the "rough deficiencies, flowing from the bourgeois outlook" of its American authors.[18] Later a new Library/Bibliographic Classification was developed to apply Marxist–Leninist principles to the organization of bookshelves and bibliographies.

• • •

"THE PUBLIC LIBRARY is today a weapon in the folkish life battle and therefore a political institution."[19] Like the Soviet Union, Nazi Germany saw the public library as a vehicle for the penetration of the ruling party's values into every aspect of society. To this end, the Nazis vastly increased the number of public libraries in Germany, with the goal of providing one in every community of over five hundred people. They also established libraries in border areas to counteract French, Danish, and Polish cultural influences. The concept of "the German folk" could be strengthened by increasing the hold of the German language on border populations, and the provision of German books was recognized as a powerful means to that end.

This expansion of public library service was a difficult task. Germany lagged well behind the Scandinavian countries and Czechoslovakia in the adoption of library laws and the provision of widespread access to libraries. While many places had "city libraries" dating back to the 17th and 18th centuries, their collections were of interest only to clergymen and antiquarians. Beginning in 1850, *volksbüchereien*—public libraries on the American model—were founded in Berlin and a few other German cities.

But these were neither free nor tax-supported. Upper- and middle-class Germans were accustomed to buying their own books, and thus public libraries were associated with a working-class clientele, who also patronized the subscription libraries operated as sidelines by newsstands and tobacconists. Perhaps for this reason, German librarians considered readers' advisory service the most important of their professional activities. Public libraries did not have open stacks; catalogs were difficult to use and seldom entirely up-to-date; so the librarian served as mediator between book and reader, guiding his selections from the carefully chosen collection of serious books.

This tradition made it easy to incorporate the public library into the Nazi program for the transformation of German society. Books by Jewish writers, communists, and others vilified by the Nazis were removed from library collections, while lists of Nazi-approved titles were distributed to librarians. To eliminate the influence of their competing worldview, the activities of the many Catholic libraries were severely restricted. (Both Protestant and Catholic organizations had maintained nationwide systems of small libraries, often staffed on a voluntary basis by a village clergyman or schoolmaster.) Not only were book selection and collection development subordinated to Nazi teachings: even cataloging and classification were revised to reflect Nazi views on race and nationalism. There was little resistance to the Nazification of German librarianship, though some librarians deliberately did as little as possible to conform.

AFTER WORLD WAR II, educational opportunities expanded across North America and western Europe. Inexpensive paperbacks enabled ordinary people to build their own home libraries. Television gave millions of people the opportunity to travel vicariously around the world, and brought a wide variety of both light and serious entertainment into the home.

At first these developments reduced the importance of the public library as a source of knowledge and entertainment. It was seldom thought of as "the people's university," a role now bestowed upon educational television and innovative institutions of higher education. But public libraries changed in response to their changing surroundings. They learned that television programs often stimulated demand for the books from which they had been adapted. Many of the students at newly established schools and colleges found the public library a convenient place to study. No longer were readers limited to the books owned by their local libraries. Through participation in regional networks, member libraries were able to call upon the resources of university collections and national libraries.

Time-sharing made it possible for even small public libraries to exploit the capabilities of remote computers, both for behind-the-scenes activities such as cataloging and interlibrary loan and for improving reference service to library users. As microcomputers and optical storage devices such as CD-ROM became widely available, libraries could offer access to information resources that took advantage of their rapid search capability and multimedia content. The most recent developments in access to information, the global Internet and its descendant the World Wide Web, offer another opportunity to the public library. By providing public access to the worldwide computer network, and advice in selecting from the countless information sources available in cyberspace, public libraries are replicating their original functions.

11
THE RISING GENERATION

THE IDEA OF providing libraries for the use of young readers was a long time in coming. Traditionally, the education of young children had offered little scope for leisure reading. Even when literacy became common in Europe and America, few children were offered anything other than the Bible and a simple reader by way of instructional material. Those few whose situation in life made anything beyond a primary education possible were trained to read the same works, in their native tongue and Latin, as their elders did. There was little that was written especially for children before the 19th century, and that early children's literature was concerned with the salvation of the soul. English children were offered books such as John Cotton's *Spiritual Milk for Boston Babes in either England, drawn from the Breasts of both Testaments for their Souls' Nourishment* (1646) and James Janeway's *A Token for Children, Being an Exact Account of the Conversion, Holy, and Exemplary Lives and Joyful Deaths of Several Young Children* (1671). Their contemporaries on the Continent did not fare any better.

Gradually secular as well as spiritual knowledge was offered in juvenile literature. In the 1740s British publisher John Newbery began to issue books intended for the amusement of middle-class children. During the 19th century, adventure stories and fairy tales began to appear. By the time that *Alice's Adventures in Wonderland* was published in 1865, pure entertainment had become an acceptable motive for children's reading.

But few children had access to these books. In much of 19th-century Europe, illiteracy was still widespread. Even when a child's parents could read, in many a household the only books available were a Bible, a prayer book, and an almanac. It was in America, where an educated population was essential to both the political and religious foundations of society, that the first substantial efforts to provide libraries for young readers were made.

In many American communities the Sunday schools provided young people with their only permanent year-round educational opportunities. Public schools, where these existed, often operated for only a few months during the year. And children growing up on the western frontier might not receive even this limited schooling. The American Sunday School Union provided isolated settlements with a preselected library of one hundred books and tracts, almost entirely religious in character. This ten-dollar library would be left in a local country store, or in the home of a local volunteer. Once a church had been built, the library usually occupied a bookcase in a corner of the building. Children could select books from a printed catalog, and bring them home to read during the week. While many of these books combined dullness and piety—summed up by one Sunday School historian as "memoirs of offensively pious infants, whose chief virtue was that they died young"[1]—accounts of missionary activity offered exciting tales of travel and danger in exotic lands. By 1850 there were nearly two thousand Sunday school libraries in the United States.

As the idea of free public education spread across the northern United States, many states passed legislation authorizing or requiring school districts to maintain libraries. These served both adults and children, and offered an alternative to the sectarian contents of the Sunday school collections. Henry Barnard, secretary of Connecticut's state board of education, claimed that

> The school-house is the appropriate depository of the district library, and a library of well-selected books, open to the teacher, children, and adults generally of the district, for reference and reading, gives completeness to the permanent means of school and self-education. . . .Without such books the instruction of the school-room does not become practically useful, and the art of printing is not made available to the poor as well as to the rich.[2]

This idea of the public library as completing the work of the public school was influential in the establishment of the urban public libraries that displaced the school district libraries. The Boston Public Library's founders conceived it as

> the crowning glory of our system of City Schools . . . an institution, fitted to continue and increase the best effects of that system, by opening to all the means of self culture through books, for which these schools have been specially qualifying them.[3]

Because the first public libraries saw themselves as agencies for enabling school graduates to continue the educational process on their own, they directed their collections and services to adults. Some displayed signs warning "children and dogs not admitted," and most libraries refused entry to anyone under fourteen years of age. Books were not lent for home use; the reference and reading rooms were crowded with adult users. There was doubt as to the propriety of allowing children to mingle with grown men and women, and concern that they might disturb their elders. It was not until the 1890s that public libraries really began to serve children.

But the problems of urban life convinced social reformers that children needed wholesome alternatives to the street-corner and saloon. The same impulses that led civic-minded men and women to found settlement houses in poor neighborhoods, and brought college students and middle-class women to volunteer to work in them, led the more imaginative public librarians to extend their services to young readers. Indeed, some of the earliest public library children's services were located in settlement houses.

Child labor came under increasing regulation, and compulsory education laws were more stringently enforced. The number of children with both the ability and the leisure time to read increased substantially. In response to this, public libraries began to make service to children a high priority. By 1896 more than a dozen American libraries had reading rooms or lending services for children. Many libraries hired young women, who were thought to have a special aptitude for work with children.

In cities with large foreign-born populations, the enthusiasm with which public libraries strove to help in the assimilation of immigrants extended to work with their children. Librarians were eager not only to foster their integration into American life but also to encourage children to retain those aspects of their cultural heritage that were considered compatible with Americanization.

After World War I, public library service to children became widespread, and was extended even to those who were too young to read. To encourage preschool children to find enjoyment in books, libraries offered picture book collections and story hours. Films, puppet programs, and other activities enticed children and their parents into the library. For older readers there were book discussion groups, hobby programs, and visits from writers. The goal of the children's library, explained a distinguished children's librarian, was

> to provide children with good books supplemented by an inviting library environment and intelligent and sympathetic service and by these means to inspire and cultivate in children love of reading, discriminating taste in literature, and judgment and skill in the use of books as tools.[4]

Librarians were concerned with the packaging as well as the content of children's books. They encouraged inviting covers and attractive illustrations. Because they represented a substantial portion of the market for children's literature, publishers were eager to oblige.

It took librarians many years to get over their insistence on hard covers. Although the dime novels of the 19th century and the pulp magazines of the 20th were widely read by older children and adolescents, they were stigmatized by schoolteachers and librarians as literary trash. This disparaging attitude carried over to the paperback novels that began to appear on American newsstands in the 1940s. But a generation of readers arose for whom paperbacks were the most natural form of reading. Publishers eager to reach them issued an immense range of paperback titles, many of undisputed high quality. American libraries began to collect paperbound books, finding that these often had more appeal for young readers than did clothbound editions of the same titles.

• • •

CHANGING TRENDS IN teaching methods and the increasing availability of well-written books for children provoked an interest in extending library service to children in their schools. The indefatigable Benjamin Franklin had proposed in 1749 that the "Academy for the Education of Youth" soon to be opened near Philadelphia be

> furnished with a Library (if in the Country, if in the Town the Town Libraries may serve) with Maps of all Countries, Globes, some mathematical Instruments, an Apparatus for Experiments in Natural Philosophy, and for Mechanics; Prints, of all Kinds, Prospects, Buildings, Machines, &c.[5]

Like the curriculum Franklin proposed for the Academy, its library was to be both pragmatic and eclectic in its content. But Franklin was ahead of his time. Few American communities had the resources to support anything so ambitious. The one-room schoolhouse gave many children all the formal education they were ever to receive, and even those who went beyond the primary level studied a narrow range of subjects. When an entire classroom worked from a single textbook, there was little need for school libraries. But as the curriculum became more diversified, and greater attention was paid to the individual needs of students, the need arose for access to wider book collections.

Many public libraries established full-scale branches or small deposit collections in school buildings. Others lent books in large numbers to teachers for classroom reading. These outreach efforts, directly primarily at students in the upper grades, were effective in convincing educators of the value of in-school library service. In 1900 the first high school librarian was appointed, in Brooklyn, New York. Four years later the state created a Division of School Libraries to encourage and supervise library services to schoolchildren.

Elementary school libraries were slower to develop. Although both teachers and librarians favored them, their growth was halted by the Great Depression of the 1930s. It was not until after World War II that libraries became common in American primary schools. The growth of suburbs and the consolidation of small rural schools—two phenomena made possible by the postwar increase in highway construction and automobile owner-ship—led to the construction of thousands of new school buildings. Many of these had both the student enrollment and the taxpayer support needed to make possible the provision of school libraries.

By the middle of the 20th century a consensus had been reached in America that schools should provide libraries of their own, the better to offer books and (increasingly) other media to supplement textbook read-ing. The launch of the first artificial earth satellite by the Soviet Union in 1957 galvanized American concern for the adequacy of the nation's schools. The National Defense Education Act of 1958 provided abundant funding for the development of improved curricula, and offered local school districts support for the establishment of new school libraries and the improvement of existing ones. Where in 1960 only 31 percent of American elementary schools had libraries or media centers, by 1978 that proportion had reached 83 percent.

These were staffed by people trained in both pedagogy and librarianship, whose duties usually extended to instructing pupils in the skills of library use. As filmstrips, motion pictures, audio- and videotapes, and later computers became part of the school's educational resources, the school librarian—often renamed "instructional media specialist"—assumed the responsibility for their selection, housing, and maintenance.

In 1941 the American Library Association and the National Education Association issued a joint statement on school library service. Ever since then, standards for school libraries have evolved to keep pace with new trends in pedagogy and new forms of educational media. Accrediting agencies began to include adequate libraries among the requirements that they laid down for both elementary and secondary schools, but these have not been uniformly adhered to. The American practice of local control of public education, and the vast difference in financial resources available to public school systems, have prevented the uniform attainment of any standard.

If the school librarian was both teacher and librarian, he or she would (at least at the secondary level) ideally be qualified as both, with a bachelor's degree in teaching followed by a master's degree in library science. Training for American school librarians was provided both by colleges of education and by library schools. Many of these programs lacked the accreditation by the American Library Association that would qualify their graduates for positions in academic or public libraries. But this hardly mattered: school librarians thought of themselves more as teachers than as librarians. Many did not join library associations or attend their meetings. They had their own professional infrastructure of organizations, publications, and conferences, and school librarians often found little in common with librarians who worked in other settings.

ONE AREA THAT they did have in common was a concern for media selection and censorship. The arguments for restricting access to materials in a library collection are more easily made, and more easily defended, when those whom such restrictions would affect are children rather than adults. Long after the ideals enunciated in the Library Bill of Rights were adopted by librarians and widely supported by library trustees and politicians, there continued to be strong support for keeping young readers from books and other library materials that might expose them to knowledge that was deemed unsuitable for them. (Although the Library Bill of Rights was adopted in 1939, it did not address the intellectual freedom of children until 1967, when Article 5 was amended to read, "The rights of an individual to the use of a library should not be denied or abridged because of his age, race, religion, national origins or social or political views."[6]) "Unsuitable" knowledge usually meant sex. "Librarians who work with children, whether in public libraries or elementary schools, have more trouble with sex education materials than with any category of materials they buy."[7] This statement, written in 1977, can be viewed as a mark of progress against censorship. Fifty years before, only the most extreme of social reformers would have argued that materials on sex education had any place at all in a children's library.

Sex was not the only controversial area in book selection for young people. The children's library—and especially the school library—has been expected to play a role in education: not only in teaching facts and reading skills, but also in inculcating the values that children were desired to absorb. The nature of these values changed greatly over time. Where a 19th-century librarian might be worried about books containing

> false views of life, making it consist, if it be worth living, of a series of adventures, hair-breadth escapes; encounters with tyrannical schoolmasters and unnatural parents; sea voyages in which the green hand commands a ship and defeats a mutiny out of sheer smartness; rides on runaway locomotives, strokes of good luck, and a persistent turning up of things just when they are wanted . . .[8]

one hundred years later an eminent library educator asked

> Do we, in the name of intellectual freedom, contribute to making nonwhite and female children feel like second-rate human beings because they were not born white males?[9]

Adults might be deemed fully capable of deciding for themselves what side to take on controversial questions. Indeed, one of the missions of the public library was to provide a wide range of opinion on the issues of the day. But there was much less consensus on the provision of a wide range of viewpoints to young readers.

Regardless of their political philosophy, both conservatives and radicals have been inclined to demand that their views be represented in the library collection. Often they have gone on to demand that competing views be excluded. Whether it was the American Legion demanding the ouster of "un-American" material, or the Council on Interracial Books for Children urging the elimination of books containing "racism and other anti-human content,"[10] there has been no shortage of advocacy groups wishing to impose their values on the library collection.

IN GREAT BRITAIN, public library service to children was established for the same reason that it had been advocated for adults. Middle-class reformers sought to turn potential delinquents into useful members of society. One librarian in Manchester described his prospective juvenile patrons as children of parents whose poverty draws them perilously near to the border-land of crime, but they are still too young to have crossed that border them-selves. It is just such lads as these whom it is essential to detach from vicious companions, and to surround with every possible influence that can tend to moral and social improvement, if they are to be made into useful men and good citizens, and rescued from absorption into the pauper and criminal classes.[11]

By 1898, over a hundred British libraries offered some form of children's services, and over the next twenty years this became almost universal. By the end of the 1930s, separate children's rooms were becoming a common feature in new library buildings, and story hours and other special pro-grams were offered to attract children to the library.

As in America, librarians took an interest in providing books and pro-grams to schools. Many public libraries deposited book collections in classrooms, and played host to visiting parties of schoolchildren. In sev-eral places the public libraries actually operated libraries in the schools, usually (but not always) with some financial support from the local edu-cation authorities.

Since the end of World War II, children's library services in Britain have developed much along the lines of the American experience. The same social forces—suburbanization, television, concentrations of ethnic minori-ties in poor inner-city neighborhoods—have affected young people and the library's ability to serve them. In both Britain and America, as in Canada, Australia, and New Zealand, service to children has become one of the leading purposes of the public library.

OUTSIDE THE ENGLISH-SPEAKING countries, libraries were much slower to extend their services to young readers. In the industrial cities of 19th-cen-tury Germany, a few public libraries offered children's programs and read-ing rooms. Their motivation was more sociological than educational: to keep young people away from saloons and trashy literature. By the end of the century, educators began to look closely at literature for young people. They came to view the shaping of young readers' literary tastes as a task equally important to that of keeping idle youngsters out of trouble.

The development of children's library services in Germany was heavily influenced by the American experience. Several 19th-century German library leaders brought back ideas from their visits to libraries in the United States. But the German view of librarianship emphasized rigid standards of book selection, and a strong role for the librarian in advising readers. In many German libraries it was the father of the family who held the library card and selected the reading matter for the entire household.

Since the end of World War II, library service to young people in Germany has followed the Anglo–American pattern. Well-chosen collec-tions, placed on open shelves, are intended to accustom children and adolescents to read for pleasure, with the goal of instilling reading as a life-long habit.

Before World War I, the only children's libraries in France were small collections distributed to primary schools. These resided in locked cup-boards except on the rare occasions at which books were distributed. A French librarian, recalling his schooldays in the 1890s, wrote:

> Only once was the door opened to me [that led] to where the 2000 or 3000 books, dressed in black binding, were lined up as if for a funeral procession. . . . We were made to pass by the shelves. Each one of us received a book, and chance attributed to me an antiquated edition of the *Travels of Marco Polo*. It was the only book I took from a school library. . . . Three weeks later I returned it unread.[12]

In 1924 a group of American women opened a model children's library in Paris. Patterned on the American public library, l'Heure Joyeuse offered children and young teenagers a selection of attractive books on open shelves, a program of story hours and book discussions, and an opportu-nity to participate in the day-to-day operation of the library. It was extremely successful, and influenced library service to adults as well as to young people.

The Soviet Union had extensive networks of children's libraries and youth libraries, both operated separately from the public libraries serving adults. In addition, trade unions, youth clubs, and other organizations pro-vided library services, and more than 150,000 school libraries served edu-cational needs. All this was intended to support the "development of the personality"[13] of Soviet youth along communist lines. The head of the Moscow State Youth Library declared that

> The foundation, the heart of all idea-educational work is the formation of the Marxist–Leninist concept of the world. To this most important task are tied without exclusion all strands of the educational work. To formulate the com-munist idea-complex means: to arm the komsomols [Young Communist Leagues], boys and girls, with a deep understanding of the laws of social development, a knowledge of the history of the work of the Communist Party, the history of the revolutionary fight and the socialist construction. To teach them to choose independently among the complex and diverse phenomena of the present reality. To implant into them a boundless faithfulness towards the party of Lenin, a pride in the great accomplishments of our country, intransi-gence towards the bourgeois ideology, to inoculate the communist attitude to work, the trend to become a zealous housekeeper, to multiply the fame of our country through work, to enrich untiringly their minds with every knowledge, which mankind has accumulated; to develop in the young boys and girls a civil ripeness and a readiness, to obey strictly the principles in the moral codex of the builders of communism.[14]

With this in mind, both children's libraries and school libraries worked to instill in children good reading habits, so that they could play their parts as workers and as citizens in Soviet society. Librarians paid careful attention to advising them on their choice of reading, and discussed books with children when they returned them.

In recent years many of the Soviet children's libraries were integrated into general public library systems. With the devolution of the Soviet Union and the diminution of the Communist Party's role in public life, the future of library services in Russia and the other ex-Soviet states is uncertain. As they shed their emphasis on the inculcation of Marxist–Leninist ideology, they will increasingly resemble the libraries of western Europe.

In most of Asia, Africa, and Latin America, there were until recently few young readers to be served by libraries. In many of these countries, educational opportunities were limited to the children of upper- and middle-class families, at least until the end of World War II. Even where an attempt was made to provide a primary education to the masses, the resources seldom existed to fund widespread library services. Many a child who had learned to read lost the skill in adulthood, for want of practice. One colonial administrator in Africa noted in 1954 that "the libraries are still in the stage of creating the demand for reading matter rather than meeting an existing demand."[15]

In their postwar modernization programs, several Asian countries sought to ensure universal primary education and universal literacy. School libraries came into being in their thousands, though these often consisted only of a classroom "book corner" or a hallway bookshelf. The education ministries of many countries issued standard book-lists for school libraries, and some governments even supplied the books. In 1973, Indonesia provided a collection of a hundred new titles to each of the nation's sixty-two thousand primary schools. Even where such direct assistance was not supplied, central agencies supplied guidance, often using model libraries to demonstrate the type of service to which a local school or public library could aspire.

In the poorer countries the situation has been bleaker. Children's libraries, where they exist at all, are limited to the national capital and perhaps the larger cities. There is seldom a good selection of books and magazines in the national languages. Even where children can read a European language the necessity to import books from overseas and the lack of foreign exchange make it very difficult to build up an adequate book stock. And in many of the developing countries there are hardly any trained children's librarians, and no facilities for training any.

ADOLESCENTS AS WELL as younger children came under the 19th-century reformers' concern. The middle-class mind found it easy to imagine the vice and depravity that lay ahead of the unguided working-class youngster. As young people left the farm to find office or factory work in the city, there was concern to provide them with the possibility of living a safe, clean, moral life. The Young Men's Christian Association was founded in Boston in 1851 to provide teen-agers on their own in the city with a decent place to live and a Christian way of life. A similar organization for girls was founded fifteen years later.

Adolescent workers were encouraged to use public libraries for self-improvement; indeed, one of the reasons advanced to encourage business support for them was that they would enable ambitious youngsters to learn what they needed to advance them in their trades or careers. Recreational reading was encouraged less as an end in itself than as a desirable alternative to the poolroom or the corner saloon.

As nations became wealthier, they increasingly prolonged the years of education: by the 1930s in America and most of Europe a boy or girl in the middle teen years was expected to be in school rather than in the workplace. The public library's service to this age group evolved into a supplement to the school curriculum and a provider of recreational reading. Under the pressure of national standards and accrediting agencies, high schools increasingly had libraries of their own, often duplicating the facilities and resources of public libraries. With the increasing sophistication of young people, and the saturation of popular culture with images originating in music, film, and television, there was an increasing tendency to provide teenagers with practically unlimited access to the adult collections. Special resources, ranging from a designated bookshelf in a small library to an entire branch of the New York Public Library system, were provided to accommodate their particular interests and concerns.

As television became the dominant medium of information and entertainment in America and Europe, the public library's appeal to adolescents diminished. Students used public library resources for their schoolwork, and a small number of middle-class adolescents borrowed books for recreational reading. But librarians realized that the great majority of their younger patrons were lost to the public library after their mid-teen years.

To counteract this, many libraries changed the nature of their service to young people. They placed less emphasis on traditional book-centered programs—book talks, book discussion groups, literary magazines—and more emphasis on subject-oriented activities based on a broader conception of adolescents' information needs. In urban libraries, special attempts were made to attract young people from ethnic minorities and poor neighborhoods. Often these outreach programs were more concerned with bringing people into the library than with getting them to use library resources for self-improvement or personal enjoyment. In recent years, some libraries have tried to attract young people by offering access to computer networks and multimedia resources. But the high cost of providing this service has limited it largely to libraries in wealthy communities.

The essential dilemma faced by "young adult librarians" (as those who work with adolescents like to call themselves) is that most teen-agers in the affluent West have many other things to do than read books, and see little reason to use public libraries except when school assignments require it.

PUBLIC AND SCHOOL libraries have had a major influence on the development of children's literature. "Librarians can make you or break you," said one best-selling writer.[16] Collectively they represent an enormous share of the market for children's and adolescent books—70 percent in America. In many developing countries the publication of children's books would be financially impossible without assured sales to libraries.

When Massachusetts educator Horace Mann drew up a list of approved books for school-district libraries, he based his selections on the educational value and literary qualities of the books, and omitted sectarian tracts from his list. Following in his footsteps, librarians choosing books for their collections attempted to balance the desirability of the content with the appeal of the books to young readers.

They have also sought to exert a larger influence on the books available to children and adolescents. In France, the librarians at l'Heure Joyeuse advised publishers who sought to improve their juvenile books, and served on the jury for Le Prix Jeunesse, the leading award for excellence in children's literature. Librarians also serve on the jury that selects the winners of the Hans Christian Anderson Award given by the International Board on Books for Young People. The John Newbery Medal has been awarded since 1922 by the American Library Association to "the author of the most distinguished contribution to American literature for children." Another ALA award, the Caldecott Medal, is presented to "the artist of the most distinguished American picture book for children." Like similar prizes in Canada and Great Britain, these awards not only recognize excellence in children's writing but also provide a strong financial incentive for the production of good books. Awards are proudly proclaimed on the covers of winning books, and sales to schools, libraries, booksellers, and parents usually rise substantially.

Librarians have had less of an impact on adult reading. The early public librarians aspired to provide an uplifting influence upon their communities and to guide the reading of adults bent upon self-improvement and self-culture. This gave way to the reality that—in prosperous democracies, at least—few adults looked to the library for much more than a free source of light entertainment. The availability of good cheap paperback books, cultural and educational programs on radio and television, and vastly expanded access to higher education provided many alternatives to the public library's role in adult education. The library's public increasingly supported it out of a mixture of civic duty and concern for young people. Its marginal importance to the community was tolerated because it consumed an unimportant proportion of the total public expenditure.

• • •

IN DEVELOPING COUNTRIES the public library still fulfills much of the role envisioned by the library pioneers of England and America. Poverty and lack of other educational opportunities make libraries attractive to ambitious youths and adults. In most of these countries there are very few public libraries outside the main urban centers. Book collections are small, and their contents outdated. The heavy use they receive wears them out quickly. A children's library in Rio de Janeiro reported that its books were often checked out more than thirty times in one year.

In many of these countries there was no organized book trade or distribution system outside the largest cities. Few publications were available in the national languages, and these were often published by missionary presses whose interests did not necessarily match that of their intended audience. Most books were in the language of the former colonial power. Even when vernacular books were available these were often shunned by ambitious young readers who saw European languages and European learning as the road to advancement. A French colonial official observed that

> The African does not read to "kill" time. He does not read for the mere pleasure of reading. He reads for a purpose. As one reader remarked to me: "I can't imagine myself reading without a purpose or reading without thinking of what I'm reading."[17]

If his purpose was to learn more about his country, the library had little to offer. Titles on the history or geography of Britain and France were easier to find than books about Africa or Asia. Books for children were especially scarce. With the development of national cultures after independence this gradually changed, but even today library collections are heavily Western in content.

Readers in rural areas, if they received any library service at all, got their books through the mail or borrowed them from small collections deposited at local schools or health centers. These were provided by regional or national library agencies, and transport conditions often called forth considerable ingenuity on the part of the providers. In many African countries book shipments were sent by rail or truck or river boat; or library vans, equipped with makeshift accommodation for their staff, traveled from village to village on circuits that might take several weeks.

In some countries public library service has been considered a marginal need in comparison with economic development. The limited resources available for library purposes have gone for the provision of technical information to government officials involved in national development. Demonstration projects in several countries, funded by UNESCO or by charitable foundations, have shown that well-stocked public libraries will attract an enthusiastic clientele. But when the donor organizations withdrew their funding, it was seldom replaced by adequate local support, and the libraries withered away. Where illiteracy is widespread—as is the case in most developing countries—radio, television, and film offer the possibility of educating multitudes who could derive little benefit from a collection of books.

Often the only libraries accessible to the public are those maintained by foreign governments: the United States Information Agency, the British Council, the Alliance Française. These seldom lend books, but that hardly matters: for many who live in the crowded housing of teeming cities, a quiet place to read is almost as important as the reading matter itself. Western travelers in tropical countries, where evenings are always dark after six o'clock, have remarked the sight of young students reading outdoors by the light of street lamps.

The welcome for these libraries was not a unanimous one. Some in the developing countries considered Western libraries an agent of cultural imperialism.

> The African who accepted the bibliophilic philanthropy of the British Council, the Carnegie Corporation, and similar donors was also abandoning his soul and oral tradition, and becoming ripe to be psychologically assailed and manipulated and then plucked by the technologically stronger Western civilization.[18]

The United States Information Agency was seen by some as a front for the Central Intelligence Agency, and its library activities viewed with suspicion by those inclined to doubt American motives. USIA libraries were often attacked during anti-American protest demonstrations, testimony to their symbolic importance.

SOCIAL HISTORIANS SPEAK of the "discovery of childhood" as a recent event in human history. The idea that children were not merely adults in miniature, but had developmental patterns of their own, arose in Western society just as that society entered upon a period of accelerating technological and cultural change. In the 20th century it has become apparent that children will spend their adult lives in a world substantially different from that into which they were born. The role of the school and public library has been to help young people to equip themselves to face that uncertain future. Attacks upon libraries are demonstrations that someone recognizes their importance. In those countries that are still in the process of developing their national traditions, every medium of education and communication is judged by its contribution to the establishment of national unity and the attainment of national goals. This is as true of libraries as of any other institution.

In most Western democracies there is little public controversy about the content of library collections for adults. The role of the library in shaping the opinions and behavior of adults is seen as limited at best, nonexistent at worst, and adults are considered able to decide such things for themselves.

But even in the most liberal societies there is wide public concern for the formation of the rising generation. The education of youth is a perennial subject of controversy; and to the extent that libraries play a role in education they share in the public scrutiny. Those who feel that young people require more rather than less guidance in making decisions tend to look with disfavor on the availability of books that advocate ideas or portray situations that do not conform to their desired norms. Those who believe that young people should have access to the information they need to form their own opinions naturally encourage the widest possible representation of viewpoints in the library collection and the widest possible provision of library service. The tension between these attitudes is eloquent testimony of the importance of library service to young people.

12
PUTTING KNOWLEDGE TO WORK

THE LIBRARIES OF antiquity were shaped by the desires of kings and the needs of the state; and those of medieval Europe existed to serve king or pope, cathedral or monastery. Even when universities were founded across Catholic Europe, their libraries were usually devoted to theology, and were used primarily by members of the faculty. But after the Renaissance men began to believe that many events heretofore considered to lie entirely within God's hands were in fact amenable to human action. As geographical and scientific knowledge grew, so did the number of professions devoted to their application. With them arose opportunities and occasions for the development of specialized libraries to serve them.

After the Industrial Revolution, the scale of economic activity increased. Work which had been performed by individuals or small groups increasingly was undertaken by large, often widely dispersed organizations. Their activities became more dependent upon the application of technology; and the application of technology was increasingly dependent upon the exchange of information. Knowledge that had once been transferred by word of mouth now needed to be recorded, preserved, and transmitted in a more organized manner.

With the growth of science and technology, more facts came to be known about the way in which the world worked and the ways in which those facts could be applied to the improvement of the human condition. Physicists began to understand how matter and energy interacted; chemists discovered the elements and their properties; biologists learned how life evolved and functioned. These discoveries were applied to agriculture, medicine, mining, and manufacturing. There was so much to know, and so many ways to apply that knowledge.

Scientists recorded their inventions, discoveries, and theories in journal articles, and gathered their knowledge into treatises. Their accomplishment was distilled into handbooks, which engineers used as the basis for their designs. As scientific thinking and its engineering applications transformed the relationship between humanity and nature, they became applied to a wider realm of human activities: to commerce, to politics, to the art of war. The traditional knowledge-based professions—medicine, divinity, law—served as models for new areas of endeavor, whose adherents established societies, training programs, and social–legal structures based upon the acquisition and application of a defined body of knowledge. To maintain this body of knowledge, special libraries were called into being.

These were distinguished not only by their concentration on collecting the literature and serving the informational needs of a particular field, but also by the expanded range of materials with which they dealt. This reflects their concern with all stages of the information cycle, not just the finished product—the aspect that traditionally concerned public and academic librarians.

THE INFORMATION CYCLE begins in the laboratory and workshop, where scientists and engineers record new data in notebooks, graphs, and computer files. The lessons learned from these data are summarized in technical reports, which are duplicated in limited quantities and distributed to that small number of people whose interest and affiliation warrants it. They may be presented to a wider audience at conferences, whose proceedings may be printed in full or summary form for distribution to attendees and other interested parties. If they are significant enough to justify the expenditure of intellectual and financial capital, the results will appear in a more formal medium: a peer-reviewed journal article, whose publication is dependent upon the approval of colleagues expert in the subject under discussion, or a patent application, in which the new information is made available to all in exchange for a temporary monopoly on its use.

Once the information is published, abstracting and information services bring it to the attention of potential users. Literature reviews incorporate a brief summary into an account of contemporary work in the field as a whole. And the most significant findings are incorporated into the received wisdom of the discipline, as recorded in handbooks for the daily use of practitioners and textbooks for the training of future workers.

Only a small portion of this information cycle consists of materials traditionally collected by public or academic libraries. These build their collections largely from books and journals—materials deemed to have both intrinsic worth and permanent reference value. After all, the dominant ethos of such a library is the selection and preservation of material for the permanent use of a wider community. But the special library's concerns are more immediate. The maintenance of the historical record is not one of its functions, except as it serves an essential corporate purpose. The true concern of the special library is the information that its clientele will need today and tomorrow. If the special library is doing its work effectively, its clients' needs will change rapidly, in response to the ever-changing environment that it has helped to create.

The term "special library" came into use at the beginning of the 20th century, to distinguish those libraries dedicated to serving a particular clientele from the public and academic libraries which were (at least in the English-speaking countries) becoming so widely spread as to define in the public mind the idea and function of a library. But the idea of the special library goes back thousands of years.

MEDICAL LITERATURE IS almost as old as writing itself. Saving only the propitiation of the gods, no topic was of as much interest to king and slave alike as the maintenance of health and the cure of sickness. The Edwin Smith Surgical Papyrus, the works of Hippocrates and Galen, the herbals compiled by monastic botanists—all testify to the perennial interest in the science of healing. As the scientific method began to be applied to medicine and surgery, the role of medical literature became more important. Where once medicine was learned through apprenticeship, the education of physicians and surgeons now took place in the laboratory and the library.

In the modern period another factor enters the picture. In many countries, malpractice liability heavily influences the practice of medicine. Failure to remain current with the latest practices and techniques is often considered—and punished as—a form of malpractice, so physicians have strong incentive to become familiar with accepted practices and keep up with new ones. The medical literature plays a large role in this. Physicians, nurses, and other health professionals read current journals on a regular basis, and search the published literature for earlier papers directly relevant to individual cases as they arise.

The first modern medical libraries were maintained by schools of medicine and medical societies. Medical schools were often located in university towns away from major population centers, making their libraries inaccessible to most practicing physicians and surgeons. Medical practitioners assembled private libraries, ranging in size from a handful of books to quite large collections. Thomas Linacre, physician to Henry VIII, bequeathed his medical books to the College of Physicians of London, of which he was a founder. His example was followed by many English medical bibliophiles. By 1660 its library contained thirteen hundred volumes, ninety percent of which were destroyed in London's Great Fire six years later. The loss was made up when the Marquis of Dorchester presented thirty-two hundred magnificent volumes to the College. Its library survives to this day, with a large collection primarily devoted to historical material. By contrast, the library of the Royal College of Surgeons of England, founded in 1800, has remained a resource for the working practitioner.

The world's greatest medical library, the National Library of Medicine, began as a small collection of books in the office of the surgeon general of the United States Army. This officer supervised physicians and surgeons at army posts across the country, and was responsible for providing them with essential journals and reference works. A catalog compiled in 1840 lists 134 titles, eight of which were journals, in the library of the surgeon general's office. Some of these were intended for distribution to army posts, but others were for reference use.

While the army's main duty was to pacify the western frontier, its surgeons were seldom called to perform unusual or extensive work; but the immense numbers of casualties in the Civil War transformed the Medical Department. In 1864, a young assistant surgeon was assigned to the surgeon general's office. A year later John Shaw Billings was placed in charge of the medical library, which now numbered over two thousand volumes. It was at first a spare-time job, but Billings soon became an enthusiastic collector of medical literature. "I wish in time to make the Library of this office as complete as possible . . ." he told a London bookseller.[1]

He had no authority save his own for styling his collection the "National Medical Library," but Billings proceeded as though he had been commissioned to establish one. His plan was "to make it a counterpart to the Library of the Royal College of Surgeons in London"[2] and to that end he solicited current subscriptions and back issues from medical editors and publishers across the country. He enlisted a network of physicians to locate and obtain obscure material for him, encouraging them to visit retired colleagues and doctors' widows in pursuit of medical literature. Billings did not confine the search to orthodox medicine. In addition to the literature of allied disciplines, such as dentistry and veterinary medicine, and the reports of hospitals, asylums, and other institutions and organizations, he sought out the publications of the "irregulars": the botanic, Thomsonian, eclectic, and homeopathic practitioners who were shunned by orthodox physicians. To obtain foreign material, Billings retained agents in the leading European publishing centers, and wrote to American consuls in other countries, as well as missionaries and other American physicians residing abroad. He offered Army Medical Department publications in exchange for wanted books and journals: the multivolume *Medical and Surgical History of the War of the Rebellion*, compiled at the library, was in particular demand.

After the Civil War the library was opened to civilian as well as military readers. Housed in Ford's Theater, a site no longer used for performances after Abraham Lincoln was assassinated there, the rapidly expanding library soon outgrew the space available, which it had to share with the Army Medical Museum. Physicians from Philadelphia and Baltimore traveled by train to use the library, and more distant readers were served by interlibrary loan, or by correspondence: simple questions were answered by letter, and more substantial service was provided on a fee basis by independent copyists, translators, and researchers (some of whom were library staff working after hours).

To make the contents of the library more accessible, Billings began a subject index of its periodical collection. By the summer of 1875 he and his assistants had prepared tens of thousands of index cards. (Not all of this work was done at the library. Volunteers, ranging from bored army surgeons at sleepy frontier posts to a bedridden Confederate general, were supplied with journals to index and a list of subject headings.) The result of this work was the *Index–Catalogue of the Surgeon-General's Library*, an enormous listing of "everything which contains either a new fact, a new idea, or a new way of stating old ones."[3] In 1879 another publication, *Index Medicus*, began to offer "a monthly classified record of the current medical literature of the world."

Ever since, the library's role as the world's leading medical bibliographer has been even more important than its status as the world's largest collection of medical literature. In 1956, its *de facto* status as a national resource was officially acknowledged, and the Armed Forces Medical Library was renamed the National Library of Medicine and transferred to the civilian Public Health Service. Five years later, it moved from downtown Washington to a new building at the National Institutes of Health campus in suburban Bethesda, Maryland, where for the first time in its history it had space adequate to house both its collection and its readers.

Having achieved this, the library undertook to decentralize access to medical literature in America. Early experiments with computerized indexing led to the establishment of MEDLINE, a database distributed on tape to other medical libraries and later made accessible to anyone with access to a computer terminal and the necessary communications equipment. This revolutionized medical literature searching: no longer did one need to consult the bulky cumulations of *Index Medicus* to identify papers; and the ability to combine search commands made it possible to locate material with a precision previously unattainable.

This led to a substantial increase in the demand for copies of journal articles and for the interlibrary loan of books. To cope with this, the library developed a national network of local and regional medical libraries, serving as the provider of last resort for materials unavailable at the local or regional level. No matter how remote from the centers of medical research, a physician could now identify and obtain whatever literature existed that might help to diagnose and treat his patients. With the spread of microcomputers into offices and homes, it became possible for individuals, whether health professionals or members of the public, to use these services without using local libraries as intermediaries. The library developed software that simplified the search process and allowed users to order copies of journal articles by computer. A rapid response service was developed, using facsimile transmission to deliver copies of essential publications when medical emergencies required them.

The library's role as a leader in medical librarianship and communication techniques was sustained with funding for experimental programs and the creation of the Lister Hill National Center for Biomedical Communications, dedicated to the application of new technologies to medical research and education. Thus the pioneering role established for the library by John Shaw Billings continues into the 21st century.

OF ALL HUMAN institutions, the law relies the most upon the compilation and consultation of written documents. Ever since Hammurabi proclaimed the laws of Babylon, lawgivers have prepared codes intended to set forth all of the regulations governing persons and property and their relations to each other and to society at large.

There is no lawyers' equivalent to the National Library of Medicine. Medicine is a universal science, but the law varies from place to place; a new drug or an innovation in surgical technique will have worldwide application, while a court decision or a new development in legal theory may be entirely irrelevant to the concerns of anyone outside the jurisdiction in which it originated. While diplomats and those involved in international finance or commerce might be interested in the legal literature of foreign countries, to most lawyers around the world concern for the literature of their profession has usually stopped at the national frontier.

Continental Europe derived its legal system from the *Corpus Juris Civilis*, which was compiled and codified under the Roman emperor Justinian in the +6th century. The study of jurisprudence in the universities led in the 16th century to what historians call the "Reception," the supplanting of customary law by Roman law in the countries of western Europe. The rationalistic spirit of the Enlightenment led to the compilation of modern legal codes: France adopted the *Code Napoléon* in 1804, and the German civil code was published in its final form in 1895. These influenced legal systems across Europe and around the world.

In Civil Law systems judges play a relatively minor role in legal innovation. There is, in theory, no role for judicial participation in interpreting and extending the law, and no obligation that a judge be guided by precedent in deciding a case. The records of cases previously decided can help a judge to reach a decision, but they do not constrain his ruling. It is the legal scholar, the professor in the university school of law, whose writings shape the growth and development of the legal system. Thus in European law libraries, legal treatises and theoretical journals have always been much more important to the collection than in Anglo–American libraries. Libraries as a whole have played a lesser role in Civil Law countries. The independent law library is an essential fixture of the American law school, but in Civil Law countries legal books and journals are integrated into the general university library. It is only in specialized institutes devoted to legal research that we find dedicated law libraries.

An eminent English judge described the Common Law as "a system which consisted in applying to new combinations of circumstances those rules which we derive from legal principles and judicial precedents."[4] In those countries whose legal system was based on the Common Law of England—essentially the entire English-speaking world—lawyers and judges do not find the law by consulting the statute books. By searching the published reports of previously decided legal cases, they find precedents applicable to the situation at hand. (Edmund Burke once remarked that "to put an end to reports is to put an end to the law of England."[5]) These decisions are binding on judges considering future cases, unless they are overturned by statute, and serve as the basis for the legal advice rendered by attorneys to their clients. Even when a judicial decision is not binding in a particular jurisdiction, the reasoning behind it might be persuasive when cited in a lawyer's brief; so the wider the range of case law available to the lawyer, the more scope he has in constructing his arguments.

In the early years of the American republic there were many backwoods lawyers whose entire law library was a well-worn copy of Blackstone's *Commentaries on the Laws of England*; but in any more settled community access to a larger collection of legal literature was essential to the practice of law. The Law Library Company of the City of Philadelphia was established in 1802 to provide that city's lawyers with access to federal and state statutes, reports of American and British cases, and legal treatises. It soon found imitators in other major cities. (Earlier lawyers had to rely upon their own collections or upon books borrowed from colleagues. John Murray, an affluent lawyer in pre-Revolutionary New York, augmented his income by renting books out from his extensive private library to other lawyers.)

"The entire body of municipal law which governs and regulates society is contained in printed books," a prominent law librarian observed in 1876; but as statutes and court decisions accumulated over the years, and treatises and law reviews multiplied, it became evident that "few lawyers, indeed, can procure by their own private resources all that they need for their investigations."[6] American attorneys found two ways to gain access to the literature of the law. In every state capital a substantial library was maintained for the use of the legislature and the state government, and (where a separate Supreme Court library did not exist) for the judiciary as well. Members of the bar enjoyed access to these, as well as to the more limited law libraries maintained at county court houses for the use of local judges. In addition, in those cities whose bar was extensive or affluent enough to support them, law associations maintained reference libraries for their members and (as a courtesy to the bench) the local judiciary. These libraries typically included the statutes of the United States and those of the state in which they were located, as well as published reports of legal cases from the higher federal and state courts. The best-equipped libraries also included English statutes and the reports of English, Irish, and Scottish courts, and the major American and British legal treatises. Because American courts often take legislative intent into account in making their decisions, law libraries often collected legislative hearings, reports, and other publications.

As large law firms came into existence across America, they maintained their own law libraries. These were managed by law librarians trained in both librarianship and the law, who could help the firm's practicing lawyers to search the legal literature more effectively. In Great Britain, where the practice of the law has been conducted on a smaller scale, such large private law libraries have not developed. Instead most lawyers rely upon the libraries of the Inns of Court, the traditional centers of training in the Common Law, and the Incorporated Law Societies.

Cases decided under Civil Law had no value as precedent in Common-Law countries, and vice versa. Thus there was little reason for law libraries (other than those assembled to support the academic study of comparative law) to collect the literature emanating from alien legal traditions. The great exceptions to this were documents and treatises pertaining to international law, and materials on commercial law of major trading partners. But growing economic interdependence among nations and the expansion of international trade and finance have increased the importance of transnational law. In Europe, the expansion of the European Union's membership and of its sphere of jurisdiction will inevitably elide the distinction between the Common Law and Civil Law systems. For an increasing number of law firms and corporate legal departments, the demands of daily practice require access to the legal literature of many countries.

This is provided not only by collecting publications from a multitude of countries and jurisdictions but even more by a reliance upon electronic media. In law as in medicine the urgent need for current information is matched by a willingness to pay the cost of providing it, especially as this cost (often with a healthy markup for overhead) can be directly charged to clients. Many legal publishers, as well as other firms in the information industry, have developed extensive collections of legal material to which access is sold either by subscription or on a metered basis. Law schools, provided with subsidized access to these resources, train their students to find the law electronically; thus a profession renowned for its veneration of tradition finds itself in the vanguard of the information age.

ONE OF THE first special libraries to serve the new professions was the Hamburger Kommerzbibliothek, the Hamburg Commercial Library. In 1735, the "Honorable Merchants" of the Hamburg Chamber of Commerce (*Kommerzdeputation*) resolved to establish a library of publications on trade and commerce. They ordered from Holland books and atlases, especially charts and engravings of harbors. The library soon began to receive many gifts, and to purchase books at auction. (A special effort was made to obtain English books on commerce and navigation.) Other books were selected from booksellers' catalogs. At first the collection was placed under the chamber's recording secretary. By 1750 a catalog of the collection's 1,016 volumes had been printed, in an edition of 100 copies. With its help—and, as one user put it, "great pains"[7]—an accomplished scholar could find the book he wanted.

As the library grew, it became something of a symbol of Hamburg's eminence in commerce, and consequently a source of pride to the city and its ruling class. The scope of its collection gradually expanded, embracing trade and geography, maps, travel descriptions, and navigation—precisely those information sources most useful to a city whose prosperity had depended for centuries on international seaborne trade. Books were ordered from England, France, Holland, Russia, Italy, and Sweden—anything having to do with commerce or navigation was wanted.

The library became one of the city's leading points of interest, and was visited by princes and nobles who came to Hamburg. But it was essentially useful rather than ornamental: there was no hesitation about selling off superfluous rare books or duplicates, or replacing old books with newer or better editions. As Hamburg grew into the leading port of a powerful German empire, the Kommerzbibliothek grew with it. The library had been expanded to include material on law, political science, statistics, and history. By 1943 it had grown to two hundred thousand volumes, of which one hundred seventy thousand were destroyed that year in the Allied bombing of the city.

The Kommerzbibliothek was well known outside Germany, and was seen by librarians in other countries as a model to be emulated. It was cited as an example of successful library service to business at the hearings before the British Parliament's Select Committee on Public Libraries in 1849. At those hearings, library advocate Edward Edwards urged that industrial collections be established at public libraries to provide for the needs of local businesses.

This was done in Britain and America, but in continental Europe public libraries have traditionally had little to do with the provision of information required by business and industry. European firms without libraries of their own relied upon the resources of universities, research institutes, and scientific and professional societies. In the socialist countries, small technical libraries were established in many factories, to provide technicians with information to help them improve production. (In 1969 there were two thousand "factory technical libraries" in Czechoslovakia.) In addition, most factories maintained collections of recreational reading for employees and their families: the socialist concept of the workplace made it the provider of a wide range of social as well as economic services.

In the industrialized countries of the world, most major commercial and manufacturing enterprises maintained library services. Many of these were quite extensive, often including separate libraries for legal, financial, and technical literature. Companies with offices or manufacturing facilities in several locations often operated coordinated library systems with branch libraries at each site. The majority of small- and medium-sized firms made no provision for the information needs of their employees, and often failed to recognize that any such need existed. A few handbooks, some recent copies of a trade magazine, and a shelf of vendors' catalogs were often the only collection of technical literature available to the engineer or technician. But as industry became ever more dependent upon a rapidly changing technology, and as the impact of industry standards and government regulations upon all aspects of corporate operations increased, the need for timely access to information grew stronger.

A leading purpose of the industrial library is to avoid the inadvertent duplication of research. (There is no point in expending time and money to discover anew the properties of a material that has been described fully in the scientific literature. Likewise, industrial espionage is not needed to learn details of a competitor's research program that can be found in its published patent applications.) In industrial firms, libraries are often responsible to the director of research; their libraries are viewed, and funded, as part of the corporate research and development effort. They are expected to pay for themselves by making those directly concerned with the primary functions of the firm—design, production, marketing—more effective in the performance of their daily work.

Companies in those industries concerned with rapidly evolving technologies are most likely to maintain extensive libraries. The nuclear, aerospace, and pharmaceutical industries—which are among the most heavily regulated of manufacturing industries—have been the foremost providers of library facilities to their personnel. This is also true of consulting firms (such as Arthur D. Little, Inc., and the Battelle Memorial Institute) whose stock in trade is the analysis of technologies and the application of specialized knowledge.

Many professional societies and trade associations maintain libraries and information bureaus. In addition to collecting the specialized literature of their fields, these groups often operate abstracting and indexing services. This form of institutional cooperation among competitors serves not only their own information needs but also helps academic, governmental, and other users.

WHILE MERCANTILIST GOVERNMENTS granted monopolies to the well-connected, the United States Constitution of 1787 set forth a stronger justification for the practice: "To promote the Progress of Science and useful Arts, by securing for limited Times to Authors and Inventors the exclusive Right to their respective Writings and Discoveries." To receive a patent, an applicant needed to demonstrate both the utility and the novelty of his invention. To evaluate these, a patent examiner needed the resources with which to understand the existing state of the art and the extent to which the proposed invention surpassed it.

For this purpose, the patent offices of industrial nations established libraries of technological publications. These included specialized periodicals devoted to various industries; treatises on materials, machines, and processes; and domestic and foreign patents. More general materials, such as encyclopedias, scientific journals, and engineering society transactions, provided the theoretical knowledge that enabled patent examiners to do their work.

In 1876, the librarian of the U.S. Patent Office Library declared that the twenty-three thousand volumes in his collection constituted "the best technological library in the country."[8] It was heavily used by scientists and engineers as well as inventors, attorneys, and patent examiners. As patent office collections grew in size and importance, their utility to those outside the patent field was recognized. The British Patent Office Library evolved into the National Reference Library of Science and Invention, and became a constituent part of the British Museum. Its mission was to build a definitive collection of publications in science and technology (with the exception of student textbooks) and to make these resources available to scientists and engineers. In addition to books and periodicals, the collection emphasized British and foreign patent specifications as well as trade literature and catalogs.

Patent offices are not the only government agencies to maintain extensive libraries in order to assemble materials needed to accomplish their mission. Even when a great national library exists in the capital city, most executive agencies have libraries of their own. Some of these, such as the library of the Foreign and Commonwealth Office in London or the Department of the Interior in Washington, are among the world's greatest collections in their special areas of interest, and their published catalogs are leading bibliographical resources for scholars. Many of these libraries are open to the public; some have evolved to the point where external service is more important than service to the parent agency's own staff.

Libraries with extensive collections of scientific and technical literature are frequently called upon to supply materials to distant users, and many have devoted their resources especially to this purpose. The British Library maintains a Document Supply Centre at Boston Spa in Yorkshire. In a building that resembles an immense warehouse more than a conventional library, 104 miles of shelving house a collection of three million books and two hundred forty-seven thousand serial titles, as well as nearly four million technical reports on microfilm. There is hardly any accommodation for readers or borrowers at Boston Spa. Instead customers throughout the world use the post, facsimile, or electronic mail to request books on loan or photocopies of journal articles. The entire operation of the BLDSC is geared to the efficient fulfillment of requests from distant users. Even in a country as rich in library resources as the United States, many users find the BLDSC to be the fastest, cheapest, and surest way of obtaining the publications they need.

IF SCIENTIFIC AND technical information is valuable during peacetime, it is essential in time of war. World War II was won by the application of new technology. The successful development of the atomic bomb depended upon the acquisition and application of scientific literature—from both Allied and enemy sources. Progress in electronics, cryptography, and aeronautics was also aided by the use of technical literature.

Before the war neither side was self-sufficient scientifically. German science underlay much British and American technology, while German industry collected scientific journals and patent literature from the United States and the United Kingdom. When the war broke out, Germany, Britain, and the U.S. all developed programs to collect technical publications from enemy countries. Though at first much of this could be done openly in neutral nations (whose booksellers happily supplied monographs and journal subscriptions to all comers), as the war progressed the collection of enemy literature became increasingly a clandestine operation. Intelligence services recruited librarians and documentation specialists to coordinate the gathering and dissemination of technical literature; they employed the new technology of microfilm both to conceal the effort and to facilitate the rapid transport of extensive amounts of material by air. (Speed was not the only consideration; hard-won literature shipped by sea might be lost in a submarine attack.) Many of these journals were then reprinted for distribution to libraries supporting the war effort.

Despite censorship on both sides designed to prevent enemy scientists from gaining useful information, both Allies and Axis were able to speed development of military technology by using information published openly in foreign journals and patents. The availability of German scientific papers on nuclear fission experiments helped to make the American atom bomb a reality in 1945. And the unsuccessful German attempt to develop a nuclear weapon relied upon information published in *Reviews of Modern Physics* and *Physical Review*. In 1944 a German submarine landed two agents and a microfilm camera on the Maine coast. They were apprehended by the Federal Bureau of Investigation before they could accomplish their mission of photographing scientific journals at the New York Public Library.

After the war, the American and British governments set up programs to collect, classify, and use captured enemy technical documents. The success of the Manhattan Project and other massive wartime technological undertakings led to the establishment of permanent government-sponsored research and development enterprises. These were provided with extensive library facilities and with the technology necessary to store and access immense quantities of scientific and technical information. It was the needs of these projects, and the substantial resources made available to meet these needs, that led to many of the pioneering developments that have shaped bibliography and librarianship today.

SPECIAL LIBRARIES COLLECT many types of material besides books and journals. Often described as "grey literature," these information resources include patents, standards and specifications, trade catalogs, technical reports, internal documents, translations, reprints, and dissertations.

Patents are granted by governments to inventors, not only to encourage the process of invention by assuring to inventors a temporary monopoly of the use of their inventions, but also to encourage the publication of their discoveries. Anyone who wishes to learn the newest techniques or processes must read the patent literature of his field; and anyone concerned with the activities of competitors will find it essential to monitor their patent activity. In addition, it is essential to avoid infringement upon the patents of others. For all these reasons, a collection of patents—or at least the ability to search the patent literature and obtain copies of interesting patent documents—is an essential part of many industrial libraries.

The peer-reviewed scientific paper is nowadays less a medium for communicating new research results than a method of establishing priority of discovery and of archiving the findings of researchers. For those whose concern is the application of science rather than the establishment of priority, it is important to communicate the lessons learned from observation and experiment. The technical report, which embodies the lessons learned, is often circulated on a restricted basis, as it may contain proprietary information or material classified as sensitive to national security. Because technical reports are seldom publicized outside their intended audience, the role of the industrial library in collecting them and making their content available to those whose work might require it is especially important, and many corporate and governmental libraries have established elaborate internal abstracting and indexing services to serve their clientele.

Standards are promulgated by governments, engineering societies, trade associations, and other organizations to assure the safety and interoperability of products and processes. They are important for legal as well as technical purposes: the extent of conformity to safety standards can be important in product liability cases, for example. In many cases international standards exist; in others, an enterprise doing business in several countries will need to comply with national standards in each country. Specifications are often issued by government agencies and large corporations to ensure that their suppliers offer products that meet precisely defined requirements. These documents are seldom publicly available, but they are essential to vendors seeking to do business with their issuers.

Few companies make every component and provide every service that go into their products. In order to decide whether to make or to buy something, design engineers need to know what is on the market and how well their needs can be met by outside suppliers. A comprehensive collection of catalogs, product documentation, and price lists is needed to ensure that well-informed "make or buy" decisions are made. In addition, such a collection is an invaluable resource for assessing the strengths and weaknesses of competitors and customers.

Some of the most important documents in an industrial library are those produced by the parent company itself. In many organizations, the role of the library as the "corporate memory" is as important as its provision of a gateway to external information resources. A company's own technical reports document the trial and error of laboratory work and testbed activities. Laboratory notebooks and project files are more than just the raw data from engineers' observations and calculations. If properly maintained, they can serve as invaluable legal records, documenting priority of invention or safety testing. In many companies the corporate library is charged with the preservation and indexing of internal documentation, as it already possesses the expertise and the infrastructure to do the job competently.

Many industries and government agencies operate in an international environment, in which essential information is produced in a range of languages. In English-speaking countries, few businessmen or engineers are fluent in foreign languages; and in those countries whose educational systems ensure that any high-school graduate speaks three or four languages fluently, there is no assurance that a crucial publication will have been written in one of them. Even when a translation is almost certain to appear, as in the case of a patent application that will be filed in many countries, there is often a need for immediate access to the content, and so a translation will be undertaken or commissioned. Some large libraries have staff members assigned to the task of translating essential documents; others hire translators or translation services as needed. In most cases the translations are retained as part of the library's collection, in case of further demand for the material; and sometimes they are shared with others through cooperative ventures or national translation centers.

Most authors of scientific papers receive reprints of their papers from the publishers, or make photocopies in lieu of reprints. These they send to other scientists who request them. This is not just a matter of courtesy to fellow researchers. The easier one's work is to obtain, the more likely one's fellows are to cite it in their own publications; and citation is a step toward reputation, tenure, and the other desiderata of the academic life. Scientists routinely send reprints of their work to collaborators and other colleagues; often this is done before the actual publication. Many a scientist uses a desk-drawer file of reprints and preprints as the heart of his working library; such papers are apt to be highly relevant to his specialty. In many industrial libraries, subscriptions to essential journals are supplemented by reprint files, to help counteract the scattering of publications among the tens of thousands of journals published around the world. And in places without substantial libraries, a shelf of handbooks and a few drawers of reprints may well be all the technical library that is available.

In order to earn a doctorate in most fields, a candidate must demonstrate an ability to conceive and execute a substantial piece of original research. The hypotheses, methodology, results, and significance of the work are set forth in a dissertation, which is then examined by a committee of experts and, if approved, made available to the scholarly world. Dissertations vary in length, from a few pages for some mathematical papers to hundreds of pages for historical or literary studies, and they vary in readability, from the merely turgid to the utterly incomprehensible. But they are often the most comprehensive and most recent investigations of a phenomenon that may be of extraordinary interest to specialists; and many industrial libraries regularly search for and obtain dissertations relevant to the interests of their clientele.

SPECIAL LIBRARIES HAVE been among the foremost adaptors of new library technology, whether it be microfilm or computerization. There are several reasons for this. Unlike academic libraries, they do not consider the instruction of their clientele in research skills to be one of their missions: they exist solely to make expensive professional workers more effective at what they do. The same economic considerations that supply the special library's reason for existence in the first place argue for the application of any means that will ensure that users receive all the information they need as quickly as possible. And when the case can be made that applying technology to this end will repay the costs involved, the necessary money is likely to be found. As information technology becomes common in the executive suite as well as in the laboratory, it has become easier for management to understand the rationale for library automation.

It is one thing to assemble a library; it is another to provide intellectual access to its contents. In public and academic libraries the patron is expected to perform much of the intellectual labor of locating precisely the material that he needs. But the special library user is expected to spend the minimum possible amount of time on searching the literature. It is the job of the library, and of the librarian, to do the searching: special librarians spend much of their time keeping up with new information sources and new ways of using existing ones.

So in designing a catalog for the special library, ease of use by the untrained patron is not the consideration that it is in the public or college library. The essential element is the ability to find precisely what is needed, and to omit nothing essential. A complex catalog, understood only by the library staff, is in these circumstances superior to a simpler but less comprehensive one.

Before the computer age, the classified catalog was preferred to the alphabetical subject catalog usually found in academic and public libraries. Because it listed the library's contents in a systematic way, it was better at bringing together related materials. (The classified catalog was especially popular in Europe, as it better served users speaking different languages. A single arrangement of entries would serve everyone equally, and an alphabetical subject index to the classification scheme could be prepared for each language spoken by patrons.) This issue has faded into insignificance with the development of computerized catalogs. The ability to search for material by any of a wide range of characteristics—author, title, key word, subject, date, report number, and many more—and to use elaborate search techniques to specify with increasing precision what the user requires, have made the computerized catalog a necessity in almost every large special library.

The variety of formats in which special libraries collect materials, and the need to locate precise items of information, have led many libraries to catalog their collections in greater depth than has been the custom in other types of libraries. It is common to include individual journal articles, patents, and technical reports along with books in the library catalog; and many libraries have developed their own indexing vocabularies and classification schemes in order to reveal the intellectual content of their collections to their users' greatest advantage.

This emphasis on placing the right piece of information in the right hands at the right time is the distinguishing characteristic of the modern special library. The Special Libraries Association's slogan, "Putting knowledge to work," summarizes the role of the special library past and present in applying technical information to the problems of the world.

13
THE CRAFT OF LIBRARIANSHIP

To THE ANCIENT Babylonians and Egyptians, the care of libraries was an aspect of the scribal art. The Greeks and Romans likewise had no concept of librarianship as a special branch of knowledge, nor did the Byzantines and Arabs who inherited their intellectual tradition. No professor in the medieval universities of Europe expounded the principles of library management, no textbooks existed to impart the rudiments of library economy, and no bibliothecal philosopher had proclaimed a theory of library science.

Until the 19th century there was little concept of librarianship as a profession. Very few people consciously set out to become librarians, and most of the eminent librarians of an earlier age became librarians more or less by accident. In the Benedictine monastery a monk with an aptitude for scholarship might be appointed librarian, and in the medieval university the administration of the library was either assumed in rotation by members of the faculty or delegated to a college treasurer.

After the rebirth of learning, an educated man who did not enter medicine, law, or the Church might find employment as librarian to a prince or a bibliophilic nobleman. For such a post presentability was as much a qualification as bibliographic knowledge. Mastery of the social graces was important: a major component of the librarian's duties was the reception of eminent visitors. These were to be shown the collection's high points, while being discreetly supervised to ensure that these treasures remained in the collection.

A knowledge of languages was essential. Scholarship in those days was an international affair, and a scholar's career might well take him across Europe. The librarian needed the Latin universal among the educated, and also the other literary languages: Greek and perhaps Hebrew for the theologically inclined, French and Italian for those interested in modern literature and scholarship.

A personal acquaintance with the great writers and their works, and a wide background in reading, were needed in a time when bibliographic aids scarcely existed. Even when working with a collection that had already been cataloged, the librarian had to rely largely upon his own knowledge of literature to identify important books that were needed to fill gaps.

Though some medieval books, such as Richard de Fournival's 13th-century *Biblionomia* and Richard de Bury's 14th-century *Philobiblon*, dealt with book collecting, it was two 17th-century books that introduced European readers to the principles of library organization. Gabriel Naudé's *Advis pour dresser une bibliothèque* (Instructions concerning the erecting of a library), a guide for the wealthy but untutored book collector, was widely circulated across Europe, not only in its original French but also in English and Latin. Naudé held that a library should be universal in scope but highly selective, arranged systematically and carefully cataloged for the benefit of users. John Dury, a Scottish divine, published the *Reformed Library-Keeper* in 1650. An educational reformer, Dury wished to transform librarians from mere custodians of books to advocates for their use and educators of their users. Most university librarians, he observed, were required "to look to the books committed to their custody, that they may not be lost or embezzled by those that use them, and this is all." They seldom took part in the selection of books for their libraries, nor were they expected (or even qualified) to provide advice and guidance to readers. But if salaries could be offered that "might maintain a man of parts and generous thoughts," then a library keeper might be expected "to keep the public stock of learning, which is books and manuscripts; to increase it, and to propose it to others in the way which may be most useful unto all; his work, then, is to be a factor and trader for helps to learning, and a treasurer to keep them, and a dispenser to apply them to use, or to see them well used, or at least not abused."[1]

The 18th century was characterized by an enthusiasm for knowledge. Reason began to make serious headway against superstition, observation and experiment began to supersede inherited authority, and men of learning began to regard the discovery of new knowledge as a more valuable activity than the reiteration of the old. Led by the *philosophes* of France, an international network of correspondence, publication, and travel united the intellectual life of Europe and America.

The ideal 18th-century librarian was a scholar's scholar whose knowledge of books and their contents was truly encyclopedic. With this knowledge he could build a collection that could meet the intellectual needs of the expanding scholarship that characterized the Enlightenment. And he could catalog this collection, so that its riches would serve the needs of scholars who could no longer keep up with the vastly increasing output of learned literature. Thus the librarian must not only be familiar with publications ancient and modern, in Latin and in the major living languages of Europe; he must also know something of the principles of bibliographical method.

During the 19th century librarians began in earnest to define the principles governing the organization and management of libraries. Textbooks on librarianship by the German librarians Martin Schrettinger and

Friedrich Adolf Ebert emphasized the rapid acquisition of books and the ability to find them quickly in the library collection. This practical approach offended the Danish librarian Christian Molbeck, who could not envision a library science that was not based on the "constant perfecting of the scientific or the encyclopedic system of order."[2]

These early library philosophers were concerned with the principles governing the selection of books in library collections, and the cataloging and arrangement of those collections. One issue was that of who would select the books. How was the university library to prevent the more influential or more conscientious professors from distorting the balance of the collection? The best defense against this, it was agreed, was the appointment of a librarian learned enough to be able to discuss scholarly literature on equal terms with professors, and strong enough not to be intimidated by them.

Not every possessor of an important library saw the importance of a good librarian. The aristocrat who had inherited a book collection from a scholarly ancestor, or the university whose curriculum had not changed appreciably over the centuries, often looked on the care of the library as an unimportant task to be dealt with as cheaply as possible. An impoverished graduate who had failed at his other endeavors, or an indolent professor willing to undertake nominal duties for an equally nominal augmentation of his salary, was often appointed librarian. The position frequently lacked prestige as well as profit. When Giovanni Jacoppo Casanova accepted the post of librarian to a Bohemian nobleman, he was chagrined to learn that he was to take his meals in the servants' hall.

Many of the most eminent librarians of the Renaissance and Enlightenment periods owed their renown far more to their writing than to their library work. The 17th-century German philosopher and mathematician Gottfried Wilhelm Leibniz began his library career at the age of twenty-six. Though under his direction the ducal collections at Hannover and Wolfenbüttel ranked among the finest court libraries in Germanic Europe, his reputation rests upon his role as one of the inventors of the differential calculus. Casanova, a Venetian adventurer, served for fourteen years as librarian to the Count von Waldstein: but his fame derives from the twelve volumes of his memoirs and the amorous escapades he recounts in them. Johann Wolfgang von Goethe, whose dramatic poem *Faust* is the masterwork of modern German literature, became court librarian at Weimar in 1797 and later served as chief librarian at the University of Jena.

Few of the builders of the great national libraries were especially trained for library work. Antonio Panizzi received a law degree from the University of Parma; after he fled political persecution in his native Italy he eked out a living as a language teacher and literary journalist until he secured an appointment in the British Museum. Ainsworth Rand Spofford, who began the transformation of the Library of Congress from a small book collection serving the needs of the national legislature into America's largest library, had been a bookseller and journalist before becoming librarian at the Smithsonian Institution. John Shaw Billings, who built the modest library in the surgeon general's office into the world's leading repository of medical literature, was trained as a surgeon.

AS SCIENTIFIC KNOWLEDGE accumulated, and the scientific method of inquiry became formalized and ever more widely applied, the social structure of scientific activity changed. Where in the 18th century scientific investigation was the avocation of a small group of rich hobbyists, during the 19th it became a profession. The word "scientist" first entered the English language in 1840, but by that time there were very few "scientists" left. The age of specialization had begun, and scientific workers thought of themselves as botanists or geologists, physicists or chemists, astronomers or zoologists. Though there were (as there are today) general organizations such as the British Association for the Advancement of Science and its American counterpart, and journals such as *Science* and *Nature* that embrace all the fields of science, most scientific communication was conducted within disciplinary boundaries that over the decades grew smaller and smaller.

In emulation of this, those devoted to the study and application of "political economy" became increasingly more specialized in their methodology and subject matter. In the *hautes ecoles* of post-Revolutionary France and especially in the research-oriented German universities, young men from Europe and America became familiar with the literature and imbued with the ethos of the newly emerging scholarly disciplines of the social sciences. Likewise those who studied languages came to think of themselves as philologists, no mere gatherers of folklore but practitioners of a science whose principles could be established through the same careful gathering and analysis of evidence that characterized zoology or botany.

Learned societies multiplied. In the United States, over two hundred were founded in the 1870s and 1880s. Much of this activity was part of the national stock-taking that accompanied the centennial of American independence in 1876.

A group of librarians led by Charles Coffin Jewett had issued a call to convention in 1853, "for the purpose of conferring together upon the means of advancing the prosperity and usefulness of public libraries, and for the suggestion and discussion of topics of importance to book collectors and readers."[3] The resulting meeting drew 82 people to New York, where they discussed the indexing of periodical literature, the management of small libraries, and the cataloging rules recently adopted by the Smithsonian Institution library. But no permanent organization was founded until Melvil Dewey called upon American librarians to gather in Philadelphia in connection with the Centennial Exposition. At that meeting he organized not only the American Library Association but also groups devoted to two other favorite Dewey causes: the Spelling Reform Association and the American Metric Bureau.

The U.S. Bureau of Education, in its 1876 report on *Public Libraries in the United States of America: Their History, Condition, and Management*, revealed the diversity of library collections in the United States while drawing attention to severe deficiencies in the availability of library resources to many Americans. (Its authors, like most librarians of the day, used the term "public library" to mean any library whose books might be consulted by members of the public. The "free public libraries, established and maintained in the same principle that free public schools are,"[4] were a recent development, treated as a novelty worthy of wide emulation.)

The American Library Association, proclaiming that "the difficult and delicate art of library management rested upon a science,"[5] proposed to apply that science to the betterment of humankind and to foster cooperation toward the increase and improvement of libraries. At its initial meeting, Charles Ammi Cutter proposed his rules for a dictionary catalog, to make library collections more accessible to nonscholarly readers, and Melvil Dewey outlined the Decimal Classification that he had devised at Amherst. Clearly there were many theories and much experience to be shared among librarians. To this end Dewey established the *Library Journal*, the world's first periodical publication devoted to what was then called "library economy." Many of the new techniques that Dewey and his colleagues advocated involved the use of printed forms and manufactured equipment designed specifically for library applications, and Dewey established the Library Bureau as a commercial enterprise to supply them.

All this activity inspired comparable developments in Great Britain, where the Library Association of the United Kingdom was founded in 1877 and its journal, the *Library Association Record*, in 1899. Continental Europe was slower to adopt the Anglo–American model of professional organization, but by 1920 there were library associations and journals in France, Germany, and other European countries.

Because there are so many different types of libraries in the 20th century, and such a variety of activities within them, a profusion of specialized organizations and publications has emerged. Many of these have operated as divisions of broad national library associations: the American Library Association, for example, publishes an annual *Handbook of Organization* to sort out its abundance of divisions, committees, task forces, round tables, and caucuses. Others, identifying more with their subject orientations than with librarianship in general, have existed independently: this is typically true of groups representing legal, medical, and other special libraries. Each of these has evolved its own apparatus of local chapters, special interest groups, and publications.

Many observers have doubted the need for all this, and it has often been suggested that very little of what appears in library journals is worth reading. This has not deterred the multiplication of specialist publications. An apparatus of secondary literature, including the continuing bibliography *Library Literature* and the *Library and Information Science Abstracts* database, has evolved to make this material intellectually accessible. This is a necessity; by 1998, there were in existence several hundred journals devoted to librarianship and information science.

AS LIBRARIANS CAME together in professional associations, they concerned themselves with the training of newcomers to the field. In 1882, the Library Association devised a program of three certificates to which British librarians might aspire. A Preliminary Certificate, attesting to competence in English language, literature, and history; arithmetic; and a foreign language, would be prerequisite to beginning in library work. After at least a year's experience, a library worker might earn a Second Class Certificate by passing an examination in English literature; one of the continental literatures; the basic principles of bibliography, cataloging, and library administration; and a "cataloging knowledge" of two foreign languages. The First Class Certificate required at least a second year's library experience and a more detailed examination in the same subjects, as well as a knowledge of library history and the ability to catalog material in at least three foreign languages. Candidates had to prepare for these examinations on their own, although beginning in 1893 they could take correspondence courses or summer schools.

In America, preparation for library work took a different course. Melvil Dewey, who had become chief librarian of Columbia College in New York City, persuaded the Columbia trustees to offer instruction in librarianship. The School of Library Economy opened in January 1887 with an enrollment of twenty students, seventeen of whom were women. Their four-month course of study included lectures on

> Library Economy, the Scope and Usefulness of Libraries, the Founding and Extension of Libraries, Government and Service, Regulations for Readers, Administration, Libraries on Special Subjects, General Libraries, Libraries of Special Countries or Sections, Reading and Aids, Literary Methods, Bibliography, and Catalogs of General Collections.[6]

The teaching of the seven instructors, all of whom were on the staff of the Columbia College Library, was supplemented by specialized bibliographical lectures given by faculty members from other schools at Columbia and by distinguished librarians and bookmen who served as guest lecturers.

All this broke new ground for Columbia. The trustees, caught up in an existing controversy over the provision of undergraduate education for young women, encouraged the removal of the school to Albany, where Dewey had been appointed to a high position in the New York state educational system. (The New York State Library School returned to Columbia in 1926 through a merger with the Library School of the New York Public Library. The resulting School of Library Service, the world's oldest library school, was abolished by the trustees of Columbia University in 1993, one of many library school closings in America.)

The New York State Library School attracted students from nearly every state in America and from many foreign countries. Like the library schools founded at several American universities, it had a great influence on library practice and library education both at home and abroad, especially in those countries that did not have strong native library traditions. Gradually the university-based library schools supplanted those operated by large public library systems and YWCAs, and the bachelor's degree became a prerequisite for admission. With the founding of the University of Chicago's Graduate Library School in 1928, education for librarianship took on a professional character modeled after schools of law and medicine.

The training of European librarians was conducted mainly by the libraries themselves. In many countries academic scholarship was both the prequisite for library work and the primary purpose for the existence of libraries. As in the Renaissance, a knowledge of languages and of learned literature was the most important qualification for the aspiring librarian. Where the seminar library was predominant, as it was in German universities, a degree in a particular subject rather than the study of library science was the prerequisite for a library appointment. Even in public libraries a high level of academic training was required.

In 1834 the German librarian Martin Schrettinger proposed that a special school for educating librarians be established at the principal library of each country. Forty years later, Friedrich Rullmann, librarian of the University of Freiburg, urged that "at one of our universities, gradually perhaps at several, lectures on library science should be delivered by competent men." The course he proposed was considerably more rigorous than the program Dewey established thirteen years later at Columbia. In addition to the German, French, Latin, and Greek that he would have learned in the *gymnasium*, the aspiring librarian should acquire a reading knowledge of Hebrew, English, Italian, and Spanish—though these languages should "be pursued outside of the lecture room." Lectures on general history and collateral studies; the nature and extent of the various sciences; literary history; the history of manuscripts, printing and pictorial reproduction, and the book trade; the principles of library science; major libraries of the world; administration and financial management; cataloging and classification; and the management of archives would qualify the student to be examined by "a special committee composed of the professors or persons lecturing on library science," and if successful to receive a certificate of qualification that would be prerequisite to a position as librarian.[7]

So rigorous a program held little appeal in countries whose librarians served the broader public rather than the scholar. Canada and Scandinavia followed the American pattern of library education, in which a course of specialized classroom study following a liberal arts degree from a four-year college led to a diploma or degree in library service. Librarians in the British empire and the subsequent Commonwealth sought qualifications patterned after those recognized by the Library Association. Toward the end of the 20th century the American pattern had become dominant. University-affiliated library schools had been established in most industrialized nations and at several places in the developing countries. The first British library school was founded at University College, London, in 1919. Although the university librarian at Göttingen had held the title of Professor of the Library-Auxiliary Sciences since 1886, the first formally constituted German course in library education was not offered until 1905, when one was begun at the Court and State Library of Munich.

Library schools and professional examinations permitted entry to basic professional positions. At both the lowest and highest ends of the library hierarchy, alternative forms of entry existed. Those working in essentially clerical positions, and many who ran smaller libraries, received most of their training on the job. Library associations and government agencies responsible for public libraries offered informal workshops and courses, often leading to a certification that recognized basic competency in library work.

At the other end of the spectrum, leading research collections and national libraries often chose their directors for their scholarly attainments rather than for their education or experience in librarianship. This has often been decried by library associations. When Franklin D. Roosevelt appointed Archibald MacLeish to be the Librarian of Congress in 1939, the American Library Association formally opposed his selection: "Mr. MacLeish could not qualify for the librarianship of any collection or public library in America which attempts to maintain professional standards."[8] But their protests were unheeded. To many scholars a librarian, no matter how skilled in his craft, is essentially a technician. The leadership of a major scholarly resource, they feel, should be entrusted to one of their own peers.

The increasing application of computers and other new information technologies to libraries, and to scholarship and publication generally, has further brought into question the nature and purpose of education for librarianship, while the emergence of information science as a field of scholarship offers both a theoretical underpinning for library science and a potential replacement for it in the university.

• • •

THE CATALOGING OF library collections was a task that even the most disputatious of professors was happy to leave to the librarian. Libraries had been cataloged for centuries, of course, but the purpose of that effort had changed over time. The first library catalogs were compiled to serve as inventories of valuable property, though by the 13th century they were deemed equally important as finding aids. (There were even attempts at union catalogs, in which the book holdings of several libraries were listed in a single volume, with a code indicating in which library a particular book might be found.) There was no single, obvious way of listing the contents of a library for the benefit of readers. Some catalogs were arranged by author; others by subject; in still others books were listed in order of accession to the collection.

As literature multiplied, and the formats in which it was produced grew ever more diverse, it became necessary for libraries to ensure that their books were cataloged uniformly. The Bodleian Library at Oxford University adopted cataloging rules in 1674. These recognized that the most important fact about a book is its intellectual origin; that is, in most cases, its author. The Bodleian rules called for all books by a single author to be listed together in the catalog, regardless of the attribution of authorship contained in the book itself. In the 19th century cataloging codes were developed for two very large libraries. Anthony Panizzi's 92 rules for the printed books of the British Museum (1841) and Charles Coffin Jewett's 39 rules for the Smithsonian Institution's library (1853) were widely viewed as applicable to other collections as well. They greatly influenced the more complex "Rules for a Dictionary Catalog," which Charles Ammi Cutter published in 1876. This code of 205 rules was abridged in the American Library Association's *Condensed Rules for an Author and Title Catalog* (1883).

The dictionary catalog, in which author names, book titles, and subject headings were listed in a single alphabetical sequence, had the virtue of simplicity. In theory, the user was required to bring to the catalog only a knowledge of alphabetical order and some idea of what it was that he wanted. In practice, things were not that simple. Establishing precisely who was the author of an anonymous book, or one published by a corporate entity (such as a government agency or a society), was not a straightforward task. No matter how carefully designed the rules governing a decision, there were always readers who could make no sense of the thought processes librarians used to establish them.

Subject cataloging posed even greater problems. In a language replete with synonyms, which of several equally plausible terms should be chosen to express a concept? Even in languages with less copious vocabularies there was often a choice to be made between scholarly terminology and that used more widely by the common people. Should a book treating of several subjects be listed under all of them, or only under one; and, if the latter, how was that one topic to be chosen? Should there even be a list of subject terms to be assigned by catalogers, or should the author be regarded as the best judge of his subject matter and cataloging terms be taken from those he employed in his title?

Many librarians, and their more scholarly users, argued that a dictionary catalog subjected those who would find a book on a particular subject to the caprices of the alphabet and an arbitrary choice of subject terms. They preferred a classified subject catalog, in which a logical sequence of the major divisions of knowledge was subdivided into ever-finer distinctions between subjects. This would describe each book not only in terms of its own subject content, but also place it into a relationship with those books taking a narrower or a broader approach. Ideally the classed catalog would be accompanied by an alphabetical index to its classification scheme, guiding users to the correct place to search for books on a subject regardless of the terms they had in mind when beginning their search.

The arrangement of books on library shelves had originally been governed by the locations recorded in catalogs. These were seldom based on any feature of the book other than its size, or the order in which it came into the collection. Even when some division of the collection by subject was employed, there was seldom any attempt at close classification. But as libraries began to give their users direct access to their bookshelves, they employed schemes such as Dewey's Decimal Classification to arrange the books in some logical order by subject.

If the books themselves were placed on the shelves in a classified order by subject, what purpose was served by the classed catalog? This question was often answered by the abandonment of the classed catalog and its replacement by the dictionary catalog or (in larger libraries) by a divided catalog with separate author/title and subject sequences. The role of the classed catalog in facilitating subject access could better be served by the publication of specialized subject bibliographies which could list all relevant works, whether included in a particular library collection or not. The same argument was employed against the detailed cataloging of such little-used classes of publications as doctoral dissertations, technical reports, and government documents. Similarly, the process of analyzing collective works in the library catalog was replaced by the purchase of printed indexes that could guide readers to individual articles in periodicals and stories or essays gathered in books.

The development of cataloging codes has led to an increasing uniformity of practice. By the middle of the 20th century two major systems existed: the *Anglo–American Cataloguing Rules* jointly compiled by the major library organizations of the English-speaking world, and the continental codes descended from the "Prussian Instructions." (These differ principally in their treatment of corporate authorship, where the European tradition has been to enter such works under their titles as with anonymous publications.) This standardization, together with economic realities and the growing realization that the fine points of cataloging practice had little to do with the way readers actually used library catalogs, led to various forms of centralized and cooperative cataloging. The sale of printed cards by the Library of Congress, which began in 1902, in effect made that library the centralized cataloging agency for thousands of American libraries, while commercial vendors provided catalog cards suited to the needs of the smaller school and public libraries. The development of computers made true cooperative cataloging a reality, with entities such as OCLC (founded as the Ohio College Library Center) and the Research Libraries Group maintaining immense databases of bibliographical records contributed by member institutions. Instead of cataloging a newly received book from scratch, a cataloger could determine if someone else had already entered the necessary information, and then use it with or without modification. If no record for the book were present, that cataloger's work would be input to serve colleagues in other libraries.

THE CAPABILITIES AND requirements of the computer have caused the modification of many library procedures, and have even brought into question the need for maintaining libraries in the traditional sense of the word. As the growth of literature and the expense of maintaining collections increased, even the most ambitious of librarians came to realize that no single collection could house everything that its clientele might ever demand. The assurance of access to needed materials began to replace outright ownership as the measure of a library's utility. As both raw data and the results of research were increasingly produced in electronic form and circulated over computer networks rather than as printed documents, forward-looking librarians began to see their task as that of cataloging the evanescent literature of cyberspace, guiding patrons to the resources best suited to their purposes, and ensuring the preservation of information that existed only in electronic form. In short, they applied the principles that had well served the management of manuscripts and printed books to the new electronic medium.

Just as the development of printing did not render existing manuscripts valueless, so new electronic forms of publishing do not make print obsolete. An enormous amount of material has been printed since Gutenberg's day, and much of importance to our culture exists in holograph and typescript form. The creators of this material might have hoped that their thoughts would last through the ages, but all too often the media in which they were fixed has a much shorter life expectancy. Books and manuscripts produced on acid paper, films on nitrate stock, recordings in formats for which playback equipment no longer exists—all these have challenged the ability of libraries to make the words of the past available to those in the future who would use them. The application of physical and chemical technology to the preservation of library materials has become a major concern of librarians. Library agencies conduct and sponsor research into the most effective preservation techniques for arresting the gradual deterioration of fragile materials and for rescuing library resources subjected to natural or manmade disasters.

All but the most extreme preservationists acknowledge that the purpose of a library is to make its resources available to those who would use them. Much of the thinking behind library science is devoted to better ways of doing this. By studying the ways in which readers and scholars actually seek and use information, researchers have attempted to ensure that librarians' efforts, whether in collection development, cataloging and classification, or direct interaction with library users, have the intended results. Methodologies borrowed from such disciplines as psychology, sociology, and economics have been employed in this process. In recognition of this interdisciplinary approach, its practitioners often call themselves "information scientists."

Two of the primary concerns of information scientists have been information retrieval and bibliometrics. The former is concerned with understanding the ways in which those who produce and those who use information define its content and use their definitions to describe and identify it. The latter is concerned with the ways in which information is used in the process of creating more information. While these may be studied in highly theoretical ways, they have very real practical consequences. They have informed not only the design of computer interfaces, bibliographical databases, and library collections, but have also been applied to issues of personnel selection and research funding.

As AN EMERGING field with interdisciplinary origins, information science does not have a universally accepted definition. It might be compared to economics: where the latter discipline is concerned with the production and exchange of goods and services, information science deals with the production and transmission of knowledge. Though it acquired its name in the middle of the 20th century, its origins lay in the documentation movement that began among European scientists in the 1890s. Concerned with the rapid growth of scientific activity and the corresponding growth of the scientific literature, they began to consider ways of facilitating the communication of scientific discoveries and avoiding the duplication of research.

Beginning in 1665 with the French *Journal des scavans* and the Royal Society's *Philosophical Transactions*, the scientific journal had established itself as the leading medium in which scientists might report their findings and establish priority of discovery. As journals multiplied, abstracts and indexes were produced to enable scientists to keep up with the work of their colleagues and to identify those papers that they wanted to read. These "secondary publications" were the projects, not of librarians, but of scientific societies and entrepreneurial publishers.

By the end of the 19th century it became apparent that existing bibliographical projects, even when combined with the resources of great libraries, were inadequate to the task of making scientific literature readily accessible to those who needed it. The growth of industries based on applications of science made the solution to this problem a matter of urgency. In 1895, the Belgian lawyers Paul Otlet and Henri La Fontaine founded the International Institute of Bibliography (IIB) in Brussels for the purpose of compiling the *Répertoire bibliographique universel*, a card index of world literature. They devised a modification of Dewey's Decimal Classification, using greatly expanded class numbers and a variety of typographical symbols to indicate relationships between them. (This Universal Decimal Classification, though difficult to use as a shelf arrangement for a collection of books, was well suited to producing a classified bibliography of scientific and technical literature. Because an alphabetical index to the classification can be prepared in as many languages as needed, while a single numerical sequence can be used by readers of any language, the UDC has been widely used in Europe to surmount the language barrier posed by an alphabetical subject arrangement.)

The inadequate resources available to Otlet and La Fontaine, and the disruption of scientific communication caused by World War I, nearly put an end to this international bibliographic activity. But interest in universal bibliography and international cooperation remained strong. The IIB evolved into the Federation Internationale de Documentation (International Federation for Documentation, known universally as FID), and expanded its concerns into the areas of document reproduction and distribution.

The application of new technologies to the management of information fascinated their disciples. The first of these new technologies was microfilm. The dispatch of scientific communications via airmailed microfilm offered a great advantage in speed over traditional printed journals sent across the world on steamships and railroads. In 1934, R.H. Draeger invented a camera that could make fast, cheap microfilm copies from books and journals. This offered a convenient substitute for interlibrary loan, and made it possible for the resources of noncirculating collections to be made widely available to scientists and scholars. No longer would a library risk losing part of an unbroken run of a journal to the vagaries of the post or the conscience of the borrower; no longer would a distant patron need to hire someone to copy out a rare volume's contents in longhand. The development of machinery for locating a desired section of a long microfilm roll inspired further attempts to provide for the more precise location of specific information within a substantial text.

The use of abstracts to represent the content of journal articles was originally intended as a way of alerting readers to interesting publications that they might otherwise overlook, especially because of language barriers. This need became urgent after World War II, when American military intelligence experts had to index 1,750 tons of captured German technical reports. It was realized that a collection of brief document surrogates, whether abstracts or lists of key words, could be used as part of a mechanical system to identify which documents met certain criteria of subject matter. In one such system, each document in the collection was represented by a card bordered with small holes. The presence of a particular concept in a document was indicated by cutting a notch from a designated portion of its card's edge. When a rod was passed through the deck of cards representing the collection, those cards notched to indicate the concept sought would drop from the deck.

The next step was to use this method to find the co-occurrence of several concepts within the same document. While only a relatively simple search could be performed mechanically, the same principles could be used by computers. As the application of digital computers was extended from mathematical problems to those involving textual material, information scientists began to experiment with using computers for bibliographical searching.

The development of computer-driven photocomposition as a substitute for mechanical typesetting encouraged the producers of abstracts and indexes to enter their bibliographic information on magnetic tape. This not only made the production of periodic cumulations much easier; it also produced a database that could be searched by using the pattern-matching techniques invented by computer scientists. Searches could be performed only by submitting a set of instructions to the computer, giving it time to perform the search, and then examining the results. These were often unsatisfactory, requiring a revision of the search commands and another try. The high cost of computer memory limited the amount of information that could be contained in a particular system. But these limitations soon were overcome. Interactive searching became a possibility; desktop terminals and, later, microcomputers made it possible to conduct a search from libraries and offices; and the speed and flexibility of searching steadily increased.

As the 20th century progressed, it became increasingly difficult to speak of an all-embracing "library profession." While some functions and activities were common among libraries and librarians, the basic motivation behind their work varied greatly. There came to be several competing philosophies of librarianship.

The traditional concept of the librarian as a scholar with a special competence in bibliography continued to be the dominant one in continental Europe, and in many Anglo–American research libraries. The director of a leading research collection in history and literature was more likely to have the letters Ph.D. after his name than M.L.S.; those trained as librarians might be hired to perform the technical tasks of cataloging and to provide assistance to readers, but the making of library policy and the development of its collection remained in the hands of the scholar.

Two alternative views emerged from the American library movement at the end of the 19th century. Melvil Dewey saw librarianship as essentially a managerial function, one that could be made much more efficient through the use of the technology of the day. Thus the library could serve the informational needs of the entire community, rather than minister only to those scholars with sufficient leisure and education to extract what they needed from the library's treasures. Charles Ammi Cutter's dictionary catalog sacrificed the cumbersome precision offered by an elaborate classification scheme for the patron's ease of use. The card catalog was more up-to-date than the printed book catalog; it was easier for the library's patrons to use, but copies could no longer be sent to other libraries where scholars could use them to locate books they might want to consult. The scholar was but one of the constituencies to be served by the library, now a utilitarian institution devoted to providing the greatest (literary) good to the greatest number.

By contrast, other American librarians saw their work as essentially a missionary enterprise. The same impulses and circumstances that led to the emergence of social work as a profession in the 1880s caused many librarians to view themselves as engaged in a program of social betterment among those less fortunate than they. In Britain and America, the first public libraries were founded, in large part, to encourage working people in habits that would make them more valuable to the ruling classes as employees, while at the same time diverting them from radical politics and social delinquency. The influx of university-trained middle-class women onto the library scene produced many librarians who saw themselves as advocates for the working classes. To them, what was important in librarianship was not the provision of scholarly works to professors or the effective management of book collections, but rather the opportunity for the downtrodden urban masses to make a better life for themselves and their children. This viewpoint was especially well represented among public and school librarians, the majority of whom were female; but it also manifested itself in the emphasis on interlibrary cooperation that made the resources of many academic and special libraries available to readers who had no legal call upon them.

The conviction that information ought to be freely available to all who might want it had underlain both the tradition of scholarly communication that has evolved since the 17th century and the idea of a democratic society in which public policy is determined by a well-informed electorate. Thus it was entirely natural that it should become a fundamental principle of librarianship. But a conflict began to arise between that concept and another equally fundamental principle, that information is a valuable resource which amply repays the costs incurred in its production and dissemination.

As special librarians labored to justify the devotion of corporate or institutional resources to the provision of library services, they attempted to establish a way of measuring the value their work added to their parent organizations' basic activities. By preventing the inadvertent infringement of a competitor's patent, by finding needed technical information in print so that engineers did not have to rediscover it, by alleviating the need for market researchers to conduct expensive surveys, they made it possible for their parent organizations to function more efficiently in a competitive environment. As it became possible to work out the costs and benefits of providing library services, information increasingly was seen as a resource no more to be shared promiscuously than any other valuable property.

The demand for information increased as the application of technology and the social sciences played an ever-greater role in government, commerce, and industry. The entrepreneurs who collected and packaged this information developed increasingly sophisticated technologies, which they had no motivation to give away. Advances in information science and technology were as often the products of corporate as of academic research; and as the idea of an "information industry" arose the capitalist values of the corporation competed with the eleemosynary values that pervaded the academy and the public library.

The traditional library principle, that information is inherently a public good that should be freely available, has come into conflict with the conviction held by many that information is a valuable resource, most efficiently allocated through the workings of the marketplace.

LIBRARIES AND LIBRARIANS have always existed at the margins of the societies they served. The central function of the medieval monastery was prayer; that of the university, education; and that of the prince's household, the power and pleasure of the prince. In all of these settings the library played a supporting rather than a central role. In the 19th century, as the university, the corporation, and the institutions of government itself adapted to a society increasingly shaped by technological change, libraries were seen as essential to the well-being of their constituencies. But even then they were assigned a subordinate role. Professors, not librarians, determined the curriculum. The working classes preferred to choose their reading at the newsstand rather than the public library.

The "feminization of librarianship" is often adduced as the essential reason for the marginalization of the field in America. In 1852, the Boston

Public Library hired its first female clerk; by 1878, two-thirds of American library workers were women; and by the 1920s that figure had reached nearly ninety percent. During those years the leaders of the most important libraries—like the top people in every field—were men; but most of the staff that a library user would encounter were female. This was praised by many: "Instead of the barkeeper and his satellites, we find modest and pleasing young women dispensing books over the counter," J.P. Quincy wrote in 1876.[9] But, like the spinster schoolmarm, the female librarian became in popular culture a figure of fun mixed with scorn: the old maid, grey hair in a bun, shushing anyone who dared break the silence with which she surrounded herself.

In one sense, the lack of respect that libraries and librarians have endured can rightly be traced to the feminization of librarianship. The first women to become librarians in England and America were imbued with the middle-class notion that women were a civilizing force in society with special feminine abilities to work with the young, the sick, and the poor. Under their leadership, libraries became identified with underprivileged and marginal elements of society. To many of those who controlled the country's purse strings and set its priorities, that made the library into a societal luxury—inexpensive enough to maintain at a limited level, but irrelevant to the real needs of those who mattered. The low repute that has been the constant companion of the pedagogue has also had its impact. Despite librarians' attempts to be viewed as educators, it is the prestige of the schoolteacher rather than that of the professor that has become attached to them.

Especially in the United States, the social-work impulse has continued to be pervasive among librarians. Most are imbued with a missionary confidence in the importance of reading, but have little interest in assessing or dealing with the economic importance of information. Much of the leadership in developing new ways of access to information has come from chemists, computer scientists, economists, linguists, philosophers—from people whose professional interest in information science has not been shaped by the library schools and the library literature.

But this is nothing new. The librarians at Alexandria never went to library school, and nobody at Urbino ever read a library journal. The craft of librarianship is not so narrowly defined. For many centuries a love of literature and a respect for learning have been the essential qualifications of the effective librarian. Books, and libraries, have changed over the thousands of years since the invention of writing. The pace of change accelerated with the invention of printing, and again in the age of the computer. But the essential task of the librarian has remained the same: to collect and preserve the record of human accomplishment and imagination, and to put this record in the hands of those who would use it.

14
LIBRARIES OF THE FUTURE

OF THE SEVEN Wonders of the Ancient World, one was located in Alexandria. The Pharos was an immense lighthouse, whose four-hundred-foot tower was topped by a perpetual fire reflected by metal mirrors, casting a light visible for thirty miles. The Greek poets and historians who enumerated the Seven Wonders were well aware of the Library of Alexandria, but they did not account it the equal of the monuments whose grandeur they commemorated. It did not capture the imagination in comparison with the Hanging Gardens of Babylon or the Pyramids of Egypt. To a poet or a historian, the gathering together of the world's literature in one place might be an immense achievement; but to his audience it was just an immense collection of scrolls.

If the Alexandrine library embodied man's ability to transcend the bounds of time, the Pharos symbolized his mastery over night and distance. Both were monuments to man's ability to project human achievement across time and space. And both have provided inspiration to the generations that followed.

The librarians of Alexandria gathered books from across the known world. They acquired the literature of Hellenic culture, and the writings of the Egyptians, Jews, and Persians. Had they known anything of China—where the emperor Wu Ti was collecting classical texts for the Imperial Library—they would surely have sent emissaries in search of the Confucian Classics.

Since their day there has been no diminution of the creation of literature, and an immense addition to the number of literary languages and cultures. The libraries of the world have traditionally taken upon themselves the task of Alexandria—the collection and preservation of the world's literary heritage. But their future role may well be that of the Pharos—to help their users navigate the seas of information that increasingly impact on their lives.

THERE ARE MANY who maintain that paper will soon be obsolete as a means of transmitting and recording information. Messages will be sent, and literature preserved, in digital form. No longer will the reader be required to follow the order of the writer's argument or the style of his editor. No longer will the publisher, the bookseller, the librarian stand between writer and reader. All of literature, past, present, and future, will be available through worldwide computer networks, and neither economics nor geography will restrict access to the wisdom of the ages or the latest literary sensation. In the "paperless library" all users will be equal, and neither wealth nor location will pose a barrier between the reader and the information he needs.

There are obvious objections to this scenario. In whose interest will it be to make all these resources freely available? How will the authors of literary works or the compilers of reference works be compensated for their efforts? How will readers discover and locate the literature they want?

Even if the most optimistic dreams of the technophiles were to come true, there would still be a place for the old-fashioned library of printed books. No miracle of digitization will lessen the aesthetic value of a medieval illuminated manuscript or a Grolier binding. No historian of the book arts will accept an electronic substitute for a Kelmscott Chaucer or a Gutenberg Bible. The need to preserve, catalog, and exhibit the masterworks of the book arts will not be abolished by the progress of computer science.

ONE OF THE tasks of the library of the future will be the preservation of material whose original form is too fragile to survive. The poor quality of the paper on which many 19th- and 20th-century books and manuscripts were produced has caused a crisis for the libraries that own them. The pages of many a book crumble at even the most careful reader's touch. Despite the most stringent environmental safeguards, many volumes face certain disintegration.

An extensive technology has arisen to ensure the protection of precious documents, and great strides have been made in preservation technology. The development of chemicals to remove destructive acids from book paper, and the provision of acid-free materials for the repair and storage of book and manuscript pages, offers the opportunity of halting—and even reversing—their deterioration. But these methods are extremely expensive. It may be worth the cost to apply them to the most valuable items in a library collection, but it would be far too expensive to extend them to the thousands of ordinary books and journals in equal danger of deterioration. In the majority of cases, the preservation of the literary artifact is an impossibility. The best that can be hoped for is to protect the information contained within the artifact.

It may be the humble technology of microfilm that will offer the most reliable form of preservation. The process of filming paper documents is a simple one, and the machinery to read it is inexpensive to manufacture and easy to use. Experience has proven that silver halide microfilm can last for decades, and there is no reason to suppose that it cannot last indefinitely.

Two recent technological developments have made it possible to store bulky, fragile, or valuable publications in digital form. Scanners can convert the markings on a page into a pattern of dots in a computer's memory, and optical character recognition software can convert those dots into a digital representation of text. Unlike microfilm, which preserves entire page images in miniature, digital texts can be searched, manipulated, and reformatted to meet the needs of readers and scholars.

An increasing amount of material is not published at all, in the traditional sense of the word. In many scholarly disciplines and scientific specialties, highly specialized research materials exist only in digital form, and are transmitted over computer networks among the few who need them. On a larger scale, a multimedia publishing industry is attempting to discover what mass market there might be for information and entertainment in digital form, and how best to reach it. Some of this material combines text, images, sound, and animation in unprecedented ways. But much of the information produced in digital form, whether scholarly or commercial in nature, is comparable to the textual documents that libraries have been collecting ever since the Sumerians. Librarians will have to adapt their theories and practices to these new media, just as their predecessors have come to terms with the scroll, the codex, and the phonograph record in their time.

But there are dangers in relying upon digital technology. The machinery used to convert printed publications to machine-readable form, and the media on which the resulting electronic data are stored, rapidly become obsolete. The software which interprets the electronic data is also subject to rapid change. And librarians have no experience by which to judge the permanence of electronic data. Words written on paper, parchment, or papyrus five hundred, a thousand years ago, and more, can still be read in their original form today; but we have no sure way of knowing whether a diskette or compact disc produced today will be intelligible in ten years' time.

While it may be possible to transfer electronic files to new media as old ones become obsolete, this will be a time- and resource-consuming endeavor. Choices will have to be made, and future readers may wish that those choices had been made otherwise. Nearly two thousand years ago, when the codex replaced the scroll as the preferred medium for Western literature, many books that we would like to have today did not survive that transition.

Instead of recopying files whenever a new technology came into use, libraries might decide to preserve carefully, not only the data themselves, but also the complete range of machinery needed to read them. Such a preservation project would need to include the expertise necessary to use the hardware and software: user documentation and repair manuals, and descriptions of searching and indexing procedures. Those in charge would have to understand the assumptions and methodology employed in producing the information in the first place. This would help to ensure that the unanticipated information needs of future generations would be met, without requiring prescient decisions as to what was worth preserving.

There will certainly be a need to deal with these issues of data preservation. Valuable scientific data, from environmental studies, space probes, and astronomical observations, are accumulating at enormous rates. These data, the conclusions that scientists draw from them, and the applications of this knowledge by engineers have created an enormous literature which shows no signs of diminishing in volume. Scientific and technical publications have grown at exponential rates for over 250 years; every ten years there is a doubling in the total number of scientific papers ever published. As the developing countries of Africa, Asia, and Latin America produce their own scientific and technological infrastructure, they will make their own contribution to increasing its bulk. (But there are inherent limits to exponential growth. Otherwise, as Derek de Solla Price has observed, "we should have two scientists for every man, woman, child, and dog in the population."[1] This would leave nobody to collect, preserve, and catalog their publications—much less read them.)

IF THIS IMMENSE profusion of information is to be of any use in performing the work of the world, there must be some mechanism for making it available to those who would act upon it. This requires that the materials so carefully collected and painstakingly preserved by librarians be cataloged and classified, at increasingly more detailed levels. And it requires that the results of this bibliographical work be readily available to those who would use the knowledge they describe.

The Internet had its origins in a telecommunications network established for the use of American scientists working on military research projects. Its expansion to the academic community worldwide, and more recently to commercial users and the general public, has vastly increased the opportunities for scholarly communication and a wide range of other activities. By offering an easy-to-use graphic interface, the World Wide Web has broadened both the appeal and the utility of the Internet. Just as the automobile's effect on 20th-century society went well beyond the facilitation of personal transportation, we can expect that the communications revolution embodied in the Internet and the World Wide Web will have far-reaching socioeconomic consequences for 21st-century civilization.

Among the institutions to be affected by this revolution in telecommunications is the library. The development of the Internet has made an immense range of specialized bibliographical databases available to users worldwide. It has also encouraged a profusion of numerical, textual, and other databases containing information itself, rather than merely directions to its location. These may be consulted by anyone with access to the Internet, regardless of geographical location. Many of them are freely available at no cost to the user. Increasingly this wealth of publication has made access to information, rather than ownership of documents, the real role of the library.

This has not solved the problems of library growth and the increasing cost of publications. Old habits die hard, and many scholars and scientists are reluctant to give up immediate access to their favorite publications in printed form. In many scientific disciplines, knowledge becomes obsolete so quickly that few publications are ever read more than five years after they appear. But in the humanities and social sciences, scholars and students need continued access to older publications.

Two great problems are posed by the substitution of access for ownership. What will be the economic incentive for continued production and publication of the literature? How can we ensure that at least one library undertakes the responsibility of acquiring, preserving, and making permanently available the content of each publication?

Many specialized journals depend upon academic institutions as subscribers. This means that their customers find themselves paying for research twice: by funding its performance in the first place, and by paying to read its results. This has created a great interest in alternatives to the existing system of scientific communication.

In many academic and scientific specialties, the journal has lost much of its function as a medium for communicating current research. The handful of specialists worldwide who are working in a particular area communicate their findings to one another by exchanging manuscripts or preprints by mail or (increasingly) over the Internet. By the time this material appears in print, its interest is more archival than current.

This being the case, there seems less and less reason for libraries to continue to expend ever-greater proportions of their budgets upon acquiring and housing specialized journals. A generation of young scientists and scholars, trained from their schooldays in the use of the computer as an essential communications tool, is emerging from the universities. As they assume positions of leadership in their fields, they will look with increasing favor upon the replacement of expensive printed journals by cheaper ones produced and distributed in digital form over computer networks. The editorial process, and the system of peer review that is meant to ensure that the work published conforms to the methodological criteria of the discipline, can function just as well for a digital journal as a printed one. By eliminating the substantial cost of producing and transporting printed journals, publishers will be able to make their contents more readily available to potential readers, even while collecting sufficient revenue to maintain the editorial process and to earn a decent profit. If they are not nimble enough to do that, they will be replaced by academic consortia and scientific societies.

The library's role in this process will be twofold. First, it will continue to be responsible for maintaining the relationships with publishers that result in access to the content of the journals needed by their patrons. Second, it will be responsible for ensuring that some provision is made for the permanent availability of noncurrent material. Some form of interinstitutional cooperation—or possibly entirely new institutions—will be required so that future needs for access to material published in the past will continue to be met. This will help to lend sufficient credibility to the digital journal to allow the decline and eventual extinction of its printed counterpart.

Whether in digital or printed form, the ever-increasing flood of published literature must be brought to the desktops of those who would use it. The task of document delivery depends upon the maintenance of comprehensive library collections; but that does not mean that the library itself must deliver the documents to the end user. Many years ago, retailers realized that the merchandise they sold could be delivered to their customers by specialist firms more efficiently and cheaply than they could do it themselves. Similarly, many libraries have decided that the provision of documents from their collections should be contracted out to others. This would allow them to concentrate their efforts on collecting, preserving, and cataloging the intellectual resources that provide their reason for existence.

Cataloging is an expensive process, one that lends itself to being shared among libraries. We can expect to see a continuation and expansion of the trend toward cooperative cataloging, and of the trend toward the adoption of international standards. These will increasingly reflect the capabilities and requirements of the computer, and incorporate methods taken from outside the library field.

Toward this end, an International Standard Book Description (ISBD) was devised during the 1970s by the International Federation of Library Associations and Institutions, as part of its ambitiously named program for Universal Bibliographic Control. The second edition of the *Anglo–American Cataloguing Rules* (1978) used the ISBD as the basis for its prescribed presentation of the bibliographical details of books and other library media. Similarly, the International Standard Book Number (ISBN) and International Standard Serial Number (ISSN) were devised as unambiguous ways of identifying publications for commercial as well as bibliographical purposes. New uses have been found for them. A code incorporating the ISSN for each title is used for keeping account of royalty payments due to publishers whose journals are photocopied in libraries. As new forms of publication and distribution emerge, similar coding schemes will facilitate the imposition and collection of fees for the use of documents or parts of documents. Other codes, embedded in the electronic text of the document itself, will prevent unauthorized changes to the text, ensuring that the reader sees what the document's publisher intended. The development of unique, unambiguous identifiers for individual periodical articles and book chapters will encourage the decentralization of scholarly literature, accelerating the trend to making the individual article or chapter, rather than the book or journal as a whole, the basic bibliographic unit.

• • •

KINGS AND SCHOLARS might have needed little guidance in their reading, but as libraries opened their doors to a wider public the need was felt to provide patrons with some help in choosing books. Public libraries no longer place the emphasis on "reader's advisory services" that they did earlier in the century, when neither broadcasting nor higher education offered widespread opportunities for learning. But reference librarians have always been willing to help individual users to select the books or other resources appropriate to their information needs.

During the 1970s many American and British public libraries set up information and referral centers. These attempted to combine the function of the reference librarian and the social worker, by matching individuals with whatever resources—bibliographical or organizational—existed in the community to meet their needs. This movement was short-lived, but like the earlier reader's advisory service was often absorbed into the daily work at the reference desk. The concept may yet be revived as the library's response to the profusion of electronic information resources.

The multiplication of Internet resources has made available to an ever-increasing number of people a wide range of information sources, containing material of infinite variety and extremely variable quality. It is easy and cheap to publish on the Internet, and no mechanism exists to ensure that the information appearing there is accurate. The considerable investment required to publish in traditional book or journal form has tended to limit print publication to material whose publishers are confident that its quality will attract an audience sufficient to reward the effort. Peer review is intended to ensure that scientific and scholarly literature is methodologically and factually valid, and an extensive apparatus of book reviewers exists to place on the record any concerns about the merit of published books. The cost of buying, processing, and storing print publications gives librarians ample motive to be selective in what they choose to add to their collections.

No doubt similar mechanisms will evolve to monitor the Internet. But the lack of any intermediary between author and user removes the filters offered by the publisher, bookseller, and librarian. The Internet user may not be able to find the reviewing media that could help him to evaluate the information he finds; and, even if he does, how is he to evaluate the reviewers?

Herein lies the opportunity for the library. An increasing number of school and public libraries offer their patrons some form of access to the Internet, while academic and special libraries have been at the forefront of electronic access to information resources. If the library offers counsel as well as access, it will become indispensable to Internet users.

THE FUTURE ROLE of the national library is essentially a dual one. One of its priorities will be the preservation of the nation's literary patrimony, including its share of the common treasure of world literature. The other will be the coordination of an increasingly extensive (and expensive!) network of intellectual resources. All this will be accomplished largely by leverage: by using limited resources of money, personnel, and political influence to encourage other libraries to play a role in creating and maintaining a national system.

We can expect to see an increase in scientific research on the conservation of library materials, with a special emphasis on ways of preserving large quantities cheaply. National libraries and library asociations will also play an important part in developing physical as well as bibliographical standards for library materials.

Like the Imperial Library of T'ang China, the national library of the future will be as much a publisher as a storehouse. It will bear the responsibility for making available to potential users the massive statistical, epidemiological, and geographical databanks created by government agencies in the course of their duties. As changing technologies make the existing mechanisms for collecting, publishing, and distributing information economically impossible for commercial publishers, many publications will have to be regarded as a "public good" and disseminated by a nonprofit agency such as a national library.

Like the national library, the academic library of the future will have two basic missions. It will continue to provide students and faculty with access to a wide range of material for education and research. But an increasing proportion of this material will not reside in the library. "Access to information" has already begun to replace "ownership of information" as a desideratum, at least for the more esoteric research material. The efforts that academic libraries now expend on collecting, cataloging, and housing their collections will increasingly be diverted to ensuring that arrangements exist for the permanent archiving of important research materials. New interinstitutional arrangements will be undertaken to ensure that this task is shared out fairly, and that those institutions that serve as hosts for publicly accessible files are compensated for their efforts.

A major challenge to the academic library will be the changing composition of the academic community that it serves. Young people just out of secondary school will make up an ever smaller portion of full-time enrollment, and a larger number and wider variety of part-time students will reflect the increasing need of people in knowledge-based occupations for periodic upgrades to their skills. As full-time teachers are encouraged to hone their technical knowledge by engaging in professional practice and consulting, and as full-time practitioners are coaxed onto campus as adjunct faculty, the boundaries between campus and industry will become more permeable. This will tend to lessen the distinction between the academic and the special library.

The second basic mission of the academic library will be the training of its users (both students and faculty) in the skills needed to discover, access, and evaluate information. A particular challenge to the academic library will be the provision of support to distant learners, especially to those whose primary interaction with the campus is electronic. This support will have to go well beyond making the library's collections available to students off campus. A major role of the academic library will be to play an active part in their educational experience.

More than any other type of library, the future of the special library lies in the expertise that it can bring to tapping the proliferating wells of information in both printed and electronic form. As the nature of published information grows more complex, and as the stakes grow higher (as for example in matters concerning the ownership of patents and other intellectual property), this expertise will become more important. But it may not continue to exist within an institutional framework. Like many other specialized services, the information needs of the corporation will increasingly be met by recourse to outside experts retained as consultants rather than by permanent employees.

WHAT IS THE future of the public library?

In developed countries, there are increasingly many rivals to the book as a source of entertainment and information. What were once mass media are increasingly personal. Videocassettes, compact discs, and CD-ROMs allow the individual to see a movie, listen to music, or interact with a multimedia resource at a time and place of his own choosing. This is eroding the traditional advantage of the book over other methods of packaging information and education. But the book is far from dead. Unlike videotapes and CD-ROMs, books do not require an expensive display apparatus before they can be used. Nor do their display systems tend to become obsolete quickly. So long as literacy is widespread, the printed book is capable of benefiting a much wider portion of the community than the newer media.

Although many public libraries have added materials in these new media to their collections, the library is far from being the only source for them. People have become accustomed to renting videotapes from commercial enterprises, and an increasing number of outlets are now renting books on audiotape. Some observers wonder, now that the public has become used to paying for the privilege of borrowing its home entertainment, for how much longer will they see a reason for providing one form of home entertainment—the book—at the taxpayers' expense? What will be the justification for providing the public with recreational reading free of charge, while expecting users of other recreational media to pay for them?

In those communities where there is a substantial number of people who read for pleasure, a market may develop for private subscription libraries such as the London Library or the Boston Atheneum. Perhaps the commercial circulating library will make a comeback, prompted by the commercial success of firms that rent audiotapes largely to people who listen to them while driving or using public transport.

If the continued existence of the free public library is to be justified, it will have to be as an educational rather than a recreational institution. The public library collection will have to reflect the long-term needs of the society it supports rather than the transitory desires of that small portion of the public that reads books for amusement. This will fit in with the increasing need that an information-based society will have for lifelong continuing education.

The public library of the future, then, will in many ways represent a return to the original concept of the free library: a people's university, whose serious purpose justifies its public support. In the developing countries, where a rapidly increasing population will strain the limited resources for formal education, the public library's role as an educational agency will be even stronger.

As an adjunct to its basic educational role, the public library will increasingly serve as an access point to the resources of other libraries as well as to nonlibrary sources of publicly available information. In those societies that place an importance upon a freely informed citizenry, libraries and librarians wishing to expand their role in equipping and supporting their public in the art and science of information gathering will be able to create such a role for themselves. Those without this desire will find themselves relegated to the status of antiquarians, whose maintenance will be seen as a luxury easily forsaken in hard times.

Until utopia is realized, there will still be societies whose rulers will attempt to control access to information. They will have to balance this desire with the realization that technological progress and economic development require extensive access to information resources. In these societies, the public library can serve (as it did in Nazi Germany and Soviet Russia) as a carefully controlled gateway to the world's information resources.

THE FUTURE WILL certainly bring substantial changes in the ways in which information is produced, transmitted, and preserved. The continuing advance of computer technology will increase the flexibility of access to, and use of, recorded information. This will render readers increasingly independent of the library and the librarian, at least with regard to obtaining information. But paradoxically it will also increase the importance of such traditional library functions as cataloging and reader guidance. The ease and economy of producing and transmitting documents in electronic form will transform the economic and sociological structure of publishing, and the library's role in the selection and preservation of texts.

The functions of the librarian have always been to select the material that his constituents will require; to catalog it so that those who would use it can know what is available and where it is kept; and to preserve it so that both contemporary readers and those who will follow will be able to use it. With the opening of libraries to a wider public, another task fell to the librarian, that of helping the patron to choose the library materials most appropriate to his needs.

None of these tasks will disappear with the emergence of the electronic library. Somebody will have to perform them: if not the librarian, then his replacement. The anarchy of the Internet may be daunting for the neophyte, but it differs little from the bibliographical chaos that is the result of five and a half centuries of the printing press. The same science that produced the *Anglo–American Cataloguing Rules* and the Universal Decimal Classification can be applied to the World Wide Web. The same cooperative spirit that has informed interlibrary loan and cooperative acquisitions programs can ensure the establishment and maintenance of digital archives. And the expertise in bibliographical instruction and reader guidance acquired by generations of librarians can be as well applied to electronic media as to printed publications.

So long as human beings continue to use the knowledge they have inherited from their ancestors and learned from their contemporaries, so long as human ingenuity and creativity increase the store of information, there will be a need for persons and institutions to collect, to catalog, to preserve, and to guide. Books, and libraries, have changed over the thousands of years since the invention of writing. The pace of change accelerated with the invention of printing, and again in the age of the computer. But the essential task of the librarian has remained the same: to collect and preserve the record of human accomplishment and imagination, and to put this record in the hands of those who would use it.

These tasks will continue to be of importance, and they will be performed. It is up to the initiative of libraries and librarians to determine if they shall be the ones to perform them.

NOTES

1 The Earliest Libraries

1. Dalby, "The Sumerian Catalogs," 476.
2. "In Praise of Learned Scribes," quoted from Papyrus Chester Beatty IV, in Pritchard, *Ancient Near Eastern Texts*, 431.
3. "In Praise of Learned Scribes," quoted in Pritchard, *Ancient Near Eastern Texts*, 432.
4. "The Instruction for Merikare," in Lichtheim, *Ancient Egyptian Literature*, 1:97 ff.
5. Inscription from Weshptah's tomb at Abusir, quoted in Breasted, *Ancient Records of Egypt*, 1:112.
6. Diodorus Siculus, *Bibliotheca Historia*, 1:75; in, *Diodorus on Egypt*, 99.
7. Great Abydos Stela, quoted in Breasted, *Ancient Records of Egypt*, 1:333–34.
8. Diodorus of Sicily, *Bibliotheca Historia*, 1:49; trans. C. H. Oldfather (Loeb Classical Library, *Library of History*).
9. Ahmed, *Southern Mesopotamia in the Time of Ashurbanipal*, 42, 156, 160–61.
10. Quoted in Pfeiffer, *State Letters of Assyria*, 179–80 (no. 256).
11. Quoted in Weitemeyer, "Archive and Library Technique in Ancient Mesopotamia," 228.
12. British Museum, *Babylonian Story of the Deluge*, 21.
13. Assurbanipal, quoted in N. K. Sandars, ed., *The Epic of Gilgamesh*, rev. ed. (Baltimore: Penguin Books, 1964), 8.

Biblical quotations are from *Tanach* (Philadelphia: Jewish Publication Society of America, 1985).

2 Libraries of Classical Antiquity

1. Aulus Gellius, *Noctium Atticarum* 7.17.1–2, trans. John C. Rolfe (Loeb Classical Library, *Attic Nights*).
2. Strabo, *Geographica* 13.1.54, trans. Horace Leonard Jones (Loeb Classical Library, *The Geography of Strabo*).
3. Pfeiffer, *History of Classical Scholarship*, 97.
4. Plutarch, quoted in Canfora, *The Vanished Library*, 18.
5. Vitruvius, *De Architectura* 5.11.2, quoted by Jones in *The Geography of Strabo*, 8:34n (Loeb Classical Library).
6. Strabo, *Geographica* 17.1.8, trans. Horace Leonard Jones (Loeb Classical Library, *The Geography of Strabo*).
7. Durant, *The Life of Greece*, 636.
8. John Malalas, *Chronographia* 235.18–236.1, quoted in Downey, *A History of Antioch in Syria*, 132.
9. Cicero, *Ad Atticus* 4.8.2, trans. E. O. Winstedt (Loeb Classical Library).
10. Seneca, *De Tranquillitate Animi* 9.4–7, trans. John W. Basore (Loeb Classical Library, *Moral Essays*).

11. Pausanias, *Attica* 1.18.9, quoted in Pinner, *The World of Books in Classical Antiquity*, 51.

3 Lanterns of the Dark Ages

1. *Vita S. Galli*, chap. 12, quoted in Clark, *The Abbey of St. Gall*, 27.
2. Quoted in Menzies, *Columba of Iona*, 25.
3. Bede, quoted in Duckett, *Anglo–Saxon Saints and Scholars*, 276.
4. Alcuin, "Versus de Sanctis Eboracensis Ecclesiae," lines 1535–61, trans. Andrew Fleming West in his *Alcuin and the Rise of the Christian Schools*, 34–35.
5. Einhart, *Vita Karoli Magni*, ch. 33, quoted in Christ, *Handbook of Medieval Library History*, 122.
6. Charlemagne, *Karoli Epistola de Litteris Colendis*, quoted in Duckett, *Alcuin, Friend of Charlemagne*, 125.
7. Alcuin, *Epistulae* 4:239, quoted in Duckett, *Alcuin, Friend of Charlemagne*, 20.
8. Eadbeorht, epilogue to the St. Gall Codex of the *Collectio Canonum Hibernensis*, quoted in Clark, *The Abbey of St. Gall*, 62–63.
9. *Rule of St. Benedict*, chap. 48, trans. Christopher Fry, *RB 1980*.
10. Abridged from Hildemar, *Expositio Hildemari*, chap. 48, in Horn and Born, *The Plan of St. Gall*, 1:149.

4 Libraries of the Orient

1. Wu, "Libraries and Book-Collecting in China," 239.
2. Li Ssu, "Memorial on the Burning of Books," *Shih chi* 87:6b–7a, in De Bary et al., *Sources of Chinese Tradition*, 155.
3. Herbert, "From *shuku* to *tushugan*," 98.
4. *Han shu* 30/1b, quoted in Tsien, *Written on Bamboo and Silk*, 13.
5. Wu, "Libraries and Book-Collecting in China," 243.
6. Juan Yüan, *Shan-tso chin-shih chih* 10/21b, quoted in Tsien, *Written on Bamboo and Silk*, 79.
7. *Wen Hsien Thung Khao*, chap. 174, 1506–7, quoted in Tsien, *Paper and Printing*, 136.
8. Quoted in McMullen, *State and Scholars in T'ang China*, 212.
9. Ibid., 9 (paraphrasing *Thung Chien Kang Mu* chap. 3, p. 46b).
10. *T'ai-ping kuang chi* 187/1404–5, quoted in McMullen, *State and Scholars in T'ang China*, 236.
11. Quoted in Kuang, "Chinese Library Science," 365–67 passim.
12. Cheng T'an, quoted in McMullen, *State and Scholars in T'ang China*, 100.
13. Trans. John Timothy Wind in Victor H. Mair, ed., *Columbia Anthology of Traditional Chinese Literature* (New York: Columbia University Press, 1994), 273.
14. Quoted in Reischauer and Fairbank, *East Asia: The Great Tradition*, 382.
15. Watters, *On Yuan Chwang's Travels in India*, 1:386.
16. Hui-li, *The Life of Hsuan-Tsang*, 107–9.

17. "Regulations for Students of the Mountain School," in Tsunoda et al., *Sources of Japanese Tradition*, 134.

18. Hatsuo Nakamura, in *Encyclopedia of Library and Information Science* 13:222, s.v. "Japan, Libraries and Information Centers in."

5 Libraries of the Islamic World

1. Al-Mutannabi, *Diwan*, quoted in Pinto, "The Libraries of the Arabs," 46.

2. Al-Kalkashandi, *Subh al-A'sha fi Sina'at Al-Insha*, quoted in Elayyan, "The History of the Arabic–Islamic Libraries," 126.

3. Yakut al-Himawi, *Mu'djam al-Udaba* 15:157, quoted in Elayyan, "The History of the Arabic–Islamic Libraries," 127.

4. Al Ma'arri, quoted in Mackenson, "Four Great Libraries," 291.

5. Al-Makrizi, *Khitat*, 1:458, quoted in Pinto, "The Libraries of the Arabs," 59.

6. Eche, *Les bibliothèques arabes*, 250.

7. Ibid., 327.

8. Ibn al-Furat, quoted in Pinto, "The Libraries of the Arabs," 66.

9. Al-Mukaddasi, *Ahsan al-takasim fi ma'rifat al-akalim*, quoted in Pinto, "The Libraries of the Arabs," 59–60.

10. Ibn Hayyan, quoted in Pinto, "The Libraries of the Arabs," 67.

11. Ibn al-Furat, quoted in Pinto, "The Libraries of the Arabs," 67.

6 The High Middle Ages

1. Humphreys, *The Book Provisions of the Medieval Friars*, 131.

2. Quoted in Thorndike, *University Records and Life in the Middle Ages*, 167.

3. Ibid., 167.

4. Ibid., 259.

5. Petition to Humphrey, Duke of Gloucester, quoted in Clark, *The Care of Books*, 171–72.

6. *The Observances in Use at the Augustinian Priory of S. Giles and S. Andrew at Barnwell*, ed. J. W. Clark (Cambridge, 1897), 15, quoted in Clark, *The Care of Books*, 71.

7. Hubert of Romans, *Instructiones de Officiis Ordinis*, in his *Opera*, ed. J. J. Berthier (Turin, 1956), 2:263, quoted in Rouse and Rouse, *Authentic Witnesses*, 357.

8. Quoted in Thorndike, *University Records and Life in the Middle Ages*, 319.

9. Ibid., 317.

10. Ibid., 168.

11. Council of Paris, 1212, quoted in Clark, *The Care of Books*, 74.

12. Quoted in Dolbeau, "Les usagers des bibliothèques," 401.

13. Hugh of St. Victor, *De tribus maximus circumstantiis gestorum*, quoted in Bowen, *A History of Western Education*, 2:70.

14. Richard Aungerville de Bury, *Philobiblon*, chap. 8, trans. E. C. Thomas (London: De la More Press, 1903), 56–57.

15. Ibid., chap. 8, 54.

16. Quoted in Buzás, *German Library History*, 143.

7 Gutenberg's Legacy

1. Petrarch, *De remediis utriusque Fortunæ*, lib. 1 dial. 43, p. 42, quoted in Symonds, *The Revival of Learning*, 129–30.
2. Quoted in Schottenloher, *Books and the Western World*, 57.
3. Quoted in Thompson, *The Medieval Library*, 454.
4. Quoted in Buzás, *German Library History*, 200.
5. Quoted in Newman, *Leibniz (1646–1716) and the German Library Scene*, 47.
6. Quoted in Strauss, *Historian in an Age of Crisis*, 90, 69.
7. Hakluyt, *Voyages*, Everyman ed., 1:19.
8. Vespasiano da Bisticci, *The Vespasiano Memoirs*, 104.
9. Vat. Urb. MSS. no. 1248, f. 58, quoted in Dennistoun, *Memoirs of the Dukes of Urbino*, 1:167–68.
10. Quoted in Dennistoun, *Memoirs of the Dukes of Urbino*, 1:241–43.
11. Quoted in Edwards, *Free Town Libraries*, 262.
12. Sixtus IV, *Ad decorem militantis Ecclesiae*, quoted in *The Vatican Library: Its History and Treasures*, 13.
13. Quoted in Koch, "The Vatican Library," 30.
14. La Bruyere, *Caracteres* (1688), quoted in Eisler, "Jean Grolier and the Renaissance," 33.
15. Naudé, *Instructions concerning erecting of a library* (Evelyn translation), 33.
16. Quoted in Newman, *Leibniz (1646–1716) and the German Library Scene*, 18.
17. Luther, "To the Councilmen of All Cities in Germany," 373.
18. Ibid., 375.
19. Ibid., 375–76.
20. Quoted in Schottenloher, *Books and the Western World*, 165.
21. Ibid., 151.
22. John Bale, *Laboryouse Journey of John Leylande*, leaf B1 recto, quoted in Oates, *Cambridge University Library*, 77.
23. Richard Layton, in *Original Letters Illustrative of English History*, ed. H. Ellis, 2d ser., 2:61–62, quoted in Oates, *Cambridge University Library*, 78.

8 Treasuries of the Book

1. A.-A. Renouard (French bookseller), quoted in Hobson, *Great Libraries*, 273.
2. Quoted in *Dictionary of American Biography*, s.v. "Morgan, John Pierpont."
3. Quoted in Pomfret, *The Henry E. Huntington Library and Art Gallery*, 54.
4. George E. Hale, quoted in Pomfret, *The Henry E. Huntington Library and Art Gallery*, 57.
5. Martin Lister, quoted in Edwards, *Memoirs of Libraries*, 2:256.

6. Quoted in Hobson, *Great Libraries*, 130.

7. Edwards, *Memoirs of Libraries*, 2:277.

8. Quoted in Miller, *Prince of Librarians*, 134.

9. Ibid., 156.

10. Ibid., 275.

11. Paraphrased in Esdaile, *National Libraries of the World*, 14.

12. George Ticknor, to his wife, July 4, 1857; Ticknor, *Life, Letters, and Journals*, 2:359.

13. Quoted in Barwick, *The Reading Room of the British Museum*, 141.

14. Quoted in Simsova, *Lenin, Krupskaia, and Libraries*, 63.

15. Carlyle, to Jane Welsh Carlyle, in *The Collected Letters of Thomas and Jane Welsh Carlyle*, Duke–Edinburgh ed., 24 vol. (Durham, N.C.: Duke University Press, 1970–), 5:146.

16. Thackeray to Antonio Panizzi, 10 March 1850, in *The Letters and Private Papers of William Makepeace Thackeray*, ed. Gordon N. Ray, 4 vol. (Cambridge: Harvard University Press, 1945–46), 2:651.

17. J. G. Kohl, *Russia and the Russians in 1842* (London, 1842), 1:290, quoted in Stuart, *Aristocrat-Librarian in Service to the Tsar*, 135–36.

18. Boston *Independent Chronicle*, May 13, 1790, quoted in Goodrum and Dalrymple, *The Library of Congress*, 9.

19. Jefferson, quoted in Goodrum and Dalrymple, *The Library of Congress*, 14.

20. Quoted in Goodrum and Dalrymple, *The Library of Congress*, 14.

21. John Russell Young, quoted in Goodrum and Dalrymple, *The Library of Congress*, 31.

22. Archibald MacLeish, quoted in Goodrum and Dalrymple, *The Library of Congress*, 46.

23. Magda Jóboru (Director-General of the National Szechenyi Library), "The Function of the National Library in the Hungarian Library System," *Libri* 23:155–65 (1973), 158.

24. Abdoul Aziz Diallo (Director, Bibliothèque Nationale du Mali), in *Encyclopedia of Library and Information Science*, 45:247, s.v. "Mali, National Library of."

25. Evans, *A Tropical Library Service*, 161–62.

26. Amoussou H. Noël, in *Encyclopedia of Library and Information Science*, 44:27, s.v. "Benin. The National Library of the People's Republic of Benin."

27. Benge, *Libraries and Cultural Change*, 194.

9 The Repositories of Knowledge

1. Quoted in Kunoff, *The Foundations of the German Academic Library*, 142.

2. Ticknor, Journal, June 15, 1836, *Life, Letters, and Journals*, 1:510.

3. Thomas Clap, *The Annals or History of Yale College*, 3–4, quoted in Shores, *Origins of the American College Library*, 21.

4. *Catalogue of Books in the Library of the College of New Jersey*, January 29, 1760, quoted in Shores, *Origins of the American College Library*, 29–30.

5. Harvard College, "Laws for the Library" (December 12, 1765), quoted in Shores, *Origins of the American College Library*, 190, 192, 193.

6. Quoted in Thomas Wentworth Higginson, "Göttingen and Harvard Eighty Years Ago," *The Harvard Graduates' Magazine* 6:8 (1897), quoted in Hamlin, *The University Library in the United States*, 103.

7. Quoted in Gaskell and Robson, *The Library of Trinity College, Cambridge*, 25.

8. John Wright, quoted in Green, *The Universities*, 205–6.

9. F .D. Maurice, *Life of Frederick Denison Maurice*, 3d ed. (London, 1884), 1:48–49, quoted in Gaskell and Robson, *The Library of Trinity College, Cambridge*, 33.

10. Herbert B. Adams, "Seminar Libraries and University Extension," *Johns Hopkins University Studies in Historical and Political Science*, 5th ser., 12:10–11 (1887), quoted in Thompson, "The Historical Background of Departmental and College Libraries," 60–61.

11. Dumas, "Bibliothèques," 427.

12. Quoted in Dawe, *Melvil Dewey*, 18.

13. Ibid., 174.

14. Robert Talmadge, "Farmington Plan Survey," *College and Research Libraries* 19:375–83 (1958), 376, quoted in Hamlin, *The University Library in the United States*, 193.

10 Libraries for the People

1. Bray, quoted in Laugher, *Thomas Bray's Grand Design*, 21.

2. Franklin, *Autobiography*, in *Writings* (Library of America), 1361–62.

3. Ibid., 1372.

4. Altick, *The English Common Reader*, 11.

5. New York State Board of Education, quoted in Edwards, *Free Town Libraries*, 277.

6. Quoted in Whitehill, *Boston Public Library*, 81.

7. E. A. Savage, *A Librarian's Memories, Portraits, and Reflections* (London: Grafton, 1952), 168, quoted in Kelly, *History of Public Libraries in Great Britain*, 172.

8. William I. Fletcher (Watkinson Library, Hartford), quoted in Lee, *Continuing Education for Adults*, 21.

9. *Return from Places in which the Formation of Free Libraries has been proposed . . .* (Great Britain, Parliamentary Papers, 1856), s.v. "Salford," quoted in Kelly, *History of Public Libraries in Great Britain*, 51.

10. Walter, *Periodicals for the Small Library*, 24–25.

11. Quoted in *Encyclopedia of Library and Information Science*, 2:459–60, s.v. "Bill of Rights, Library."

12. "Enquête: La place de la science dans les bibliothèques françaises," *Revue Scientifique* 42:1–3 (July 1, 1905), quoted in Maack, "L'Heure Joyeuse," 261.

13. Carnovsky, "The Public Libraries of Paris," 196.

14. Quoted in Chandler, *Libraries, Documentation, and Bibliography in the USSR*, 23.

15. Ibid., 16.

16. Lenin, *Complete Collected Works*, 44:422, quoted in Francis, *Libraries in the USSR*, 40.

17. Quoted in Chandler, *Libraries, Documentation, and Bibliography in the USSR*, 167.

18. Quoted in Francis, *Libraries in the USSR*, 151.

19. Heinz Dahnhardt, quoted in Stieg, *Public Libraries in Nazi Germany*, 29.

11 The Rising Generation

1. Walter, "A Poor but Respectable Relation," 738.

2. Quoted in Long, *Public Library Service to Children*, 54.

3. George Ticknor, quoted in Whitehill, *Boston Public Library*, 33.

4. Effie Louise Power, *Library Service for Children* (1929), quoted in *Encyclopedia of Library and Information Science*, 4:560, s.v. "Children's Libraries and Librarianship."

5. Franklin, *Proposals Relating to the Education of Youth in Pennsilvania* (Philadelphia, 1749), in *Writings* (Library of America), 326–27.

6. Quoted in Broderick, *Library Work with Children*, 38.

7. Broderick, *Library Work with Children*, 47.

8. Fletcher, in U.S. Bureau of Education, *Public Libraries in the United States*, 416.

9. Broderick, *Library Work with Children*, 37.

10. Editorial in *CIBC Bulletin* 9(2):3 (1978), quoted in Burress, *The Battle of the Books*, 120.

11. W. R. Credland, quoted in Kelly, *A History of Public Libraries in Great Britain*, 44.

12. Gabriel Henriot, *Des livres pour tous* (Paris: Editions Durraissiee, 1943), 32, quoted in Maack, "L'Heure Joyeuse," 263.

13. V. Petroshan, quoted in Andersen et al., *Libraries and Information Centres in the Soviet Union*, 47.

14. A. Chabisova, quoted in Andersen et al., *Libraries and Information Centres in the Soviet Union*, 47.

15. J. M. Domont, in Seminar on the Development of Public Libraries in Africa, *Development of Public Libraries in Africa*, 81.

16. Robert A. Heinlein, *Expanded Universe* (New York: Ace Books, 1980), 372 (1981 paperbound ed.).

17. J. C. Pauvert, in Seminar on the Development of Public Libraries in Africa, *Development of Public Libraries in Africa*, 71.

18. Amadi, *African Libraries*, 161.

12 Putting Knowledge to Work

1. Quoted in Miles, *A History of the National Library of Medicine*, 29.

2. Letter to Paul F. Eve, quoted in Miles, *A History of the National Library of Medicine*, 52.

3. Quoted in Miles, *A History of the National Library of Medicine*, 131.

4. Lord Wensleydale, in Mirehouse v. Mennell (8 Bing. 515), quoted in *Encyclopaedia Britannica*, 1969 ed., s.v. "Common Law."

5. Quoted in *Encyclopaedia Britannica*, 1969 ed., s.v. "Common Law."

6. Stephen B. Griswold, in U.S. Bureau of Education, *Public Libraries in the United States*, 161.

7. Baasch, "Die Kommerzbibliothek in Hamburg," 148.

8. W. P. Taylor, in U.S. Bureau of Education, *Public Libraries in the United States*, 271.

13   The Craft of Librarianship

1. John Dury, *The Reformed Librarie-Keeper*, 40–41, 43, 45.

2. Christian Molbeck, *Über Bibliothekswissenschaft*, 246, quoted in Buzás, *German Library History*, 407.

3. Jewett, quoted in U.S. Bureau of Education, *Public Libraries in the United States*, xxvi.

4. U.S. Bureau of Education, *Public Libraries in the United States*, xiv.

5. Quoted in Thompson, *A History of the Principles of Librarianship*, 113.

6. U.S. Bureau of Education, *Public Libraries in the United States*, xxv.

7. Quoted in U.S. Bureau of Education, *Public Libraries in the United States*, xxv.

8. Milton Ferguson (president of American Library Association) to Carl H. Milam, June 12, 1939, quoted in Stielow, "Librarian Warriors and Rapprochement," 524.

9. Quincy, in U.S. Bureau of Education, *Public Libraries in the United States*, 390.

14   Libraries of the Future

1. Derek de Solla Price, *Little Science, Big Science*, 19.

PRINCIPAL WORKS CONSULTED

In addition to the publications listed below, I consulted the *Dictionary of American Biography*, *Dictionary of National Biography*, *Encyclopaedia Britannica*, *Encyclopaedia Judaica*, *Encyclopaedia of Islam*, *International Encyclopedia of the Social Sciences*, *New Catholic Encyclopedia*, and *Oxford English Dictionary*.

Ackroyd, P. R., and C. F. Evans, ed. *The Cambridge History of the Bible*. Vol. 1, *From the Beginning to Jerome*. Cambridge: Cambridge University Press, 1970.

Addy, George M. *The Enlightenment in the University of Salamanca*. Durham, N.C.: Duke University Press, 1966.

Ahmed, Sami Said. *Southern Mesopotamia in the Time of Ashurbanipal*. The Hague: Mouton, 1968.

ALA World Encyclopedia of Library and Information Services. Chicago: American Library Association, 1986.

Albright, William Foxwell. *The Biblical Period from Abraham to Ezra*. New York: Harper and Row, 1963.

Alksnis, Gertrude. "Soviet Russian Children's Libraries: A Survey of Recent Russian Sources. *Library Quarterly* 32(4):287–301 (October 1962).

Allchin, Bridget, and Raymond Allchin. *The Rise of Civilization in India and Pakistan*. Cambridge: Cambridge University Press, 1982.

Allen, James Smith. *In the Public Eye: A History of Reading in France, 1800–1940*. Princeton: Princeton University Press, 1991.

Altick, Richard D. *The English Common Reader: A Social History of the Mass Reading Public, 1800–1900*. Chicago: University of Chicago Press, 1957.

Amadi, Adolphe O. *African Libraries: Western Tradition and Colonial Brainwashing*. Metuchen, N.J.: Scarecrow Press, 1981.

Andersen, Axel; J. B. Friis–Hansen; and Leif Kajberg. *Libraries and Information Centres in the Soviet Union*. Ballerup, Denmark: Bibliotekscentralens, 1985.

Ashby, Eric. *African Universities and Western Tradition*. Cambridge: Harvard University Press, 1964.

Avrin, Leila. *Scribes, Script, and Books: The Book Arts from Antiquity to the Renaissance*. Chicago: American Library Association, 1991.

Baasch, Ernst. "Die Kommerzbibliothek in Hamburg: Ein Rückblick vorzüglich auf ihre Geschichte." *Zentralblatt für Bibliothekswesen* 36:147–57 (1919).

Bagchi, Probodh Chandra. *India and China: A Thousand Years of Cultural Relations*. 2d ed. Bombay: Hind Kitabs, 1950.

Bakewell, K. G. B. *Industrial Libraries throughout the World*. Oxford: Pergamon Press, 1969.

Barnett, Stanley A., and Roland R. Piggford. *Manual on Book and Library Activities in Developing Countries*. Washington: Agency for International Development, 1969.

Barwick, G. F. *The Reading Room of the British Museum*. London: Ernest Benn, 1929.

Basham, A. L. *The Wonder That Was India*. New York: Grove Press, 1959.

Bashiruddin, S. "The Fate of Sectarian Libraries in Medieval Islam." *Libri* 17(3):149–62 (1967).

Bede. *A History of the English Church and People*. Trans. Leo Sherley–Price. Baltimore: Penguin Books, 1955.

Beeston, A. F. L.; T. M. Johnstone; R. B. Serjeant; and G. R. Smith, eds. *Arabic Literature to the End of the Umayyad Period*. Cambridge: Cambridge University Press, 1919.

Ben–David, Joseph. *Centers of Learning: Britain, France, Germany, United States*. New York: McGraw–Hill, 1977.

Benge, Ronald C. *Libraries and Cultural Change*. London: Clive Bingley, 1970.

Bermant, Chaim, and Michael Weitzman. *Ebla: A Revelation in Archaeology*. New York: Times Books, 1979.

Bischoff, Bernhard. *Manuscripts and Libraries in the Age of Charlemagne*. Ed. and trans. Michael Gorman. Cambridge Studies in Palaeography and Codicology, vol. 1. Cambridge: Cambridge University Press, 1994.

Bishop, W. J. "Some Medical Bibliophiles and Their Libraries." *Journal of the History of Medicine and Allied Sciences* 3(2):229–62 (March 1948).

Bishop, William Warner. "Some Recollections of William Lawrence Clements and the Formation of His Library." *Library Quarterly* 18(3):185–91 (July 1948).

Blum, Rudolf. *Kallimachos: The Alexandrian Library and the Origins of Bibliography*. Trans. Hans Wellisch. Madison: University of Wisconsin Press, 1991.

Bogart, Leo. *Premises for Propaganda: The United States Information Agency's Operating Assumptions in the Cold War*. New York: Free Press, 1976.

Bonner, Stanley F. *Education in Ancient Rome: From the Elder Cato to the Younger Pliny*. Berkeley and Los Angeles: University of California Press, 1977.

Bottero, Jean; Elena Cassin; and Jean Vercoutter, eds. *The Near East: The Early Civilizations*. Trans. R. F. Tannenbaum. New York: Delacorte Press, 1967.

Bowen, James. *A History of Western Education*. 3 vols. New York: St. Martin's Press, 1972–81.

Bozzolo, Carla, and Ezio Ornato. *Pour une histoire du livre manuscrit au moyen âge: Trois essais de codicologie quantitative*. Paris: Éditions du Centre National de la Recherche Scientifique, 1983.

Braverman, Miriam. *Youth, Society, and the Public Library*. Chicago: American Library Association, 1979.

Breasted, James Henry, ed. *Ancient Records of Egypt: Historical Documents from the Earliest Times to the Persian Conquest. . . .* 4 vols. Chicago: University of Chicago Press, 1906.

Briggs, F. Allen. "The Sunday School Library in the Nineteenth Century." *Library Quarterly* 31(2):166–77 (April 1961).

British Museum. Department of Egyptian and Assyrian Antiquities. *The Babylonian Story of the Deluge and the Epic of Gilgamesh, with an Account of the Royal Libraries of Nineveh*. London: British Museum, 1929.

Brockliss, L. W. B. *French Higher Education in the Seventeenth and Eighteenth Centuries: A Cultural History*. Oxford: Clarendon Press, 1987.

Broderick, Dorothy M. *Library Work with Children.* New York: H. W. Wilson, 1977.

Browne, Edward G. *A Literary History of Persia, from the Earliest Times until Firdawsi.* New York: Charles Scribner's Sons, 1902.

Bullard, Melissa Meriam. *Lorenzo il Magnifico: Image and Anxiety, Politics and Finance.* Florence: Leo S. Olschki Editore, 1994.

Burke, Redmond A. "German Librarianship from an American Angle." *Library Quarterly* 22(3):180–93 (July 1952).

Burney, Charles. *The Ancient Near East.* Ithaca, N.Y.: Cornell University Press, 1977.

Burress, Lee. *Battle of the Books: Literary Censorship in the Public Schools, 1950–1985.* Metuchen, N.J.: Scarecrow Press, 1989.

Busse, Gisela von, and Horst Ernestus. *Libraries in the Federal Republic of Germany.* Trans. John S. Andrews and Gregory Walker. Wiesbaden: Otto Harrassowitz, 1972.

Butler, Nicholas Murray. *Across the Busy Years.* New York: Scribner's, 1939.

Buzás, Ladislaus. *German Library History, 800–1945.* Trans. William D. Boyd. Jefferson, N.C.: McFarland, 1986.

Byzantine Books and Bookmen: A Dumbarton Oaks Colloquium. Washington: Dumbarton Oaks Center for Byzantine Studies, 1975.

Callmer, Christian. "Antike Bibliotheken." *Skrifter Utgivna av Svenska Institutet i Rom, Acta Instituti Romani Regni Sueciae* 10:145–93 (1944).

Canfora, Luciano. *The Vanished Library.* Trans. Martin Ryle. Berkeley and Los Angeles: University of California Press, 1990.

Cantor, Norman F. *Medieval History: The Life and Death of a Civilization.* 2d ed. New York: Macmillan, 1969.

Carnovsky, Leon. "The Public Libraries of Paris." *Library Quarterly* 22(3):194–99 (July 1952).

Carter, Thomas Francis. *The Invention of Printing in China and Its Spread Westward.* 2d ed., revised by L. Carrington Goodrich. New York: Ronald Press, 1955.

Cassiodorus Senator. *An Introduction to Divine and Human Readings.* Trans. Leslie Webber Jones. Records of Civilization—Sources and Studies, vol. 40. New York: Columbia University Press, 1946.

Cerny, Jaroslav. *Paper and Books in Ancient Egypt.* London: H. K. Lewis for University College, 1952.

Chandler, George. *Libraries, Documentation and Bibliography in the USSR 1917–1971: Survey and Critical Analysis of Soviet Studies 1967–1971.* London: Seminar Press, 1972.

Chevalier, Maxime. *Lectura y lectores en la España de los siglos XVI y XVII.* Madrid: Turner, 1976.

Christ, Karl. *The Handbook of Medieval Library History.* Ed. and trans. Theophil M. Otto. Metuchen, N.J.: Scarecrow Press, 1984.

Clark, Burton R., ed. *The Research Foundations of Graduate Education: Germany, Britain, France, United States, Japan.* Berkeley and Los Angeles: University of California Press, 1993.

Clark, James Midgley. *The Abbey of St. Gall As a Centre of Literature and Art.* Cambridge: Cambridge University Press, 1926.

Clark, John Willis. *The Care of Books: An Essay on the Development of Libraries and Their Fittings, from the Earliest Times to the End of the Eighteenth Century*. Cambridge: Cambridge University Press, 1901.

Clarke, H. B., and Mary Brennan, *Columbanus and Merovingian Monasticism*. BAR International Series, vol. 113. Oxford: British Archaeological Reports, 1981.

Clarke, Jack A. "French Libraries in Transition, 1789–95." *Library Quarterly* 37(4):366–72 (October 1967).

Cole, John Y. *Jefferson's Legacy: A Brief History of the Library of Congress*. Washington: Library of Congress, 1993.

Commons, John R. *Myself*. New York: Macmillan, 1934.

Connolly, Brendan. "Jesuit Library Beginnings." *Library Quarterly* 30(4):243–52 (October 1960).

Contreni, John J. *The Cathedral School of Laon from 850 to 930: Its Manuscripts and Masters*. Münchener Beiträge zur Mediävistik und Renaissance-Forschung, vol. 29. Munich: Arbeo–Gesellschaft, 1978.

Cornfeld, Gaalyah. *Archaeology of the Bible: Book by Book*. New York: Harper and Row, 1976.

Craster, Edmund. *History of the Bodleian Library, 1845–1945*. Oxford: Clarendon Press, 1952.

Craver, Kathleen W. "A Survey of Library Services to Children and Young Adults in Selected Developing Countries in Africa and Asia." *Top of the News* 42:33–45 (Fall 1985).

Cross, Rupert. *Precedent in English Law*. 3d ed. Oxford: Clarendon Press, 1977.

Curtis, Edmund. *A History of Ireland*. 6th ed. London: Methuen, 1950.

Dain, Phyllis. *The New York Public Library: A History of Its Founding and Early Years*. New York: New York Public Library, 1972.

Dalby, Andrew. "The Sumerian Catalogs." *Journal of Library History* 21(3):475–87 (January 1986).

Daly, Lowrie J. *The Medieval University, 1200–1400*. New York: Sheed and Ward, 1961.

Datta, Bimal Kumar. *Libraries and Librarianship of Ancient and Medieval India*. Delhi: Atma Ram and Sons, 1970.

David, René, and John E. C. Brierley. *Major Legal Systems in the World Today: An Introduction to the Comparative Study of Law*. London: Stevens and Sons, 1968.

Dawe, Grosvenor. *Melvil Dewey: Seer, Inspirer, Doer, 1851–1931*. Lake Placid Club, N.Y.: Melvil Dewey Biografy, 1932.

Dearman, J. A. "On Record-Keeping and the Preservation of Documents in Ancient Israel (1000–587 B.C.E.)." *Libraries and Culture* 24:344–56 (June 1989).

De Bary, William Theodore; Wing-tsit Chan; and Burton Watson, eds. *Sources of Chinese Tradition*. Records of Civilization—Sources and Studies, vol. 55. New York: Columbia University Press, 1960.

De Bary, William Theodore, Stephen N. Hay, Royal Weiler, and Andrew Yarrow, eds. *Sources of Indian Tradition*. Records of Civilization—Sources and Studies, vol. 56. New York: Columbia University Press, 1958.

Dennistoun, James "of Dennistoun." *Memoirs of the Dukes of Urbino, Illustrating the Arms, Arts and Literature of Italy, 1440–1630*. Ed. Edward Hutton. 3 vols. London: John Lane, 1909.

Dibdin, Thomas Frognall. *A Bibliographical, Antiquarian, and Picturesque Tour in France and Germany.* 2d ed. London: Robert Jennings and John Major, 1829.

Dickson, Paul. *The Library in America: A Celebration in Words and Pictures.* New York: Facts on File Publications, 1986.

Diodorus Siculus. *Diodorus on Egypt.* Trans. Edwin Murphy. Jefferson, N.C.: McFarland, 1985.

Ditzion, Sidney. *Arsenals of a Democratic Culture: A Social History of the American Public Library Movement in New England and the Middle States from 1850 to 1900.* Chicago: American Library Association, 1947.

Dolbeau, François. "Les usagers des bibliothèques," in *Histoire des bibliothèques françaises,* ed. André Vernet, 1:395–413. 4 vols. Paris: Promodis, 1988–91.

Donaldson, Frances. *The British Council: The First Fifty Years.* London: Jonathan Cape, 1984.

Dore, R. P. *Education in Tokugawa Japan.* Berkeley and Los Angeles: University of California Press, 1965.

Downey, Glanville. *A History of Antioch in Syria, from Seleucus to the Arab Conquest.* Princeton: Princeton University Press, 1961.

Drogin, Marc. *Anathema! Medieval Scribes and the History of Book Curses.* Totowa, N.J.: Allanheld, Osmun, 1983.

Duckett, Eleanor Shipley. *Alcuin: Friend of Charlemagne: His World and His Work.* New York: Macmillan, 1951.

———. *Anglo–Saxon Saints and Scholars.* New York: Macmillan, 1947.

Dumas, Alban. "Des bibliothèques des facultés aux bibliothèques universitaires." In *Histoire des bibliothèques françaises,* ed. André Vernet, 3:417–34. 4 vols. Paris: Promodis, 1988–91.

Dundas, Paul. *The Jains.* London: Routledge, 1992.

Durant, Will. *The Story of Civilization.* Vol. 1, *The Life of Greece.* New York: Simon and Schuster, 1936.

Durkheim, Emile. *The Evolution of Educational Thought: Lectures on the Formation and Development of Secondary Education in France.* Trans. Peter Collins. London: Routledge and Kegan Paul, 1977.

Dury, John. *The Reformed Librarie-Keeper.* Chicago: McClurg, 1906.

Eche, Youssef. *Les bibliothèques arabes publiques et semi-publiques en Mésopotamie, en Syrie et en Égypte au moyen age.* Damascus, Syria: Institut Français de Damas, 1967. (Cataloged in American libraries under: Al-'Ishsh, Yusuf)

Edwards, Edward. *Free Town Libraries, Their Formation, Management, and History, in Britain, France, Germany, and America, Together with Brief Notices of Book-Collectors, and of Their Respective Places of Deposit of Their Surviving Collections.* London: Trübner, 1869.

———. *Memoirs of Libraries, Including a Handbook of Library Economy.* London: Trübner, 1859.

Egren, Soren. "The Book in China." Lecture at Dartmouth College, 11 May 1990.

Eisler, Colin. "Jean Grolier and the Renaissance." In Gabriel Astin, *The Library of Jean Grolier: A Preliminary Catalogue,* 1–39. New York: Grolier Club, 1971.

Elayyan, Ribhi Mustafa. "The History of the Arabic–Islamic Libraries: 7th to 14th Centuries." *International Library Review* 22(2):119–35 (June 1990).

Encyclopedia of Library and Information Science. New York: Marcel Dekker, 1968– .

Erman, Adolf. *The Literature of the Ancient Egyptians.* Trans. Aylward M. Blackman. London: Methuen, 1927.

Esdaile, Arundell. *National Libraries of the World: Their History, Administration, and Public Services.* 2d ed., revised by F. J. Hill. London: Library Association, 1957.

Evans, Evelyn J. A. *A Tropical Library Service: The Story of Ghana's Libraries.* London: Andre Deutsch, 1964.

Fa-hsien. *A Record of the Buddhist Countries.* Trans. Li Yung-hsi. Peking: Chinese Buddhist Association, 1957.

———. *The Travels of Fa-hsien (399–414 A.D.), or Record of the Buddhistic Kingdoms.* Trans. H. A. Giles. Cambridge: Cambridge University Press, 1923.

Fairservis, Walter A. "The Script of the Indus Valley Civilization." *Scientific American,* March 1983, 58–66.

Fallon, Daniel. *The German University: A Heroic Ideal in Conflict with the Modern World.* Boulder: Colorado Associated University Press, 1980.

Febvre, Lucien, and Henri-Jean Martin. *The Coming of the Book: The Impact of Printing, 1450–1800.* Trans. David Gerard. London: NLB, 1976.

Fenwick, Sara Innis. "Library Service to Children and Young People." In *Reader in Children's Librarianship,* ed. Joan Foster, 5–30. Englewood, Colo.: Information Handling Services, 1978. First published in *Library Trends* 25:329–60 (July 1976).

Ferguson, John. *Libraries in France.* London: Clive Bingley, 1971.

Ferruolo, Stephen C. *The Origins of the University: The Schools of Paris and Their Critics, 1100–1215.* Stanford, Calif.: Stanford University Press, 1985.

Fletcher, Harry George, III. *New Aldine Studies: Documentary Essays on the Life and Work of Aldus Manutius.* San Francisco: Bernard M. Rosenthal, 1988.

Francis, Simon, ed. *Libraries in the USSR.* London: Clive Bingley, 1971.

Franklin, Benjamin. *Autobiography and Selected Writings.* Ed. Larzer Ziff. New York: Holt, Rinehart and Winston, 1959.

———. *Writings.* Ed. J. A. Leo Lemay. New York: Library of America, 1987.

Fraser, P. M. *Ptolemaic Alexandria.* Oxford: Clarendon Press, 1972.

Friedman, Richard Elliott. *Who Wrote the Bible?* New York: Summit Books, 1987.

———, ed. *The Creation of Sacred Literature: Composition and Redaction of the Biblical Text.* University of California Publications, Near Eastern Studies, vol. 22. Berkeley and Los Angeles: University of California Press, 1981.

Fry, Timothy, ed. *RB 1980: The Rule of St. Benedict in Latin and English with Notes.* Collegeville, Minn.: Liturgical Press, 1981.

Galt, Howard S. *A History of Chinese Educational Institutions.* Vol. 1, *To the End of the Five Dynasties (A.D. 960).* London: Arthur Probsthain, 1951.

Gardner, Frank M. *The Delhi Public Library: An Evaluation Report.* UNESCO Public Library Manuals, vol. 8. Paris: UNESCO, 1957.

Garnett, Richard. *Essays in Librarianship and Bibliography.* London: George Allen, 1899.

Garrison, Dee. *Apostles of Culture: The Public Librarian and American Society, 1876–1920.* New York: Free Press, 1979.

Gaskell, Philip. *Trinity College Library: The First 150 Years.* Cambridge: Cambridge University Press, 1980.

Gaskell, Philip, and Robert Robson. *The Library of Trinity College, Cambridge: A Short History.* Cambridge: Trinity College, 1971.

Gilmore, Myron P. *Humanists and Jurists: Six Studies in the Renaissance.* Cambridge: Harvard University Press, Belknap Press, 1963.

Goitein, S. D. *A Mediterranean Society: The Jewish Communities in the Arab World as Portrayed in the Documents of the Cairo Geniza.* Vol. 5, *The Individual: Portrait of a Mediterranean Personality of the High Middle Ages As Reflected in the Cairo Geniza.* Berkeley and Los Angeles: University of California Press, 1988.

Goodrum, Charles A., and Helen W. Dalrymple. *The Library of Congress.* 2d ed. Boulder, Colo.: Westview Press, 1982.

Gore, Daniel, ed. *Farewell to Alexandria: Solutions to Space, Growth, and Performance Problems of Libraries.* Westport, Conn.: Grenwood Press, 1976.

Gosnell, Charles F., and Géza Schütz. "Goethe the Librarian." *Library Quarterly* 2(4):367–74 (October 1932).

Grafton, Anthony. *Defenders of the Text: The Traditions of Scholarship in an Age of Science, 1450–1800.* Cambridge: Harvard University Press, 1991.

———, ed. *Rome Reborn: The Vatican Library and Renaissance Culture.* Washington: Library of Congress, 1993.

Great Britain. House of Commons. *Minutes of Evidence Taken before the Select Committee on Public Libraries.* 15 May 1849.

Green, Vivian H. H. *The Universities.* Harmondsworth, Middlesex: Penguin Books, 1969.

Greenwood, Thomas. *Edward Edwards, the Chief Pioneer of Municipal Public Libraries.* London: Scott, Greenwood, 1902.

Grendler, Paul F. *Schooling in Renaissance Italy: Literacy and Learning, 1300–1600.* Baltimore: Johns Hopkins University Press, 1989.

Griest, Guinevere L. *Mudie's Circulating Library and the Victorian Novel.* Bloomington: Indiana University Press, 1970.

Guppy, Henry. *The John Rylands Library, Manchester: 1899–1924.* Manchester: Manchester University Press, 1924.

Guy, R. Kent. *The Emperor's Four Treasuries: Scholars and the State in the Late Ch'ien-Lung Era.* Cambridge: Harvard University Press, 1987.

Hadas, Moses. *Ancilla to Classical Reading.* New York: Columbia University Press, 1954.

Hamlin, Arthur T. *The University Library in the United States: Its Origins and Development.* Philadelphia: University of Pennsylvania Press, 1981.

Hansen, Esther V. *The Attalids of Pergamon.* 2d ed. Ithaca, N.Y.: Cornell University Press, 1971.

Harris, Michael H., and Gerard Spiegler. "Everett, Ticknor, and the Common Man, the Fear of Social Instability as the Motivation for the Founding of the Boston Public Library." *Libri* 24(4):249–75 (1974).

Hayes, John H. *Introduction to the Bible.* Philadelphia: Westminster Press, 1971.

Hazeltine, Alice E., ed. *Library Work with Children: Reprints of Papers and Addresses.* White Plains, N.Y.: H. W. Wilson, 1917.

Held, Ray E. "The Odd Fellows' Library Associations of California." *Library Quarterly* 32(2):148–63 (April 1962).

Herbert, P. A. "From *shuku* to *tushugan*: An Historical Overview of the Organisation and Function of Libraries in China." *Papers on Far Eastern History* 33:93–121 (March 1986).

Herner, Saul. "Brief History of Information Science." *Journal of the American Society for Information Science* 35(3):157–63 (May 1984).

Hessel, Alfred. *A History of Libraries*. Trans. Reuben Peiss. Washington: Scarecrow Press, 1950.

Hillenbrand, Robert. "'The Ornament of the World': Medieval Córdoba as a Cultural Centre." In *The Legacy of Muslim Spain*, ed. Salma Khadra Jayyusi, 112–35. Leiden: E. J. Brill, 1992.

Hirsch, Felix E. "The Scholar as Librarian." *Library Quarterly* 9(3):299–320 (July 1939).

Hirtle, Peter B. "Historical Note: Atherton Seidell and the Photoduplication of Library Material." *Journal of the American Society for Information Science* 40(6):424–31 (November 1989).

Hitti, Philip K. *History of the Arabs: From the Earliest Times to the Present*. 9th ed. New York: St. Martin's Press, 1967.

Hobson, Anthony. *Great Libraries*. New York: Putnam, 1970.

Holmes, Urban Tigner. *Daily Living in the Twelfth Century, Based on the Observations of Alexander Neckham in London and Paris*. Madison: University of Wisconsin Press, 1952.

Homayum Farrokh, Rokn od Din. *History of Books and the Imperial Libraries of Iran*. Trans. Abutaleb Saremi. Tehran: Department of Publications, Ministry of Art and Culture, 1968. (Cataloged in American libraries under: Humayun Farrukh, Rukn al-Din)

Hopkins, Judith. "The 1791 French Cataloging Code and the Origins of the Card Catalog." *Libraries and Culture* 27(4):378–406 (September 1992).

Horn, Walter, and Ernest Born. *The Plan of St. Gall: A Study of the Architecture and Economy of, and Life in a Paradigmatic Carolingian Monastery*. 3 vols. Berkeley and Los Angeles: University of California Press, 1979.

Horowitz, Helen Lefkowitz. *Campus Life: Undergraduate Cultures from the End of the Eighteenth Century to the Present*. New York: Knopf, 1987.

Houston, Robert Allan. *Literacy in Early Modern Europe: Culture and Education, 1500–1800*. London: Longman, 1988.

Hsuan-Tsang. *Su-Yu-Ki: Buddhist Records of the Western World, Translated from the Chinese of Hiuen Tsiang (A.D. 629)*. Ed. and trans. Samuel Beal. London: Kegan Paul, Trench, Trübner, n.d.

Huck, Charlotte S., and Doris Young Kuhn. *Children's Literature in the Elementary School*. 2d ed. New York: Holt, Rinehart and Winston, 1968.

Hui-li. *The Life of Hiuen-Tsiang by the Shaman Hwui Li*. Ed. Samuel Beal. London: Kegan Paul, Trench, Trübner, 1914.

———. *The Life of Hsuan-Tsang, the Tripitaka Master of the Great Tzu En Monastery*. Trans. Li-Yung-hsi. Peking: Chinese Buddhist Association, 1959.

Humphreys, K. W. *The Book Provisions of the Medieval Friars*. Studies in the History of Libraries and Librarianship, vol. 1. Amsterdam: Erasmus Booksellers, 1964.

————. *The Library of the Carmelites of Florence at the End of the Fourteenth Century.* Studies in the History of Libraries and Librarianship, vol. 2. Amsterdam: Erasmus Booksellers, 1964.

————. "The Medical Books of the Medieval Friars." *Libri* 3(3):95–103 (1954).

Ibn al-Nadim, Muhammad Ibn Ishaq. *The Fihrist of al-Nadim: A Tenth-Century Survey of Muslim Culture.* Ed. and trans. Bayard Dodge. Records of Civilization—Sources and Studies, vol. 83. New York: Columbia University Press, 1970.

Ibn Khallikan. *Wafayat al-a'yan wa anba' abna' al-zaman: M. de Slane's English Translation.* Ed. S. Moinul Haq. Karachi: Pakistan Historical Society, 1961.

Imamuddin, S. M. *Muslim Spain, 711–1492 A.D.: A Sociological Study.* Leiden: E.J. Brill, 1981.

Jackson, Sidney L. *Libraries and Librarianship in the West: A Brief History.* New York: McGraw–Hill, 1974.

Jacob, E. F., ed. *Italian Renaissance Studies.* London: Faber and Faber, 1960.

Jaini, Padmanabh S. *The Jaina Path of Purification.* Berkeley and Los Angeles: University of California Press, 1979.

James, Henry. "The Role of the Information Library in the United States International Information Program." *Library Quarterly* 23(2):75–114 (April 1953).

James, T. G. H. *Pharaoh's People: Scenes from Life in Imperial Egypt.* Chicago: University of Chicago Press, 1984.

Japan. Department of Education. *An Outline History of Japanese Education, Prepared for the Philadelphia International Exhibition, 1876.* New York: Appleton, 1876.

Jóboru, Magda. "The Function of the National Library in the Hungarian Library System." *Libri* 23:155–65 (1973).

Kaufman, Paul. "Some Community Libraries in Eighteenth Century Europe: A Reconnaissance." *Libri* 22(1):1–57 (1972).

Kelly, Thomas. *A History of Public Libraries in Great Britain, 1845–1965.* London: Library Association, 1973.

Kenyon, Frederic G. *Books and Readers in Ancient Greece and Rome.* 2d ed. Oxford: Clarendon Press, 1951. Reprint, n.p.: Arden Library, 1978.

Kleberg, Tönnes. "Bibliophiles in Ancient Rome." *Libri* 1(1):2–12 (1950).

Koch, Theodore Wesley. "The Vatican Library: An Historical Sketch." In *The Vatican Library: Two Papers,* 15–40. Jersey City, N.J.: Snead, 1929.

Kuang, Neng-fu. "Chinese Library Science in the Twelfth Century." *Libraries and Culture* 26(2):357–71 (Spring 1991).

Kumar, P. S. G. *Indian Library Chronology.* New Delhi: Metropolitan Book, 1977.

Kunoff, Hugo. *The Foundations of the German Academic Library.* Chicago: American Library Association, 1982.

Læssøe, Jørgen. *People of Ancient Assyria: Their Inscriptions and Correspondence.* Trans. F. S. Leigh–Browne. London: Routledge and Kegan Paul, 1963.

Lancaster, Lewis R. "The Editing of Buddhist Texts." In *Buddhist Thought and Asian Civilization: Essays in Honor of Herbert V. Guenther on his Sixtieth Birthday,* ed. Leslie S. Kawamura and Keith Scott, 145–51. Emeryville, Calif.: Dharma Publishing, 1977.

Laugher, Charles T. *Thomas Bray's Grand Design: Libraries of the Church of England in America, 1695–1785*. Chicago: American Library Association, 1973.

Le Goff, Jacques, ed. *Medieval Callings*. Trans. Lydia G. Cochrane. Chicago: University of Chicago Press, 1990.

Lee, Robert Ellis. *Continuing Education for Adults through the American Public Library, 1833–1964*. Chicago: American Library Association, 1966.

Leslie, Donald D.; Colin Mackerras; and Gungwu Wang, eds. *Essays on the Sources for Chinese History*. Columbia: University of South Carolina Press, 1975.

Lichtheim, Miriam, ed. *Ancient Egyptian Literature: A Book of Readings*. 3 vols. Berkeley and Los Angeles: University of California Press, 1973–80.

Lilley, Dorothy B., and Ronald W. Trice. *A History of Information Science, 1945–1985*. San Diego: Academic Press, 1989.

Llewellyn, Karl. *The Case Law System in America*. Ed. Michael Ansaldi. Chicago: University of Chicago Press, 1989.

Long, Harriet G. *Public Library Service to Children: Foundation and Development*. Metuchen, N.J.: Scarecrow Press, 1969.

Lough, John. *Writer and Public in France, from the Middle Ages to the Present Day*. Oxford: Clarendon Press, 1978.

Luckenbill, Daniel David. *Ancient Records of Assyria and Babylon*. Vol. 2, *Historical Records of Assyria, from Sargon to the End*. Chicago: University of Chicago Press, 1927.

Luther, Martin. "To the Councilmen of All Cities in Germany That They Establish and Maintain Christian Schools." Trans. Albert T. W. Steinhaeuser. In *The Christian in Society, II*, ed. Walter I. Brandt, 339–78. *Luther's Works*, American ed., vol. 45. Philadelphia: Muhlenberg Press, 1962.

Maack, Mary Niles. "L'Heure Joyeuse, the First Children's Library in France: Its Contribution to a New Paradigm for Public Libraries." *Library Quarterly* 63(3):257–81 (July 1993).

Mackensen, Ruth Stellhorn. "Four Great Libraries of Medieval Baghdad." *Library Quarterly* 2(3):279–99 (July 1932).

Macqueen, J. G. *The Hittites and Their Contemporaries in Asia Minor*. London: Thames and Hudson, 1975.

Makdisi, George. "Muslim Institutions of Learning in Eleventh-Century Baghdad." *Bulletin of the School of Oriental and African Studies, University of London* 24(1):1–56 (1961).

———. *The Rise of Colleges: Institutions of Learning in Islam and the West*. Edinburgh: Edinburgh University Press, 1981.

Marker, Gary. *Publishing, Printing, and the Origins of Intellectual Life in Russia, 1700–1800*. Princeton: Princeton University Press, 1985.

Marshall, D. N. *History of Libraries: Ancient and Medieval*. New Delhi: Oxford and IBH Publishing, 1983.

Marshall, Margaret R. *An Introduction to the World of Children's Books*. Aldershot, Hampshire: Gower, 1982.

Martin, Henri-Jean. *The History and Power of Writing*. Trans. Lydia G. Cochrane. Chicago: University of Chicago Press, 1994.

Matthiae, Paola. *Ebla: An Empire Rediscovered,*. Trans. Christopher Holme. Garden City, N.Y.: Doubleday, 1981.

Mayer, Josephine, and Tom Prideaux. *Never to Die: The Egyptians in Their Own Words.* New York: Viking Press, 1938.

McArthur, Tom. *Worlds of Reference: Lexicography, Learning and Language from the Clay Tablet to the Computer.* Cambridge: Cambridge University Press, 1986.

McClelland, Charles E. *State, Society, and University in Germany, 1700–1914.* Cambridge: Cambridge University Press, 1980.

McColvin, Lionel R. *Public Library Services for Children.* UNESCO Public Library Manuals, vol. 9. Paris: UNESCO, 1957.

McCue, George S. "Libraries of the London Coffeehouses." *Library Quarterly* 4(4):624–27 (October 1934).

McGovern, John N. "Chinese Papermaking Technology Goes West before A.D. 751." *Tappi Journal,* August 1987, 111.

McKitterick, Rosamond. *The Carolingians and the Written Word.* Cambridge: Cambridge University Press, 1989.

McMullen, David. *State and Scholars in T'ang China.* Cambridge: Cambridge University Press, 1988.

Menzies, Lucy. *Columba of Iona: A Study of His Life, His Times, and His Influence.* London: Dent, 1920.

Merryman, John Henry. *The Civil Law Tradition: An Introduction to the Legal Systems of Western Europe and Latin America.* 2d ed. Stanford, Calif.: Stanford University Press, 1985.

Miles, Wyndham D. *A History of the National Library of Medicine: The Nation's Treasury of Medical Knowledge.* Bethesda, Md.: National Library of Medicine, 1982.

Miller, Edward. *Prince of Librarians: The Life and Times of Antonio Panizzi of the British Museum.* Athens: Ohio University Press, 1967.

Montgomery, Jack Warwick. "Luther and Libraries." *Library Quarterly* 32(2):133–47 (April 1962).

Mookerji, Radha Kumud. *Ancient Indian Education (Brahmanical and Buddhist).* 2d ed. London: Macmillan, 1951.

Moore, George Foot. "The Theological School at Nisibis." In *Studies in the History of Religions, Presented to Crawford Howell Toy,* ed. David Gordon Lyon and George Foot, 255–67. New York: Macmillan, 1912.

Munford, W. A. *Edward Edwards, 1812–1866: Portrait of a Librarian.* London: Library Association, 1963.

Naudé, Gabriel. *Instructions concerning erecting of a library, presented to My Lord the President de Mesme; and now interpreted by Jo. Evelyn.* Cambridge, Mass: Houghton Mifflin, 1903 (reprint of 1661 edition).

Needham, Joseph. *Science and Civilisation in China.* Vol. 1, *Introductory Orientations.* Cambridge: Cambridge University Press, 1965.

Neufeld, M. Lynne, and Martha Cornog. "Database History: From Dinosaurs to Compact Discs." *Journal of the American Society for Information Science* 37(4):183–90 (July 1986).

Newman, L. M. *Leibniz (1646–1716) and the German Library Scene.* London: Library Association, 1966.

Oates, J. C. T. *Cambridge University Library: A History from the Beginnings to the Copyright Act of Queen Anne.* Cambridge: Cambridge University Press, 1986.

O'Donnell, James J. *Cassiodorus.* Berkeley and Los Angeles: University of California Press, 1979.

O'Gorman, James F. *The Architecture of the Monastic Library in Italy, 1300–1600: Catalogue with Introductory Essay.* New York: New York University Press for the College Art Association of America, 1972.

Olmert, Michael. *The Smithsonian Book of Books.* Washington: Smithsonian Books, 1992.

Oppenheim, A. Leo. *Ancient Mesopotamia: Portrait of a Dead Civilization.* Rev. ed. Chicago: University of Chicago Press, 1977.

Parsons, Edward Alexander. *The Alexandrian Library, Glory of the Hellenic World: Its Rise, Antiquities, and Destructions.* Amsterdam: Elsevier, 1952.

Paulsen, Friedrich. *The German Universities: Their Character and Historical Development.* Trans. Edward Delevan Perry. New York: Macmillan, 1895.

Peter, Prince of Greece and Denmark. "The Books of Tibet." *Libri* 5(1):20–28 (1954).

Petrucci, Armando. *Writers and Readers in Medieval Italy: Studies in the History of Written Culture.* Trans. Charles M. Radding. New Haven: Yale University Press, 1995.

Pettinato, Giovanni. *The Archives of Ebla: An Empire Inscribed in Clay.* Garden City, N.Y.: Doubleday, 1981.

Pfeiffer, Robert H., ed. *State Letters of Assyria: A Transliteration and Translation of 355 Official Assyrian Letters Dating from the Sargonid Period (722–625 B.C.).* American Oriental Series, vol. 6. New Haven: American Oriental Society, 1935.

———. *History of Classical Scholarship: From the Beginnings to the End of the Hellenistic Age.* Oxford: Clarendon Press, 1968.

Pfeiffer, Rudolf. *History of Classical Scholarship, from 1300 to 1850.* Oxford: Clarendon Press, 1976.

Pinner, H. L. *The World of Books in Classical Antiquity.* Leiden: A. W. Sijthoff, 1948.

Pinto, Olga. "The Libraries of the Arabs during the Time of the Abbasides." Trans. F. Krenkow. *Pakistan Library Review* 2(1–2):44–72 (March 1959).

Piyadasa, T. G. *Libraries in Sri Lanka: Their Origin and History from Ancient Times to the Present Time.* Delhi: Sri Satguru Publications, 1985.

Pomfret, John Edwin. *The Henry E. Huntington Library and Art Gallery, from Its Beginnings to 1969.* San Marino, Calif.: Huntington Library, 1969.

Porter, Barbara Nevling. *Images, Power, and Politics: Figurative Aspects of Esarhaddon's Babylonian Policy.* Philadelphia: American Philosophical Society, 1993.

Posner, Ernst. *Archives in the Western World.* Cambridge: Harvard University Press, 1972.

Possehl, Gregory L., ed. *Harappan Civilization: A Contemporary Perspective.* New Delhi: Oxford and IBH Publishing, 1982.

Powicke, F. M. *The Medieval Books of Merton College.* Oxford: Clarendon Press, 1931.

Prasad, Anirudh. "Libraries in Medieval India." *Library Herald* 20:155–59 (July 1981–March 1982).

Price, Derek de Solla. *Little Science, Big Science.* New York: Columbia University Press, 1963.

Pritchard, James B., ed. *Ancient Near Eastern Texts Relating to the Old Testament.* 2d ed. Princeton: Princeton University Press, 1955.

Radding, Charles M. *The Origins of Medieval Jurisprudence: Pavia and Bologna, 850–1150.* New Haven: Yale University Press, 1988.

Randall, David A. *Dukedom Large Enough.* New York: Random House, 1969.

Rao, K. Ramakrishna. "Library Development in India." *Library Quarterly* 31(2):135–53 (April 1961).

Rashdall, Hastings. *The Universities of Europe in the Middle Ages.* [2d] ed., ed. F. M. Powicke and A. B. Emden. Oxford: Clarendon Press, 1936.

Ray, Colin. *Library Services to Schools and Children.* Documentation, Libraries and Archives Studies and Research, vol. 10. Paris: UNESCO, 1979.

Reichmann, Felix. "The Book Trade at the Time of the Roman Empire." *Library Quarterly* 8(1):40–76 (January 1938).

Reischauer, Edwin O., and John K. Fairbank. *East Asia: The Great Tradition.* Boston: Houghton Mifflin, 1960.

Reynolds, Leighton D., and N. G. Wilson. *Scribes and Scholars: A Guide to the Transmission of Greek and Latin Literature.* 2d ed. Oxford: Clarendon Press, 1974.

Rice, James V. *Gabriel Naudé, 1600–1653.* The Johns Hopkins Studies in Romance Literatures and Languages, vol. 35. Baltimore: Johns Hopkins Press, 1939.

Richards, Pamela Spence. "Information Science in Wartime: Pioneer Documentation Activities in World War II." *Journal of the American Society for Information Science* 39(5):301–6 (September 1988).

Richardson, Ernest Cushing. *The Beginnings of Libraries.* Princeton: Princeton University Press, 1914. Reprint, Hamden, Conn.: Archon Books, 1963.

———. *Biblical Libraries: A Sketch of Library History from 3400 B.C. to A.D. 150.* Princeton: Princeton University Press, 1914. Reprint, Hamden, Conn.: Archon Books, 1963.

Riché, Pierre. *Education and Culture in the Barbarian West: Sixth through Eighth Centuries.* Trans. John J. Contreni. Columbia: University of South Carolina Press, 1976.

Ridder–Symoens, Hilde de, ed. *A History of the University in Europe.* Vol. 1, *Universities in the Middle Ages.* Cambridge: Cambridge University Press, 1992.

Roberts, Colin H., and T. C. Skeat. *The Birth of the Codex.* London: Oxford University Press for the British Academy, 1983.

Rollock, Barbara T. *Public Library Services for Children.* Hamden, Conn.: Library Professional Publications, 1988.

Ronan, Colin A. *The Shorter Science and Civilisation in China: An Abridgement of Joseph Needham's Original Text.* 2 vols. Cambridge: Cambridge University Press, 1978–81.

Ross, Janet, trans. and ed. *Lives of the Early Medici, as Told in Their Correspondence.* London: Chatto and Windus, 1910.

Roth, Cecil. *The Jews in the Renaissance*. Philadelphia: Jewish Publication Society of America, 1959. Reprint, New York: Harper and Row, 1965.

Rouse, Mary A., and Richard H. Rouse. *Authentic Witnesses: Approaches to Medieval Texts and Manuscripts*. Notre Dame, Indiana: University of Notre Dame Press, 1991.

Rudolph, Frederick. *Curriculum: A History of the American Undergraduate Course of Study Since 1636*. San Francisco: Jossey–Bass, 1977.

Runciman, Steven. *Byzantine Civilization*. Cleveland: World, 1954.

Russell, Colin A. *Science and Social Change in Britain and Europe, 1700–1900*. New York: St. Martin's Press, 1983.

Ryan, John. *Irish Monasticism: Origins and Early Development*. Dublin: Talbot Press, 1931. Reprint, Ithaca, N.Y.: Cornell University Press, 1972.

Saggs, H. W. F. *The Might That Was Assyria*. London: Sidgwick and Jackson, 1984.

Salton, Gerard. "Historical Note: The Past Thirty Years in Information Retrieval." *Journal of the American Society for Information Science* 38(5):375–80 (September 1987).

Sandys, John Edwin. *A History of Classical Scholarship, from the Sixth Century B.C. to the End of the Middle Ages*. Cambridge: Cambridge University Press, 1903.

Sarton, George. *Introduction to the History of Science*. Vol. 1, *From Homer to Omar Khayyam*. Baltimore: Williams and Wilkins for the Carnegie Institution of Washington, 1927.

Savage, Ernest A. *Old English Libraries: The Making, Collection, and Use of Books During the Middle Ages*. London: Methuen, 1911.

———. *The Story of Libraries and Book-Collecting*. London: Routledge, n.d.

Schmitz, Wolfgang. *Deutsche Bibliotheksgeschichte*. Bern: Peter Lang, 1984.

Schottenloher, Karl. *Books and the Western World: A Cultural History*. Trans. William D. Boyd and Irmgard H. Wolfe. Jefferson, N.C.: McFarland, 1989.

Seminar on the Development of Public Libraries in Africa (Ibadan, Nigeria, 1953). *Development of Public Libraries in Africa*. UNESCO Public Library Manuals, vol. 6. Paris: UNESCO, 1954.

Shera, Jesse H. *Foundations of the Public Library: The Origins of the Public Library Movement in New England, 1629–1855*. Chicago: University of Chicago Press, 1949.

———. *Historians, Books, and Librarians: A Survey of Historical Scholarship in Relation to Library Resources, Organization and Services*. Cleveland: Press of Western Reserve University, 1953.

Shores, Louis. *Origins of the American College Library, 1638–1800*. Nashville: George Peabody College, 1934.

Simsova, S., ed. *Lenin, Krupskaia and Libraries*. Trans. G. Peacock and Lucy Prescott. London: Clive Bingley, 1968.

Singhal, D. P. *A History of the Indian People*. London: Methuen, 1983.

Sitzman, Glenn L. *African Libraries*. Metuchen, N.J.: Scarecrow Press, 1988.

Southern, R. W. *The Making of the Middle Ages*. New Haven: Yale University Press, 1961.

Spalinger, Anthony John. *Aspects of the Military Documents of the Ancient Egyptians*. New Haven: Yale University Press, 1982.

Sperry, John A. "Egyptian Libraries: A Survey of the Evidence." *Libri* 7(2–3): 145–55 (1957).

Steinberg, S. H. *Five Hundred Years of Printing.* 2d rev. ed. Harmondsworth, Middlesex: Penguin Books, 1966.

Stewart, Mary L. *Nalanda Mahavihara: A Study of an Indian Pala Period Buddhist Site and British Historical Archaeology, 1861–1938.* BAR International Series, vol. 529. Oxford: British Archaeological Reports, 1989.

Stieg, Margaret F. *Public Libraries in Nazi Germany.* Tuscaloosa: University of Alabama Press, 1992.

Stielow, Frederick J. "Librarian Warriors and Rapprochement: Carl Milam, Archibald MacLeish, and World War II." *Libraries and Culture* 25(4):513–33 (September 1990).

Stone, Lawrence, ed. *The University in Society.* Vol. 2, *Europe, Scotland, and the United States from the 16th to the 20th Century.* Princeton: Princeton University Press, 1974.

Strauss, Gerald. *Historian in an Age of Crisis: The Life and Work of Johannes Aventinus, 1477–1534.* Cambridge: Harvard University Press, 1963.

Streeter, Burnett Hillman. *The Chained Library: A Survey of Four Centuries in the Evolution of the English Library.* London: Macmillan, 1931.

Stuart, Mary. *Aristocrat-Librarian in Service to the Tsar: Aleksei Nikolaevich Olenin and the Imperial Public Library.* Boulder, Colo.: East European Monographs, 1956.

———. "Creating Culture: the Rossica Collection of the Imperial Public Library and the Construction of National Identity." *Libraries and Culture* 30(1):1–25 (December 1995).

Swaminathan, S. "Libraries in India: Yesterday and Today." In *Library Science Today: Ranganathan Festschrift,* 1:353–61. 2 vols. Ed. Prithvi Nath Kaula. New York: Asia Publishing House, 1965.

Symonds, John Addington. *The Renaissance in Italy: The Age of the Despots.* London: John Murray, 1926.

———. *The Renaissance in Italy: The Revival of Learning.* New York: Henry Holt, 1988.

Tan, Cho-Yüan. *The Development of Chinese Libraries under the Ch'ing Dynasty, 1644–1911.* Shanghai: Commercial Press, 1935. (Cataloged in American libraries under: Taam, Cheuk-woon).

Tarn, W. W. *Alexander the Great.* Cambridge University Press, 1948. Reprint, Boston: Beacon Press, 1956.

Tauber, Maurice F., et al. *Technical Services in Libraries.* New York: Columbia University Press, 1954.

Thomas, Alan G. *Great Books and Book Collectors.* New York: Putnam, 1975.

Thompson, James. *A History of the Principles of Librarianship.* London: Clive Bingley, 1977.

Thompson, James Westfall. *Ancient Libraries.* Berkeley and Los Angeles: University of California Press, 1940.

———. *The Medieval Library.* Chicago: University of Chicago Press, 1939.

Thompson, Lawrence. "The Historical Background of Departmental and Collegiate Libraries." *Library Quarterly* 12(1):49–74 (January 1942).

Thorndike, Lynn. *University Records and Life in the Middle Ages*. Records of Civilization—Sources and Studies, vol. 38. New York: Columbia University Press, 1944.

Thornton, John L. *Medical Books, Libraries and Collectors: A Study of Bibliography and the Book Trade in Relation to the Medical Sciences*. 2d ed. London: Andre Deutsch, 1966.

Ticknor, George. *Life, Letters, and Journals of George Ticknor*. Ed. George S. Hilliard. Boston: James R. Osgood, 1876.

Trehan, Girdhari Lal. *Learning and Libraries in Ancient India: A Study*. Chandigarh: Library Literature House, 1975.

Trigger, B. G.; B. J. Kemp; D. O'Connor; and A. B. Lloyd. *Ancient Egypt: A Social History*. Cambridge: Cambridge University Press, 1983.

Trithemius, Johannes. *In Praise of Scribes: De laude scriptorum*. Ed. Klaus Arnold. Trans. Roland Behrendt. Lawrence, Kans.: Coronado Press, 1974.

Tsien, Tsuen-Hsuin. *Paper and Printing. Science and Civilisation in China*, pt. 1, vol. 5, ed. Joseph Needham. Cambridge: Cambridge University Press, 1985.

———. *Written on Bamboo and Silk: The Beginnings of Chinese Books and Inscriptions*. Chicago: University of Chicago Press, 1962.

Tsunoda, Ryusaku; William Theodore De Bary; and Donald Keene, ed. *Sources of Japanese Tradition*. Records of Civilization—Sources and Studies, vol. 54. New York: Columbia University Press, 1958.

Tung, Louise Watanabe. "Library Development in Japan." Pts. 1 and 2. *Library Quarterly* 26(2):79–104 (April 1956); 26(3):196–223 (July 1956).

Ullman, Berthold L., and Philip A. Stadter. *The Public Library of Renaissance Florence: Niccoló Niccoli, Cosimo de' Medici, and the Library of San Marco*. Medioevo e Umanesimo, vol. 10. Padua: Editrice Antenore, 1972.

United States. Bureau of Education. *Public Libraries in the United States*. Washington, 1876.

The Vatican Library: Its History and Treasures. Yorktown Heights, N.Y.: Belser, 1989.

Vervliet, Hendrik D. L., ed. *The Book through Five Thousand Years: A Survey*. London and New York: Phaidon, 1972.

Vespasiano da Bisticci. *The Vespasiano Memoirs: Lives of Illustrious Men of the XVth Century*. Trans. William George and Emily Waters. London: Routledge, 1926.

Veyne, Paul, et al., ed. *A History of Private Life*. Trans. Arthur Goldhammer. 5 vols. Cambridge: Harvard University Press, Belknap Press, 1987–91.

Waley, Arthur. *The Real Tripitaka and Other Pieces*. New York: Macmillan, 1952.

Wallenius, Anna-Britta. ed. *Libraries in East Africa*. Uppsala, Sweden: Scandinavian Institute of African Studies, 1971.

Walter, Frank K. *Periodicals for the Small Library*. 5th ed. Chicago: American Library Association, 1928.

———. 6th ed. Chicago: American Library Association, 1932.

Walter, Frank Keller. "A Poor but Respectable Relation—the Sunday School Library." *Library Quarterly* 12(3):731–39 (July 1942).

Warmington, B. H. *Carthage*. Harmondsworth, Middlesex: Penguin Books, 1964.

Watson, Alan. *The Making of the Civil Law*. Cambridge: Harvard University Press, 1981.

Watters, Thomas. *On Yuan Chwang's Travels in India, 629–645 A.D.* 2 vols. London: Royal Asiatic Society, 1904–5.

Weimerskirch, Philip John. *Antonio Panizzi and the British Museum Library*. AB Bookman's Yearbook, 1981. Clifton, N.J.: Bookman's Weekly, 1982.

Weitemeyer, Mogens. "Archive and Library Technique in Ancient Mesopotamia." *Libri* 6(3):217–38 (1956).

Welch, Theodore F. *Toshokan: Libraries in Japanese Society*. Chicago: American Library Association, 1976.

Wellisch, Hans. "Ebla: The World's Oldest Library." *Journal of Library History* 16(3):488–500 (June 1981).

White, Carl M., ed. *Bases of Modern Librarianship: A Study of Library Theory and Practice in Britain, Canada, Denmark, the Federal Republic of Germany and the United States*. New York: Macmillan, 1964.

Whitehill, Walter Muir. *Boston Public Library: A Centennial History*. Cambridge: Harvard University Press, 1956.

Whitehouse, Ruth. *The First Cities*. Oxford: Phaidon Press, 1977.

Wiegand, Wayne A, and Donald G. Davis, eds. *Encyclopedia of Library History*. New York: Garland, 1994.

Winkelman, John H. "The Imperial Library in Southern Sung China, 1127–1279." *Library Quarterly* 39(4):299–317 (October 1969).

Winston, Richard. *Charlemagne: From the Hammer to the Cross*. New York: Vintage Books, 1954.

Wooster, Harold. "Historical Note: Shining Palaces, Shifting Sands: National Information Systems." *Journal of the American Society for Information Science* 38(5):321–35 (September 1987).

Wormald, Francis, and C. E. Wright, eds. *The English Library before 1700: Studies in Its History*. London: Athlone Press, 1958.

Wright, H. Curtis. *The Oral Antecedents of Greek Librarianship*. Provo, Utah: Brigham Young University Press, 1977.

Wu, K. T. "Libraries and Book-Collecting in China Before the Invention of Printing." *T'ien Hsia Monthly* 5(3):237–60 (October 1937).

INDEX